Inside the World Bank

Inside the World Bank

Exploding the Myth of the Monolithic Bank

Xu Yi-chong and
Patrick Weller

INSIDE THE WORLD BANK

Copyright © Xu Yi-chong and Patrick Weller, 2009.

First published in 2009 by
PALGRAVE MACMILLAN®
in the United States—a division of St. Martin's Press LLC,
175 Fifth Avenue, New York, NY 10010.

Where this book is distributed in the UK, Europe and the rest of the world,
this is by Palgrave Macmillan, a division of Macmillan Publishers Limited,
registered in England, company number 785998, of Houndmills,
Basingstoke, Hampshire RG21 6XS.

Palgrave Macmillan is the global academic imprint of the above companies
and has companies and representatives throughout the world.

Palgrave® and Macmillan® are registered trademarks in the United States,
the United Kingdom, Europe and other countries.

ISBN: 978-0-230-61672-1

Library of Congress Cataloging-in-Publication Data is available from the
Library of Congress.

A catalogue record of the book is available from the British Library.

Design by Newgen Imaging Systems (P) Ltd., Chennai, India.

First edition: September 2009

10 9 8 7 6 5 4 3 2 1

Printed in the United States of America.

CONTENTS

FIGURES AND TABLES

Figures

Tables

PREFACE

The World Bank (hereafter the Bank) is often criticized by governments in both developed and developing countries for either providing too much or too little assistance to the needy. It is condemned by many nongovernmental organizations (NGOs) for throwing poor countries further into debt and for undermining the sovereignty of independent states with the intrusive conditions it places on loans. It is argued to be an instrument of the U.S. Treasury and an extension of Wall Street. The Bank is accused for being too secretive, lacking the necessary transparency needed to judge its decisions. It is too dogmatic, not open to different ideas and driving an agenda dominated by the tenets of a crude brand of economics. Its critics charge it with environmental vandalism, of failing to encourage sustainability in its projects. They believe the Bank has widened the gap between the rich and the poor, both in and between nations; it pushes an agenda that operates only in the interests of the rich. And they argue its staff are arrogant, insensitive, and high handed in their treatment of countries with which they deal.

Weighty economists have joined the fray, attacking both the Bank and its Bretton Woods twin, the International Monetary Fund (IMF), for their policies and their approach. Some, like Joseph Stiglitz (1999, 2002) and William Easterly (2002), formerly worked in the Bank and talk with the insight of experience. They criticized the institutions for their ineffectiveness and their ideology. Even if their most strident critiques are aimed at the IMF, the Bank is discredited by the company it keeps.

The Bank is not alone. Other international organizations (IOs) are equally condemned for their sins and their failures. Some are taken as the instruments of powerful states, executing international injustice by imposing their will on the underprivileged, as monolithic monsters authorizing coercion, helping multinational corporations recolonize the world (Emadi-Coffin 2002), bringing down environmental and labor standards, and undermining the democratic process as well as "definitely and demonstrably caused human rights violations" (Darrow 2003:53).

And yet IOs survive, even prosper. Why the gap? In part it may be that bad news sells. Institutions like the Bank can act as the lightening rod for criticisms, a convenient scapegoat for the development failures around the world. Instead of blaming governments, the Bank is a convenient target. Its successes, often local and dispersed, are ignored.

Indeed the condemnatory public image contrasts with the responses of many people concerned about development and poverty alleviation and with many client countries. If its reputation is so dreadful, why are the Bank staff trusted and welcomed in many parts of the globe? Why do donors continue to pour development and trust funds into its coffers? Why do so many seek to take advantage of their assistance? The explanation must in part be what those Bank staff do, not in grandiose schemes or international conspiracies, but on the ground, helping countries and citizens. Assistance is not always successful, but it is sometimes. For the Bank staff, throwing their hands up in despair and giving up is not an option. So they keep trying. Let us provide some examples.

In a suburb in Jakarta, a young Bank staffer was asked to develop a program for access to justice for the poor. He had been given a grant to run a pilot program to identify what villagers saw as their priorities—property and marriage rights. He approached donors for support, assembled a team, and got the program running; the villagers benefitted.

In Chongqing, one of the four separate municipal governments in China, the population of over 30 million has led to traffic snarls. The municipality and Bank staff are working together on a program that would allow a motorist to drive across the municipality in less than eight hours.

In the West Bank and Gaza, the Bank's country director (CD) realized that there would not be improvement of life for Palestinians unless the Israelis agreed to open up the border for them to have access to jobs. Israelis would not agree to do so until they saw as safe. The CD saw this as the Bank's business to negotiate with the Israeli government to assist in opening up the checkpoints for Palestinians.

In Central America, Bank staff in urban development projects incorporated into their work crime prevention, after-school care, and post-combatant counseling all in one park design program—lights were located in the right places to reduce dark corners, a community center was included for kids after school, and a counseling center for post-combatants.

Two young Bank staff proposed links between schools in Africa and schools in the United States, creating a virtual world of connectedness. The president of the Bank had had a similar idea and encouraged them to think bigger, giving them time and funds. In a couple of years, over 3,000 schools were connected with some 35 developing countries participating.

In New Delhi, a Bank expert on the environment was developing a carbon trading program for a country where energy demands were rising while environment protection was a daunting challenge.

In the Philippines, the CD talked over some years with the country's chief justice, offering to provide assistance in a process of court reform. Despite initial skepticism, the chief justice eventually welcomed the knowledge and experience Bank staff could bring.

In Africa, the CD for the Democratic Republic of Congo was faced with a challenge: how to offer assistance and interact with a country in constant civil war, where there were no roads and all the airlines were blacklisted by the European Commission?

In Bosnia, the Mostar Bridge connecting the Bosnia Croats and Bosnia Muslim soars high across the river. The old medieval bridge, an engineering marvel, had been destroyed by shell fire in the civil war of the 1990s. The Bank's CD for the Balkans had taken the lead in bringing together donors and factions in Bosnia Herzegovina to rebuild the bridge, with the same materials and techniques used for the original. It stands today as a symbol of reconciliation and a testament to international cooperation. Keeping a stone from the old bridge in a glass-topped box in his office reminds the CD what the Bank can contribute.

In Washington, D.C., a senior economist was entrusted to develop a multi-faith dialogue, to bring the different religions into a discussion to explore the possibilities of cooperation between the Bank, the churches, and the mosques on poverty alleviation.

These are ten examples of the Bank's activities, all of which we will return to later in this book. We could give hundreds more. We could dig deep into sectors or list the variety of programs that are provided in one country or region. Our intent is simple: to show how the Bank staff see their role in development, whether it is in justice, transport, education, religion, energy, or governance. The programs listed here constitute but a sample, a tiny sample, of what they do. These examples show a small glimpse of the many faces of the Bank. They also explain why the Bank is still welcomed, why the public images are often wrong, and why new methods of exploring its activities are needed if its contribution is to be adequately understood and assessed. As many current and former Bank officials have stated, 'Maybe we have not done a good job in letting the public know what we do.'

So this book is for those who have worked at and with the Bank in Washington, D.C. and in the field in over 100 countries. They are much larger than the Bank itself.

In writing this book we have incurred many debts, particularly to those Bank staff, from executive directors (EDs), managing directors (MDs), vice presidents (VPs), and directors to those in research, operations, and corporate affairs, who generously gave us their time, information, and insight, and to some government officials working with the Bank staff telling us their side of the story. Our special thanks go to Will Martin and Nick Manning, who helped us organize our thoughts about the Bank and its people. Ian Goldin, then vice president external, and Kris Zedler helped to organize our research in Washington, D.C. The staff in field offices made us welcome and arranged interviews. We thank them for their hospitality. None of them are responsible for the outcome.

In Brisbane, Catherine Althaus and May McPhail gathered data on the Bank for us to use. Julie Howe and Shellaine Godbold helped to organize our trips and typed up our notes. May, Tara Scharf, Paula Cowan, and Michael Wesley read the draft and gave us useful comments, all of which were appreciated even if not heeded! The research was funded by an Australian Research Council Discovery Grant.

And the rest, as they say, is down to us.

Xu Yi-chong and Patrick Weller
Brisbane, December 2008

ACRONYMS AND

ABBREVIATIONS

AAA	analytical and advisory activities
ABD	Asian Development Bank
CAS	country assistance strategy
CD	country director
CODE	Committee on Development Effectiveness
DEC	Development Economics
DFID	Department for International Development
DG	director general
EAP	East Asia and Pacific
EBRD	European Bank of Reconstruction and Development
ECA	Europe and Central Asia
ED	executive director
ESMAP	Energy Sector Management Assistance Program
ESSD	Environmentally & Socially Sustainable Development
ESW	economic and sector work
EU	European Union
FPSI	Finance, Private Sector and Infrastructure
GAC	governance and anticorruption
GEF	Global Environmental Facility
HD	Human Development
HIPC	highly indebted poor country
HQ	headquarters
IBRD	International Bank of Reconstruction and Development
ICSID	International Center for the Settlement of Investment Disputes
IDA	International Development Association

IEG	Independent Evaluation Group
IFC	International Financial Corporation
IMF	International Monetary Fund
INT	Department of Institutional Integration
IO	international organization
IR	international relations
IRS	internationally recruited staff
LAC	Latin America and Caribbean
LRS	locally recruited staff
MD	managing director
MENA	Middle East and North Africa
MIGA	Multilateral Investment Guarantee Agency
NGOs	nongovernmental organizations
OECD	Organization of Economic Cooperation and Development
OED	Operations Evaluation Department
OPCS	Operations Policy and Country Services
PBD	Programming and Budgeting Department
PREM	Poverty Reduction and Economic Management
PSM	public sector management
QAG	Quality Assurance Group
RSD	regional sector director
RVP	regional vice president
SA	South Asia
SD	sector directors
SD	Sustainable Development
SSA	Sub-Saharan Africa
TA	technical assistance
TTL	task team leader
UNDP	United National Development Program
VP	vice president
WBG	World Bank Group
WBI	World Bank Institute
WDR	World Development Report
WFDD	World Faith Development Dialogue
YP	young professional

CHAPTER ONE

The World Bank's World

The World Bank is always good for an argument. Whatever the company, views are likely to be strongly held. They will range from outright condemnation to reluctant skepticism to ecstatic approval.

On the one hand there is the Bank as an ogre that attracts virulent and continuing hostility. Its sins are legion. It is secretive and undemocratic; it bolsters corrupt governments. It dictates to weak regimes and forces unfair conditions on them, driving them into unsustainable debt. It is dogmatic and rigid, hostage to a neoconservative brand of economics. It pushes an agenda that is in the interest of its rich shareholders. It is arrogant, high handed, and insensitive in its treatment of poor countries. The critics of the *bad* Bank are vocal, articulate, and persistent. They call to their cause distinguished Bank alumni (Stiglitz 1999, 2002; Easterly 2002).

On the other hand there is another story, perhaps less vocal, certainly more dispersed when some of the Bank's clients appreciate the electricity that lights their houses, the irrigation that underpins their shift from outright poverty, or the education that taught their children to read. Their reaction provides the basis for the *good* Bank that contributes to global knowledge and provides outstanding research on development issues and that is an authoritative powerhouse with a motivated and highly qualified staff.

The Bank is an institution that generates high emotion and strong views. Which is right? Neither and both. Most of these accounts share one characteristic—they oversimplify a complex, divided, and dispersed institution with many faces and functions. The Bank is praised or criticized as an organization with a single voice, a unified colossus. The Bank is personified—presented as though it is an actor with just one message. The image sticks, and the Bank staff find it hard to explain what they are actually doing and how they do it. It is easy to understand why. The Bank is seen as a presidential institution. Presidents dominate the headlines. To the public, they *are* the Bank. Therein lies the problem. Behind the myth of the all-powerful presidents, we know little about how the Bank, as a complex organization with a large bureaucracy, operates and what contribution staff make, whether good or bad.

At one level the presentation of an organization as a single unit is quite normal. Governments are invariably attributed a single identity. The U.S. government has views on everything; even the European Union (EU) presents identifiable policies. Yet, treating an organization as a single entity is no more than easy shorthand; it may refer to a policy outcome, but can never describe the process that has created it. No one seriously suggests that everyone in government agrees or that policies are not compromises. U.S. foreign policy may be contested between State and Defense departments. The EU policies are the consequence of international bargaining among member states. There is an extensive literature on the divisions within governments that can make organizations dysfunctional (Lindblom 1968, 1977; Barnett and Finnemore 2004) and on the personalities that interact to provide a final single official policy (Wilson 1981). To personify a government or organization is to accept a top-down version of its culture and purposes. It may be useful analytically, but it would be perverse to believe such a picture is the only one or even the most accurate.

Who actually decides? Accounts of national politics deconstruct cabinets to ask who the powerful players are. They uncover the rivalries— over ideologies and policy agendas, among cabinet members, between and within departments, or even interacting with the public—that fragment governments. The best accounts go behind the walls and ask who really has the skills, the levers, the opportunities, the information or the incentives to determine the outcomes that later become the official policy. That is not to propose that the broad personified accounts are wrong, but rather that, to understand the internal process of decision making, we need to disaggregate the whole by seeing how the parts fit together.

What works for cabinets can work for international organizations (IOs). If we take it as a given that IOs matter—and not all observers do—their staff, such as those at the Bank, should be treated as a collection of individuals, working together, sometimes cooperatively, at other times competitively (Claude 1971; Langrod 1963; Cox 1969; Cox and

Jacobson 1973, Xu and Weller 2008). Talented, well educated, experienced, committed—they research and argue, negotiate and agonize, fight and combine, all in the cause of the Bank. Their interpretations of the institution's mission may vary; their preferred solutions may initially clash; their own career prospects may sometimes be uppermost in their minds. They have to deliver an outcome, not only for the Bank, but also to the countries that need assistance. These decisions are neither predetermined nor inevitable; they are choices made by officers at different levels and of differing importance. They may be constrained by Bank policy, executive fiat, institutional history, the limits of the expertise, expectations, or by a host of other factors. All decisions made by anyone in an organization, including its president, are constrained. They are nevertheless *choices* that determine final outcomes.

The Bank's presidents may call on the Bank to overcome poverty, eradicate corruption as the cancer for development, launch an infrastructure action plan, contribute to an inclusive and sustainable globalization, build a knowledge bank or multi-faith development. How to define each topic, make ideas operational, gain support from governments, and eventually assess their success or failure is always subject to a process of debate and discussion. For example, when the Bank's president decided to place anticorruption on the agenda, many client governments saw it as an intrusion into their politics prohibited by the Articles of Agreement, and many Bank staff could not see how to avoid working with corrupt governments if the Bank was to continue its work in many developing countries. Fierce debates took place. The consequences are not trivial for the client countries and for Bank officials. Rhetoric into programs, wish lists into conditions or loans, ideas into projects: these are the arenas where the officials argue and decide. To explain who makes these choices, how alternatives are developed, what factors determine the delegations of authority will allow us to demonstrate the two sides of the Bank: the public monolith and many faces of the people working within.

These two images—the myriad of contested ideas at the bottom, the dominant view at the top—are not necessarily irreconcilable. The general directions sought by the Executive Board of the Bank, representing the shareholders and stakeholders, are never so specific that they can provide more than a general framework. Presidential speeches may determine the agenda for the Bank, but careful planning is required to translate general prescription into projects, to turn the 'obvious intent' into development progress. Officials of the Bank constantly choose. They design programs for delivery to over 100 countries around the world, countries that are the poorest and the neediest. The projects and programs are delivered through government agencies, national as well as subnational, through NGOs and in partnership with other donor agencies. Seen from the bottom, the Bank appears fragmented, argumentative, local, and contested; it acts as entrepreneur, partner, research center, teacher, and policy advocate.

The Bank may be a monolith to its critics. To its client countries, it is represented by those working with them who come in all shapes, undertaking a wide range of activities. After all, as a former vice president (VP) of the Bank pointed out, most people at the Bank work with clients (Ritzen 2005). The Bank's activities are therefore made up of multiple local decisions by varieties of people with an extensive range of experiences. Different parts of the Bank are organized on different principles, and its policy is a combination of bottom–up experience, contested economic thought, and top–down political directives. The Bank thus viewed is a broad and diverse body, where the whole is less than the sum of its squabbling parts.

Of course, officials work within an institution and in a broad epistemic community (Hass 1992). The 'whole profession sometimes can shift,' as in the 1980s with neoliberal economic ideas taking the dominant position. The environment may change from president to president, as attention becomes concentrated on particular priorities. There may be, at different times, a dominant frame of reference; the question is how rigid that framework is and how much discretion officers have. The Bank has certainly been described as though it had but a single message, a semireligious fervor, but that single message has seldom survived unchanged for long. Besides, those interpretations oversimplify.

It is worth getting inside the Bank to understand how decisions are made for the same reason it is worth getting inside national government. No decisions are inevitable; there are choices to be made, even within constraints. The *how* of decision making is important because it affects what decision is made and because control over decision making may be tantamount to control over the outcome. To throw light on the processes is the purpose of this book.

Frameworks for Ideas and Action

Understanding the Bank has always been a challenge. It is complex, diverse, and contested. The literature on the Bank is terrifying in its extensiveness and completely divided in its conclusions. Much of it, however, concerns the impact of the Bank, its effectiveness in reducing poverty, and the approach it takes to the poorest states. That is not the concern of this book. Others are concerned with the allocations of authority between donors and recipient countries and a debate that considers the weighted voting and proposed better modes of governance of the Bank. This may be an extension of the view of IOs, as terrain over which sovereign states fight. That is the subject for a different book.

Our interest is how the Bank works, what drives its staff, and what their expectations are. There are some internal accounts by Bank staff (Ritzen 2005; Marshall 2008), of which the most fascinating are the accounts of country directors (CDs) in *At the Front Line of Development* (Gill and Pugatch 2005).

To understand IOs, a number of approaches developed by academic colleagues provided some insights, none of which in our view are adequate for explaining the picture of the Bank that we seek to draw. Three potentially rewarding approaches to IOs can be explored:

- Principal/agent (PA) analysis seeks to identify how the Bank's political masters (the principals) can control the behavior of the staff (the agents)
- The impact of the Bank's bureaucratic and career structure on its performance and its mission
- Professionalism as ideology: how professionalism and membership of an epistemic community shapes the staff responses.

Here we will note only briefly the principal arguments and explain why they need to be extended to understand how the Bank works.

PA Analysis: The Debate over Political Controls

IOs are created by states, which delegate authorities to them to achieve something states are unable or unwilling to do individually. Many international relations theorists argue, as a consequence, IOs can do nothing that the states do not want them to do and are therefore insignificant, with no independent existence. Others, such as Kenneth Abbott and Duncan Snidal, acknowledge that, when granted "some operational autonomy," the IOs can "provide neutral depoliticized forums" where collective actions take place (Abbott and Snidal 1998). In granting authority to IOs, states become the principal, while IOs are agents.

PA analysis has identified a distinct independent role for IOs. Its main concern is that the principals need to develop mechanisms to control the agents they have created because the agents, with their initial delegation of power, can "carry out their functions independent of the influence of the member states [and] behave opportunistically, pursuing their own interests subject only to constraints imposed by their relationship with the principal" (Pollack 1997:101, 108). Principal and agent will have different interests, and both will act out of self-interest. PA analysis assumes that agents will cheat; the question is how much slippage may occur between the wishes of the two parties, and how principals can exercise greater control through mechanisms such as "detailed rules, screening and selection, monitoring and reporting requirements, institutional checks and sanctions" (Hawkins and Jacoby 2006:199).

To understand the potential for slippage, Lisa Martin distinguishes between the "formal agency which is the amount of authority states have explicitly delegated...and informal agency which is the autonomy...[IOs have] in practice" (Martin 2002:4). Abbott and Snidal too differentiate between the formal powers that have been deliberately delegated to IOs and the informal powers that are developed by the agents in practice. If IOs can have "an influence well beyond their material power which is trivial on conventional measures" (Abbott and Snidal 1998:9), we need to understand how the formal delegated powers have expanded and what role international civil servants play in the process of power expansion. Power and influence are never static; yet, they change because *people* exercise them differently.

Some PA analyses focus on whether the formal powers can determine what agents can do. For example, studies of the relationship between the Executive Boards of the IMF and the Bank and the staff of these two institutions ask how the Board as a principal limits the power of the staff (agent). In doing so, these studies provide "an *indirect* picture of agents as seen through the eyes of principals" (Hawkins and Jacoby 2006:199). It is a view through a restricted lens. However important the principal's preferences and whatever its control mechanisms, they alone cannot fully explain variations in the behavior of agents. Neither can the PA approach thus applied explain the internal politics within a particular agent. Agents, domestic as well as international, vary significantly not only because of the initial delegated authorities, but also because of their historical development and their capacity to exercise these authorities in their pursuit of multilateral cooperation. Agents, once created, develop a life of their own. How agents behave, develop, and expand; why some agents are more independent of the wishes of their principals than others; and what influence agents may have on principals' behavior and further delegations are all empirical matters that require investigation. PA studies raise questions about who the principals and agents are. First, if an IO is an agent, it has multiple principals (states) who often disagree among themselves regarding what they want to achieve, what power they want to delegate, and how they can ensure the delegated power is not abused. Where principals are in dispute, is the agent accountable to one, two, or the majority of states, to those with most political and economic power, or to those who are most affected by its actions? As PA studies have shown, the greater the divisions among the principals, the greater the discretion agents have. It is then equally important to understand how agents exercise their different degrees of discretion.

Second, the focus of these studies invariably falls on the principals; it is their interests and preferences that decide what power is delegated and what opportunities are created. Agents are treated as though they *should* be the passive recipients of the decisions of principals. Cases where they diverge from the wishes of principals are interpreted as misuse of power, preferring their own interests to those of their superiors.

However, other explanations are as persuasive and not as conspiratorial. Principals may not have the capacity to direct, even if they wanted to, requiring staff to make the choices as a necessary part of meeting their objectives. They may have lost the power to exercise what appears to be their formal authority. Formal authority should never be muddled with actual power. Authority in organizations has often leeched elsewhere through a combination of practice, convention, or expertise. Why not in IOs? We cannot assume that the nominal principals have the will or the capacity to fulfill some of the heroic roles nominally allocated to them.

Third, in any given IO, there is a series of PA relations that cascade down through the organization. Studying the IMF, Martin treats the Executive Board as the principal and the staff the agent while acknowledging that "management and staff are not the unitary actor I represent it as here" (Martin 2002:5). The management and the staff may be the agents of the member states, but the staff are also the agents of the management. Identifying an IO as an agent often misses the internal politics among international civil servants. The device of assuming a single personality for the IO may have useful analytic value, but oversimplifies often complex IOs. How do the staff reach the decision that is then negotiated with the Executive Board? How does the management team ensure the compliance of the staff? It is essential to open the box of the agent to understand the internal politics of the organization. The complexity, and richness, of the debate is lost if the emphasis is primarily on modes of command and control.

By focusing on the actions of principals, these studies accept the international relations tradition that states are the legitimate and primary actors that have created agents and delegated authority to IOs. Accounts of the Bank follow suit; their principal focus is on the relationship between shareholders, embodied in the Executive Board, and the Bank as an aggregated institution. The interest is essentially in the effectiveness of hierarchy and control, not the activity within the IO in its own right.

Bureaucratic Imperatives as Organizing Concepts

With staff numbering 10,000 in the headquarters (HQ) and around the world, the Bank cannot help but be run by bureaucratic processes. That creates what Michael Barnett and Martha Finnemore (1999, 2004) describe as "bureaucratic imperatives" that can be used to explain the active participation of IOs in international politics. They accept that "the rational-legal authority that IOs embody gives them power independent of the states that created them and channels that power in particular directions" (1999:699). Since the rational-legal authority is embedded in the bureaucracies of any IO, their study tries to understand how the structure of the organization defines and shapes actors, interests, and missions. They acknowledge that IOs are not empty shells, but rather entail sets of beliefs and agenda and create categories of actors and action. By treating IOs as bureaucracies and focusing on their authority and autonomy, they argue that rational-legal or delegated authority, moral standing, and expertise not only allow IOs to develop independent roles but also make the institutions prone to dysfunctional behavior, seen as failures to carry out their specific (or designated) missions.

In discussing the possibility of dysfunctional behavior of IOs—"the way they may fail and the ways they evolve" (Barnett and Finnemore 2004:16)—these studies highlight the internal culture, shared beliefs, and the practices of bureaucracies, all of which are defined and shaped by the organizational structure and the environment within which they operate. This approach takes us some way to interpreting the internal operations of an IO and the discretion bureaucrats have. Bureaucracies are not passive receivers of commands. The literature on domestic civil services shows they have their own life, qualities, and capacities. It has also provided ample evidence to demonstrate that organizations redefine their objectives in their own interest and can use their autonomy to serve their own ends.

Yet, when Barnett and Finnemore refer to IMF staff as agents, they speak of them collectively as a single, undifferentiated group (2004:57, 63), and therefore they have but the one view. Even though they acknowledge their empirical studies "reveal the active processes of debate and contestation within these organizations" (2004:159), exploring the implications of these factors is not the objective of their study.

While we accept that dysfunctional behavior is always a possibility, it is not inevitable. The bureaucratic condition is not necessarily improper or malign. Bureaucratic rules and procedures are necessary for a large organization. Internal dilemmas create alternative propositions about the way that the Bank should be organized. Structure and agency coexist in a dynamic duet. The continuing debate in the Bank, for instance, about how country and sectoral expertise can best be fused is but one of the arenas where structure and dominant thought provides a framework for analysis.

Bureaucracies create careers. Many stay at the Bank for the duration of their working life. Whether they are fascinated by the challenge or locked in by the superannuation arrangements does not matter. They have a past and a present, and hope to have a future, in the organization. Their personal history and their ambitions, their relations with colleagues and with clients in borrowing countries will affect the way they examine issues and may alter the outcomes at the country, regional, or organizational levels. Bureaucracies thus create networks of formal rules and procedures and informal if established conventions and practices; they develop personal relationships and antagonisms. All are required if the organization is to deliver on its mission, whether initially defined or redesigned to suit the purposes of the officials. Any single outcome is the drawing together of multiple actions from a number of staff with different perspectives.

The difference between the PA and constructivist approaches is epitomized by Martin when she contrasts her findings with those of Barnett and Finnemore. She argues, "IOs gain autonomy as the result of intentional state decisions to delegate authority, not through a careless process driven by staff" (Martin 2006:141). Both PA analysis and constructivists have opened IOs, but by their own admission they do so by using unrealistic assumptions. We seek to build on that earlier work by relaxing the strict assumption about unitary actors to develop a conceptually and empirically more diverse idea of IOs.

Professionalism as Ideology

Organizations are often credited with views on the best way to approach problems. Common ideas provide both an easy determination of what is best and what is possible. James March and Johan Olsen (1989) argue that there are expectations of how people will behave and how appropriate solutions will dominate discussion. Institutions are therefore not merely organizations within which people work, but active conveyers of orthodoxy and propriety that develop dominant traditions. This is indeed what the Bank is most criticized for: its economic ideology or economic theology.

There is no shortage of criticism of the Bank's economic ideology (Caulfield 1996; Easterly 2002; Toussaint 2008). If their argument—that the Bank's economic ideology/theology dominates its operations and can explain everything about the Bank—is valid, the PA approach is superfluous. Principals need not create any mechanism to prevent slippage; their interests will be protected because their economic models dominate decision making.

The most striking picture of a Bank driven by so-called economic theology is provided by Susan George and Fabrizio Sabelli. They argue that

> *this supranational, non-democratic institution functions very much like the Church, in fact the medieval Church. It has a doctrine, a rigidly structured hierarchy preaching and imposing this doctrine and a quasi-religious mode of self-justification.*
>
> Or, to borrow from a wholly different tradition, the Bank is reminiscent of a centralized political party characterized by opacity, authoritarianism and successive party lines. Could the Bank be the Last of the Leninists? Perhaps so: we tend however to favour the religious analogy. (italics in original; 1994:5)

The monastic picture of hierarchical obedience and orthodox belief paints an institution with a single set of views and little scope for dispute or challenge.

Others are not as radical. They argue that the Bank adheres to, and pushes, economic models and templates with the ideological imprimatur of neoliberalism onto developing countries. Ngaire Woods, for example, identifies three distinct forces that shape the operations of the Bank: (a) political influence of the institution's major shareholding country, the United States; (b) the institutional imperatives of the resident economists and bureaucrats; and (c) the nature of the relationship between the Bank and its client countries. She examines "how technical ideas are shaped by political and bureaucratic imperatives" (2006:39) at the IMF and the Bank and how the two institutions "have adapted economic ideas to fit their available resources and instruments" (2006:181). The result is a narrow pool of technocratic knowledge on which the institutions draw.

Woods argues that, even if the Bank had a broader mandate than its twin sister, the IMF, it could not help but operate the same way because it too is dominated by an economics profession. Economists as a group not only drive the decisions of the Bank but show a strong tendency to endorse one set of professional ideas, engrained with neoliberal ideology. Such institutional imperatives "reduce the discretion of staff and make it easier for the institution to maintain consistence and coherence" (Woods 2006:46).

> They [The IMF and the Bank] send professional economists who "cut through" the details of local circumstances, and "tame" the complexities of economic problems, extracting indicators and specific policy goals from what otherwise might be a morass…it makes it easier to claim they are treating all members similarly. It keeps politics out of the equation. And it brings all problems within the professional ambit of staff. (Woods 2006:54–55)

Robert Wade has also argued in many Bank-hosted settings that the Bank's work fails to take fully into account the complex realities of income distribution in its oversimplified vision of poverty. These analyses raise three key issues about the actual operation of the Bank.

First, the analysis provided by Woods makes little distinction between the Bank and the IMF. They share similar ideological orientations, draw "heavily on economic theory and a staff of expert economists" (2006:46), and therefore work in a characteristically common mode. In practice, Bank staff (particularly those who fled from the 'stifling culture' of the IMF) tell how different the two institutions are in their operations and organizational culture. On IMF missions, for example, only the leader speaks; on Bank missions, everyone gets a chance to throw in ideas—'disagreement and debates are part of our life.' No wonder after reading Woods's book, one former Bank VP raised serious doubts that the "Bank staff would recognise themselves from the descriptions given" (Ritzen 2007:576).

Second, economists may have been important throughout the Bank history. They are nonetheless not the only professionals at the Bank. At stages of its history, the Bank has been dominated by different disciplines. One account discussed the predominance of engineers up to the 1980s, then economists, followed by social scientists, and finally accountants and lawyers. That account need not be accurate; it is probably far too simple. It does draw attention to the changes in the dominant professions at the Bank and the changing ideas about the way that the Bank should work, hence there is a contestation of professional ideologies. Engineers and economists see the world differently: 'We as engineers do not think economists know how to do things and economists believe we think too narrowly.' Engineers look at projects, while economists at systems of resources. More importantly, economists rarely agree: 'The field of economics has numerous schools, and many are represented within the World Bank, which aspires to remain at the cutting edge,' explained one Bank veteran. "Countless Bank publications and conferences present widely different viewpoints, and debate can be heated and open" (Marshall 2008:143). Few question the quality of the Bank staff, economists or otherwise, and their rigorous training provides them with independent thinking. "It is more difficult to ensure that the staff is like-minded with the senior management than that it is competent" (Ascher 1983:422). Active debate among economists is a fundamental aspect of the Bank's daily life. Meanwhile, economists at the Bank, like any intellectual discipline, can move through fads and fashions. It is this process of heated debate over what the fashions should be that interests us because it shapes the behavior of Bank staff.

Third, the argument that the Bank economists imposed their models on developing countries without considering either local conditions or politics may be popular but is far from the Bank that many of its staff know. "There is very little room for local knowledge [because] local knowledge is messy, political, intractable, and very difficult to make judgments about," claimed Woods (2006:55). 'The oven-dry philosophy is only in their imagination,' commented a regional chief economist. 'You cannot do the country work without consideration of local conditions.' The Bank staff as individuals and collectively may not always have the right diagnoses or solutions, but attributing the failure to imposition of an ideology or a set of economic policies oversimplifies the operation of the Bank.

On the other hand, as in all organizations, domestic or international, there are expectations driven by organizational imperatives. The Bank has its corporate agenda, needs returns and is required to operate with some economic considerations in mind. It also expects that it will contribute to—and be well regarded by—the epistemic communities outside. The question for staff is how important those economic factors should be, and whether they should trump good but less economic development prospects.

The expertise that lies at the basis of the Bank's operations is important in the way that the Bank understands and defines problems. As the range of professions expands, as environmentalists and lawyers, accountants and sociologists join the staff, so they bring more contested interpretations of how world development should be defined.

Our Approach

This is a project about the Bank. "Who is the World Bank?" a former senior staff member asked rhetorically, "its staff is and needs to be in many respects its strongest asset" (Marshall 2008:80). The highly qualified, multiple skilled, and extensively experienced staff give the Bank its standing in the international community. We seek to ask how the Bank staff exercise their influence. We ask how the structures of power provide opportunity, how organizational arrangements create expectations and incentives, how modes of thinking and expertise shape their behavior. How they are organized, how they see their responsibilities, how they work with their superiors and client countries, all make the Bank different. We need to go beyond the insights PA and bureaucratic analyses have offered.

To regard the Bank as a single entity takes all the politics out of the organization and sees it as a black box, an approach long since discredited in the study of domestic politics. The Bank is a complex institution with "large professional-technical staffs, full-blown bureaucratic structures, and ingrained routines" (Ascher 1983:415). Its staff work over a political, organizational, and intellectual terrain that is always moving. Politics and arguments are the stuff of life. If the Bank is a living, throbbing enterprise, we need to analyze the people, arguments, disagreements, contested ideas, and a wide range of activities the staff undertake.

Much of the literature on the Bank is concerned with the details of the programs per se or the impact they have on recipients. It assesses the impact of development aid, whether in general or in particular regions or sectors. The impact of the Bank remains highly disputed terrain. That is not our concern here; we are interested in people—those working inside the Bank—the work they do, the way they operate, and the impact they have.

There are a number of ways such an investigation of staff could be undertaken. We could look at the history of the institution. The Bank itself commissioned two mammoth histories, celebrating its twenty-fifth and fiftieth anniversaries, which cover these changes and far more (Mason and Asher 1973; Kapur, Lewis, and Webb 1997). Historical studies have been done on single sectors (Collier 1984), a single region (Guhan 1995), or a single presidency (Ayres 1983; Mallaby 2004). The Bank also has its own historians recording the experiences of its people (Oliver 1995; Kraske 1996). However, the principal people who have received published attention are the presidents, reinforcing the image of the Bank as an institution dominated by its leader. These historical studies provide an initial understanding of the structure and operations of the Bank; we do not want to repeat them here.

Alternatively, we could seek to understand the staff through a series of case studies that are organized around a common theme and then try to develop some generalizations about the way the Bank works. We do provide a couple of case studies in chapters 8 and 9 to show how the Bank's processes work, but they are designed to act as illustrations of the findings of the earlier chapters. Case studies could not uncover the more elemental parts of the Bank that underpin its organization.

So we need to make our position clear. This is not a history of the Bank, although at times we delve back into its origins to explain the present. Our emphasis is on the last 15 years, seeking to illustrate how the Bank staff worked during this period and how their position has changed. We need a research design that can build on the theoretical insights we have reviewed, but allow us to go further in opening up the operations of the Bank so we can understand the people who work there. Each of the three perspectives tells us something about the way that the opportunities are provided for staff and shows where we need to go further.

First, the PA approach raises the questions of political control. The controls may be effective, may not be exercised at all, or not in the way the rules imply. They may be formal or informal. An emphasis on the command and control hierarchy is at the core of PA analysis where any deviation from the objectives or wishes of the principal is seen as problematic. The challenge is to prevent its recurrence. Rather than unrealistically complain about the failure of principals to control every facet of the Bank, we see the balance between political control and bureaucratic discretion and cascading PA relations as the inevitable consequences of any large organization. In the tradition of Hugh Heclo and Aaron Wildavsky (1974)—impressionistic, anecdotal, iterative—we seek to understand how political arrangements provide levers and opportunities for staff and internal dynamics determine many of the outcomes. Even where the broad policies are announced by leaders, the scope for decision within organizations is extensive. Graham Allison's neat adage of "Where you sit depends on where you stand" (1971) is applicable to a complex institution such as the Bank where the authority of multiple principals is diverse, fragmented, and uncertain. So we ask, how do the formal and the informal rules, the official and personal networks, shape the staff's working world? We explore connections and networks and seek to understand whether connections and trust trump formal rules.

Second, organizational expectations and routines, as illustrated by Barnett and Finnemore, provide opportunities for staff. These ideas are systematized in the institutional approach. March and Olsen discuss the logics of expectations and appropriateness. Douglass North sees expectations and routines as well as formal and informal rules as important components of institutions that are "humanly devised constraints that structure political, economic and social interactions" (1990:97). Mark Bevir, R.A.W. Rhodes, and Patrick Weller emphasize that organizational expectations, norms, and routines are not static; neither are the formal rules and patterns of behavior. They change as actors analyze, interpret, and contest the traditions that shape the expectations, routines, and thereby institutions (2003). Actors, in this book the Bank staff, are not passive recipients of preordained ideas; they may adapt to the existing rules and meet the expectations initially but will then give the traditions new meaning and applicability. Bank staff operate within a large institution, which is not static. No bureaucracy remains a single, united, and uncontested unit with an agreed interpretation of its mission. We therefore need to introduce a dynamic into the calculations. Staff will contest the way that a mission is reinterpreted and new areas of activity defined. Position will often determine perspective. The diversity of activities inevitably provides an institution with contested routines and self-descriptions. And therefore many faces.

Third, expertise and professional knowledge need not, as George and Sabelli (1994) and Woods (2006) each implies, create a monolithic intellectual climate or an unchanging intellectual position. Demands for expertise change. Information can be used for diverse purposes. Professions have divergent expectations and mores. Longevity can provide an institutional memory or innate conservatism. How do these factors empower staff? If there is a dominant line or an overarching intellectual framework at the Bank, how will it be challenged? As intellectual fashions change, ideas are weapons for battle and levers for power.

Our concern is how, and to what extent, staff shape the activities of the Bank and influence the impacts of the Bank. Each of the approaches reviewed above—the hierarchy of PA, the expectations of bureaucracy, or the intellectual fashions of the moment—provides insight, but cannot by itself provide an adequate lens to understand the constraints within which staff work and the options available to them. We need to use all three if we are to discover how staff understand their position, navigate the organizational thickets, and use their assets and knowledge. With their expertise, commitment to development, and skills the staff have an obvious impact on the intellectual climate and thus setting the framework within which priorities and policies are determined.

We would therefore expect to find, within the spaces created by limited political controls, contested bureaucratic rules, and changing intellectual trends, that staff have pervasive influence and extensive opportunity for the exercise of discretion. So, as a means of determining the influence of staff within this framework, we ask the following:

- What are the activities they undertake? What choices do they make? How much discretion do they have to interpret the world and devise solutions for the problems they encounter? How are their choices shaped by their position in the Bank?
- How are they organized? What is their relationship with their supervisors and the client countries? What capacities do they have in meeting the challenges?
- What diversity is there in the answers and proposals that they provide?

If the Bank is indeed, as we propose, complex, divided, and far from the hierarchy of legend, then the range of staff activities, their use of discretion, and the diversity of their activities will provide us with a complex picture of activities—a Bank with many products, a Bank with many faces, a staff with extensive influence.

Why does it matter? The Bank's contribution can only be analyzed if we go behind the mythology and understand what the staff do. That will provide a more adequate account of how they operate and what they can achieve. That is a necessary base for considering the impact of the Bank.

The only way to discover the perspectives of staff or the influence of routine is to ask them. There are few expositions on the way the Bank staff do their job on a daily basis; internal analyses are often formulaic; the personal is squeezed out of the accounts. Interviews have their limitations: they provide opportunities for self-justification and promotion. However, the more that are undertaken, the more reliable the picture that emerges is likely to be. Simply, there is no time (or incentive) to conspire to provide a misleading picture, not least because there was no central knowledge of who we were seeing and no one cared that much! In three trips to the Bank offices in Washington, D.C., in November 2005, May 2006, and November 2007, we talked to over 100 people, including executive directors (EDs), VPs (past and present), country and sector directors (SDs), researchers, and advisers. On occasion we talked to two or three people who had held the same job, as CD for a particular place, or as VP for the same region. We talked down the line to people involved in governance and energy issues. We also visited the Bank offices in Beijing, Jakarta, Dhaka, Delhi, and Kathmandu where we talked widely from CDs to the locally employed staff. The interviews were undertaken on the basis that the comments would not be attributable. They are used throughout the book as evidence of the way that the staff view their jobs, their options, and their influence. Where quotations appear without citation and within single quotation marks, they are drawn from these interviews. Quotes may be from individuals, but they carry certain organizational insights.

The Bank's Organizational Dilemmas

All organizations have a past. Their initial mandates have long-term impacts on the organizational structure, responsibilities, and ethos. To understand the way the Bank operates, we need to discuss the issues that concern the Bank staff themselves, the challenges they face, the opportunities they have, and the constraints they encounter. We have therefore chosen to center our analysis around a set of dilemmas that go to the heart of the philosophy, structure, and operation of the Bank—how the management has organized and reorganized to deal with these constant challenges, how the Bank staff have puzzled over these dilemmas, and how, because of their very nature of the dilemmas, they will continue to puzzle. Discussion of these continuing dilemmas will provide the central themes of our analysis.

In each of those dilemmas there are a number of options and alternative strategies that all have their own logic. No choice is likely to solve the conundrums permanently because they represent legitimately different perspectives on the organization. Choices made, however, shape the incentive structures for Bank staff, their working relations, and the Bank activities.

These continuing dilemmas are as follows:

• Sector specialists versus country experts

The Bank has dual mandates: to serve as a global institution, bringing global knowledge to its member states, and to meet the demands for development of its member states. It thereby needs both technical expertise and country knowledge—technical specialists who understand merits of projects, the ins and outs of making projects work, and country experts who understand the local politics and macroeconomic conditions and have the diplomatic skills to deal with the governments and local communities. Both are required: the question is always, what the balance should be between the two? Who should be in the driver's seat in deciding what, when, in what form, and to what extent the Bank can offer assistance in a given country? The management consequently faces constant tension between two groups of experts, between geographic and sector approaches.

Maintaining the balance required sophisticated routines and management. Yet, both views had a legitimate case. The pendulum was never at rest; advocates for greater country sensitivity or more technical rigor could compete for influence, whether expressed in organizational form or by procedural directions. The pendulum has swung, from an emphasis on projects to large area departments to a matrix schema. Determining that balance, deploying suitable staff in the right locations with the necessary array of skills is a continuing management challenge. Despite the long history of the tension between areas and sectors, its terminology and ethos today "are driven largely by a 1997 reorganization that aimed to emphasise technical excellence with global reach" (Marshall 2008:71).

• Centralization versus decentralization

In addition to balancing areas and sectors, the Bank has to decide to what degree it should be centralized or decentralized. The public image is clear. It is a presidential Bank. It is a Washington Bank. The first proposes that authority is centralized, that the presidents determine what is to be done. The second paints a picture of a bank that sits three blocks from the White House, the image of an American-dominated institution doing the U.S. bidding. The image might reflect the reality of the first half century of the Bank; neither can be taken for granted today.

Until the late 1990s, all decisions were made out of Washington, D.C. Projects and programs were designed in Washington, D.C., and supervised out of there. Almost all staff were located in Washington, D.C. They went on missions "to conduct surveys, prepare economic reports, inspect projects and evaluate progress" (Mason and Asher 1973:73). In the 1970s, the management experimented with decentralization in a few countries by sending the staff to the field. The experiment by and large failed (Lim 2005). A few country representatives in the field had little authority; their offices served as no more than post offices. The 1997 reorganization changed all this—decentralization of authority, function, and personnel took the Bank staff to the field. Most CDs are now located in the field. Project supervision, procurement, financial management, and disbursement have been given to the local offices. Authority has been significantly delegated to CDs. This has changed the whole dynamics of how decisions are made and how people see their careers.

"Centralization versus decentralization brings both philosophical and practical tension" (Marshall 2008:72). While people with local knowledge are always essential, it is equally important to prevent these people from going local. How can the country ownership and global knowledge be balanced? How can CDs as managers and the Bank as an institution ensure the working relationship between the rotating internationally recruited staff and long-serving locally recruited staff? As the number of senior staff located outside Washington, D.C., has grown, has authority gone with them?

- Knowledge for research or operations

The Bank is arguably the world's most prestigious producer of knowledge on development, hosting the largest concentrated group of highly qualified specialists, supported by million dollar research funds that dwarf almost all universities and research institutions (Gilbert and Vines 2000:49). Who generates knowledge and for what purpose? That is a dilemma that has always created tension in the Bank, never more so than when it prides itself on being a knowledge bank. The Bank's reputation for innovative research needs to be maintained in the academic circles and consequently the Bank research staff are required to publish in the best outlets of their disciplines. Meanwhile, researchers also serve operations. Operations experts, practically oriented, field hardened, and focusing on particular problems are often skeptical of the value of research that is not tied to their daily challenges. That is, what academics value may be more precise than the sometimes descriptive, perhaps messier, prescriptions that help develop successful programs. How research serves operational sections is still questioned. The research staff may be pragmatic in their approach; they are seldom pragmatic enough for the operational areas.

Who holds the soul of the Bank? How should the balance be achieved? How is the research crafted for operations or policy making? Associated questions include, should research be organized as a separate unit from operation or an integral part of the Bank's operation? Should the research department have permanent staff, or should people rotate between research and operation? The dilemma remains how to balance research and operations.

- Internal and external evaluation

The Articles of Agreement state that the Bank "shall publish an annual report containing an audited statement of its accounts and shall circulate to members at intervals of three months or less a summary statement of its financial position and a profit and loss statement showing the results of its operations" (Article V, Section 12). The question of how to make the Bank accountable is by and large left to the hands of the president and the management, who have to balance self-evaluation and external assessment.

The Operation Evaluation Department (OED) was created in 1971 to "examine the activity of their peers and their colleagues in the World Bank" (McNamara 2003:ix), to ensure the quality of its projects, to learn the successes and failures of the Bank's operations, and to defend the Bank's record from public scrutiny (Kapur et al 1997:41–43). How the OED works, what challenges it faces, what relations it has with operations staff, and what impact it has on Bank activities are all important for understanding the Bank staff and operations.

The Bank has always been under public scrutiny. As its operations have expanded, the Bank has drawn increasing attention from the public, NGOs, and even the academic community. Some are positive and constructive, but most are critical. Some are misleading or even hostile. This is what we call external evaluation. However useful or unjustifiable, it has impact on how the Bank operates and how the staff see their role. It also raises the question of to whom the Bank staff are accountable. Since the late 1990s, a particular type of internal evaluation—institutional integrity—has been watching over the shoulder of the staff. With internal, external, and integrity evaluations in place, the Bank is probably the most evaluated institution in the world. The extent and the way the staff and their work should be evaluated remains a serious challenge.

The Structure of This Book

After an overview of the evolution of the Bank mandate and players to provide a context for our analysis (Chapter 2), we will focus our exploration on the relations among the players—the Executive Board, the presidents, the management, and the staff. Our concern is to identify the conventions and practices by which they work and the limits on their capacity (Chapter 3). Then, we develop each of the four organizational dilemmas (chapters 4–7). Each of the chapters on dilemmas seeks to serve three purposes: (a) to explain the way the Bank works, (b) to explore the opportunities for the exercise of influence and the use of discretion, and (c) to show the many faces of the Bank. We then devote two case studies, energy and governance (chapters 8 and 9), to illustrating these themes (the discretion, the influence, the diversity) in action. Chapter 10 tells a story of one VP, Chrik Poortman, as an exemplar of the career of so many Bank staff; it reflects the wide variety of work they do and challenges they face.

CHAPTER TWO

The Mandates and the Players

Over 60 years, the International Bank of Reconstruction and Development (IBRD) has changed significantly. It has expanded into the World Bank Group (WBG), which contains five institutions: IBRD, International Development Association (IDA), International Financial Corporation (IFC), Multilateral Investment Guarantee Agency (MIGA), and International Centre for the Settlement of Investment Disputes (ICSID). Its membership includes 185 countries. It has about 10,000 employees. As of June 30, 2008, its total assets were over $233 billion, total lending $99 billion, and operating budget $2.3 billion. The IBRD lending commitment for FY08 was $13.5 billion. The fifteenth IDA replenishment reached $25 billion in December 2007; IDA lending was $11.2 billion in FY08. In addition, the Bank manages a wide range of trust funds ($21.4 billion at the end of FY07) through 1,015 active accounts, supported by 339 sovereign and non-sovereign donor agencies (Annual Report 2008). The Bank has become "the world's premier development institution" (Marshall 2008:1), offering an extraordinary array of services and products to developing countries. This book will focus on IBRD and IDA only and refers to them as the Bank.

This chapter highlights the mandates, formal structure, players, and, more importantly, the common features of the Bank's operations so that we can take them for granted when we start discussing the dilemmas the Bank has been facing. This chapter does not intend to provide a comprehensive and systematic discussion of the Bank, nor does it involve a historical study. It will focus on four key groups: the Board of Executive Directors, the presidents, the management team, and the staff. It will examine their selection, recruitment, qualities, management styles, career paths, and relationships with each other.

Ever Changing Mandates

When the Bank opened its door, its first president, Eugene Meyer, explained, "We had only the Articles of Agreement to guide us and they provided only the sketchiest of outlines." He continued, "We had no staff then, no clear definition of our role, no operating policies or procedures, and no established standing in the private investment market" (Chronology 2007:6–7). Meyer had to interpret what had been intended when each article was discussed.

As a public institution, the Bank has predefined objectives, a formal structure, and a well-qualified staff. All three aspects are open to discussion. Do organizations truly possess goals? Can predefined objectives (those stated in the Articles of Agreement) change? Some scholars argue organizations formulate goals after the fact to justify past actions. Others question the concept of organizational objectives as a simple construct; organizations are comprised of individuals and groups who attempt to fulfill their own goals, defined by their positions and their roles in the organization. We argue that international organizations have objectives, which are defined initially by the contract among states. These objectives, however, are not static; they develop and adapt for the survival and expansion of the organization. Therefore, "we must explain organization goals, over and above the goals of individuals" and their development (Simon 1976:257).

The Bank Is a Bank

The Articles of Agreement stipulate the purpose of the Bank as "to assist in the reconstruction and development of territories of members by facilitating the investment of capital for productive purposes." The conflicts were twofold: (1) with its limited financial capacity, should the Bank support efforts for reconstruction or development; and (2) on what conditions should assistance be provided? In essence, the question was whether the Bank was a financial intermediary or an international agency to achieve specific political objectives by distributing financial assistance. Both the Europeans and the Americans wanted to shape the IBRD as an international institution, though with different emphases: Europeans were more interested in postwar reconstruction, while the Americans stressed delivering aid for development to countries in its own backyard, such as Chile. To achieve either or both, the Bank needed financial resources.

"The World Bank is an economic, not a charitable nor a political agency," declared Meyer. His successor, John McCloy, settled the issue—the Bank was a financial institution; its sustainability lay in prudent lending and sound finance. With an initial $8 billion subscription and an understanding between the American and British governments that "most of the capital of the Bank should remain uncalled and should serve simply as a guarantee against the Bank's obligations" (Mikesell 1994:39), the Bank needed to borrow on the international financial market if it was to become an important lender. The only way to expand the capital at its disposal was to convince investors that it would be a financially sound business, able to repay its creditors. McCloy insisted that earning the trust of the financial community took precedence over meeting the wishes of the member governments. This "shaped the Bank's attitude and policies for the next two decades" and thereafter (Kraske 1996:59)—the basis of its success was the confidence of investors in the Bank's financial soundness. Raising capital by selling bonds to investors in international financial markets and lending the money to the developing countries at a slight profit are the core operations of the Bank. The profits on commercial lending, plus investment earnings generated by accumulated capital, cover the Bank's administrative costs.

That the Bank is a bank has four implications: (a) an arm's-length relationship with governments, shareholders and stakeholders alike is crucial for the operation of the Bank; (b) lending is important; (c) repayment is equally important; and (d) loan officers and lawyers were the first groups recruited into the Bank.

First, as a bank as well as a public institution, the Bank must be able to attract investors while not subjecting itself to big business and Wall Street or the pressure of governments or other international organizations. Maintaining an arm's-length relationship with its member states and making decisions on the basis of economic merits rather than political demands were seen from the beginning as necessary conditions for the Bank's survival. This "financial independence of at least part of the World Bank's operations—those that involve lending, management of its assets, and borrowing on capital markets—does give it flexibility and leeway that many other development institutions lack" (Marshall 2008:4).

Second, lending keeps the Bank alive. Lending also provides the institution with unparalleled advantages in achieving its mandated objectives: from its early years, the Bank has realized that institution building—organization, management, experienced manpower, and increasingly formal and informal rules—is a necessary component of development. Lending allows the Bank staff to combine financial resources with expertise to assist developing countries. 'Lending gives us a seat at the table—if we want to help countries develop institutional capacity and if we want to make suggestions, we need to know the system and we need to be involved in every step. Lending allows us to get involved,' stated a VP simply. This combination of financial resources and expertise has made the Bank a unique international institution.

Third, the Articles of Agreement state "loans made or guaranteed by the Bank shall, except in special circumstances, be for the purpose of specific projects or reconstruction and development" (Article 3, Section 4 [vii])—in other words, there would not be a blank check to borrowing countries. To ensure its sound finance, the Bank established principles in its very first loan to France: the borrowing country must pledge its full faith and credit and the promise that no future creditor would take precedence in repayment over Bank loans; borrowing countries were able to repay the debt and would accept the Bank's intrusive scrutiny on how they spent its loans. It was never easy to secure agreement for the Bank to impose rigorous supervision over the disbursement of funds since the borrowing countries were sovereign states that considered such supervision as intrusive. In the negotiation of that first loan to France, the French delegate asked the Bank VP, Robert Garner, "'Mr. Garner, you expect me to identify every lump of coal as to which boiler it's going into?' To which Garner replied: 'No, I just want to be sure it is not going to be diverted to a Paris night club'" (Kraske 1996:58).

Fourth, since many of the early borrowers were European countries seeking to rebuild war-ravaged economies, projects were developed by the borrowing governments. The Bank staff had to ensure the projects were financially sound and the country had the capacity to repay the loans. Thus, the first recruits to the Bank were loan officers and lawyers. After the loan officers assessed applications from technical perspectives, lawyers drafted the lending contracts as well as " 'side letters' (letters indicating the expectations of the Bank on matters less formal and precise than those usually included in covenants)" (Mason and Asher 1973:76). Lawyers were consulted about practically everything because Garner insisted that "the Bank's public character was neither excuse nor reason for standards of efficiency lower than those of private business" (Chronology 2007:9).

In 1960, the IDA was established as a "subsidized window" of the Bank—"rich countries donate money to its kitty every three years, and the money is lent out to developing nations [and] the terms of these 'soft' loans are highly generous, but the Bank does demand repayment and charge various small fees" (Mallaby 2005). IDA has its own Articles of Agreement, a separate legal entity, and its own financial resources. Yet, it has always been run as an integral part of the Bank: EDs represent countries that are members of both the Bank and the IDA. The president of the Bank is ex officio president of the IDA, and the officers and staff of the Bank serve as the officers and staff for the IDA.

Several forces drove this change. First, the dollar Bank was replaced by a Bank with varieties of investors. By the end of the 1950s, most Bank bonds were sold outside the United States. With economic recovery, many Europeans countries increased their external assistance. Eugene Black believed that these European countries could and should extend their aid beyond their traditional clients (Libby 1975:1066) at the time when political needs called for new measures and sources of assistance (Annual Report 1958–1959:9–11). The Bank, with its Triple A credit rating, could bridge the gap by bringing together countries with extra capital and those that needed resources. Creating an agency working with the Bank would bring development aid under one umbrella.

Second, at the end of the 1950s, the Bank had been operating successfully with its net profits and total reserves accumulating quickly. In 1959 alone, the Bank's net income was $46 million, and the total reserves increased from $350 million in 1958 to $420 million in 1959, a 20 percent increase in one year (Annual Report 1958–1959:3). The U.S. Congress raised questions about its further contribution to the Bank. A new yet associated institution would allow the Bank to channel its financial resources to developing countries on concessional terms without undermining its own sources of finance.

Third, since over 80 percent of its lending was funded by its borrowing on international financial markets, the Bank's credit in world investment markets was of crucial importance. Yet, its borrowing countries had increasing difficulties repaying traditional loans. If the Bank wanted to continue to promote development, it needed to provide financial assistance to those that were unable to borrow commercial loans. Grants or soft lending would help poorer countries develop the ability to borrow on commercial terms.

Fourth, in late 1950s, several international or regional institutions were established to assist the underdeveloped world. The United Nations Special Fund and the European Investment Bank both went into operation in 1958. The Arab Financial Institution for Economic

Development and the Inter-American Development Bank were approved in early 1959. These financial assistance institutions could be seen both as supplementary to the Bank operations and as competitors. Between the UN and the Bank, many shareholding countries chose the latter when the UN become bogged down into a Cold War stalemate. At the Bank annual meeting in September 1959, governors asked that an IDA charter be drafted. The Articles of Agreement, submitted in February 1960 for acceptance by member governments, were drafted in general terms, giving the IDA latitude to shape its financing to meet the needs of cases as they arose.

In the following decades, other similar ad hoc 'subsidized windows' were opened under the auspices of the Bank as some developed countries started placing their dedicated concessional financial resources under its management. The total amount of trust funds reached $21.4 billion in FY07, and the top ten agencies contributed over 75 percent of it.

The creation of the IDA and various trust funds have several implications for the Bank staff: (a) it "led a marked increase in the number of individual operations, and to a rapid increase in total staff" (Mason and Asher 1973:80); it enabled the Bank staff to do business with member countries that were no longer creditworthy (or were not yet so) under Bank standards and thus increase the volume of funds available to the Bank Group; (b) the need for the IDA to be replenished every three years means that it could be used as a vehicle for some shareholders to make demands on the Bank projects and programs; and (c) grants and soft loans from the IDA provide more room for Bank staff to develop varieties of products they can offer to the client countries.

Reinventing and Redefining Itself

All organizations try to reinvent themselves by adding and modifying initial objectives and adapting to the changing environment. Since 1944 the Bank has weathered political and economic changes too, as the demands on its services altered. Even though the Bank was created as a bank, it is unique in that it is required by the Articles of Agreement to make loans to governments only. Promoting private investment is identified as one of the objectives of the Bank in the Articles of Agreement, but little interest in that activity existed initially. In 1956, the IFC was created as part of what was later known as the WBG to facilitate private investment in developing countries.

IFC would operate on *business principles*; be an *honest broker*, bringing together investment opportunities, domestic and private capital, and experienced management; and play a *catalytic role*. Since then, the Bank has expanded its activities through IFC's lending, advisory services, and project finance.

In the 1960s, amid rising nationalization, disputes between private investors and host governments called for collective actions. EDs negotiated a multilateral treaty on the ICSID. It was an impartial international forum providing facilities for the resolution of legal disputes between investors and governments through conciliation or arbitration. In 1986, WBG added another wing, the MIGA, which provides guarantees to private investors who invest in projects in developing countries. If the Bank did not take these initiatives, these institutions would have been created anyway. It seized the opportunities.

In the 1980s and the 1990s, the Bank took more programs under its wing. Some operate within the Bank but have their own mandate or charter, such as the Global Environmental Facility (GEF) and Energy Sector Management Assistance Program (ESMAP). The expansion of the Bank's programs during the Wolfensohn presidency has been criticized as 'mission creep' (Einhorn 2001), but it was necessary creep. Shareholders demanded the Bank "take on new roles, some quite far afield from its formal mandate, such as administering funds on behalf of the Global Fund for AIDS, Tuberculosis and Malaria, leading efforts to plan for an avian flu epidemic, and comprehensive programs in post-armed conflict situations" (Marshall 2008:142).

Another example is the World Faith Development Dialogue (WFDD). After meeting George Carey, then archbishop of Canterbury, in 1998, Wolfensohn decided to launch a dialogue between the Bank and churches and mosques that had been increasingly critical and even hostile toward the Bank. He asked a hardnosed economist, a former CD in Africa, to lead this exercise. When the EDs were briefed on the initiative, they went ballistic—'religions are divisive,' they charged; 'they are dangerous, counter-development, antimodern, defunct, and emotional.' In contrast the Bank's work is 'evidence-based, research-guided professional activities.' The opposition from the Board did not stop the project because after all churches and mosques and the Bank shared the common interest in alleviating poverty and promoting justice. WFDD "was created to foster active dialogue among faith institutions" (Marshall 2008:106). The newly appointed director for the multi-faith department approached the issue in the Bank's traditional way—linking religions, culture, and faith to development and making them operational in health, education, and poverty alleviation (WDR 2000).

Like all organizations, the Bank has been constantly redefining itself. From its origin as an institution to assist in the reconstruction of Europe, the Bank moved to lending for development, providing knowledge for economic and social development, addressing social and political problems in developing countries, and addressing global issues. Some see this constant redefining as a necessary condition for the Bank to become a "'hegemonic' global institution up to the monumental task of translating global truths into global plans of action" (Goldman 2005:10). Others see it as indicative of the bureaucratic nature of a large institution. Nonetheless, reassessing and retooling are necessary for the Bank to remain relevant as an international development agency in changing international environments.

The Players in the Bank

The initial structure of the Bank has had a profound impact on its evolution. Unlike many large corporations, created by a strong figure with a centralized hierarchy, the Bank began with weak leadership and virtually no hierarchy (Galambos and Milobsky 1995). Its organizational structure was developed under its second president, McCloy, who brought two effective operators into the Bank: Robert Garner as VP and Eugene R. Black as the American ED. The trio settled "a vigorous, if unacknowledged, tug-of-war between the Executive Directors and the management [and] that the Bank would be operated on a businesslike basis by a 'non-political' management" (Chronology 9). They also centralized operations by requiring that the two newly created departments—the loan department and the economics department—report to Garner, the VP, who reported to McCloy.

Since then, intricate relationships among four sets of players—EDs, the president, the senior management, and the staff—have dominated the operation and development of the Bank.

Executive Directors

According to the Articles of Agreement, the Bank's duties are to be performed by (a) a Board of Governors, (b) EDs, and (c) a president—its management team and staff. The Board of Governors is the ultimate decision making body: "All the powers of the Bank shall be vested in the Board of Governors consisting of one governor and one alternative appointed by each member." The Board of Governors may delegate to the Board of Executive Directors any of its powers, with the exception of seven matters:

- Admission of new members
- Increase or decrease of capital stock
- Suspension of a member
- Decisions on appeals from interpretations of the Articles of Agreement by the EDs
- Making long-term arrangement to cooperate with other international organizations
- Decisions to suspend permanently the operation of the Bank and distribute its assets
- Determination of the distribution of the net income of the Bank (Article V, Section 2).

Since the Board of Governors has delegated a wide range of powers to EDs, its function may thus appear to be a mere formality, a legitimizing rubber stamp for decisions made by the management. It can serve, however, as an international forum for raising, debating, or legitimizing new or contentious issues. This is the reason the Board of Governor's annual meetings can attract so much international attention. Demonstrators, NGOs, and journalists can create an image that the Governors' decisions affect the direction of the Bank's operations or the fate of international development. This may or may not be the case in practice.

Governors are usually their countries' finance ministers. Convening Board meetings of governors is a complex matter; trying to reach agreement on issues among 185 governors in a couple of days is virtually impossible. Most differences are worked out beforehand through EDs, or discussions with government officials on formal and informal occasions. Finance ministers endorse the agenda rather than raise new issues. Political support from the Governors in public, nonetheless, is important for the Bank.

In practice, the EDs work on a regular basis in Washington, D.C., to exercise all the powers delegated to them by the Board of Governors. Initially, the Articles of Agreement prescribed 12 EDs, one from each of the five largest shareholding member states and the rest elected by groups of members. The Bank now has 24 EDs: each of the five largest shareholding countries has its own ED (France, Germany, Japan,

United Kingdom, United States); so now do Saudi Arabia, China, and Russia. Other countries belong to groups of constituent members, represented by a single ED.

EDs are "responsible for the conduct of the general operations of the Bank, and for this purpose, shall exercise all the powers delegated to them by the Board of Governors." Each ED has a single vote, carrying the weighted voting power of the member states that elected him/her. In some groups, one or two countries regularly provide either the ED or the alternate. In the African groups, EDs tend to rotate, serving no more than two years because other countries demand their turn. Frequent rotation dilutes the level of experience and undermines the ability of these people working at the Board. In other groups, EDs can serve five or six years.

The Board is created as a hybrid entity with the EDs, Alternate EDs, and their assistants appointed by their governments, but paid out of the Bank budget and working on a full-time basis in the same building as the Bank staff. It is more a parliament of country representatives than a board of directors of a normal financial institution. EDs were meant to "sort out and amalgamate the diverse interests of the owners... [and] the mixed constituencies engaged individual executive directors in mediating and consolidating owner views in advance of formal Board debates" (Kapur et al 1997:1205). While they represent the interests of a country/group of countries, they are also international civil servants, owing their loyalty to the Bank. EDs are assisted by five to ten assistants, depending on the number of countries they represent. The Board occupies two floors of the main complex, with about 250 people working there. The Board might be seen occasionally as the instrument of the rich countries (Woods 2006:190–191), EDs, nonetheless, according to close observers, 'are often independent from their own governments; they see their role as representatives of the entire institution.' They may sometimes take a position different from the management, but they share with the management the same frustration vis-à-vis outsiders. It is not abnormal to see EDs defending the interests of the Bank as an institution rather than the interest of a specific country (see Chapter 3).

The capacity of EDs depends on a series of factors: their personal status in the home political structure, experience as politicians, civil servants or even diplomats, knowledge of international development, and ability to work in a multilateral environment. They come from different backgrounds: a few are financial regulators, some are former ministers or deputy ministers, and many are civil servants. American EDs tend to be from outside the government; the position is filled by the U.S. President or Treasury secretary to repay political favours. Many OECD and East Asian countries send mid-ranking civil servants from their finance or international development departments. African EDs are often former politicians. Many have had no experience in international development. Some countries, such as Britain, tend to post their young and highflyers and use the Board as a training ground for these officials. In contrast, Canada tends to send the retiring politicians to represent a group of countries, primarily from the Caribbean. Many EDs, including the Americans, admit that they had little understanding of the Bank when they first joined the Board. Few can really match the Bank management team and staff in their knowledge of either development or the client countries. As we illustrate in Chapter 3, their impact is less through formal authority than informal networks, cooperation rather than confrontation.

Presidents

"The presidents of the Bank have always been a fascinating subject for the staff of the Bank," wrote a Bank historian. "Not only were they the source of power in the institution; they were also the ones the staff looked to for signals that would indicate the Bank's primary mission and its operational priorities in a changing world" (Kraske 1996:vii). Their foremost responsibility is for an international organization: "The President shall be chief of the operating staff of the Bank and shall conduct...the ordinary business of the Bank" (Article V, Section 5). In doing so, the president holds "a strong position with respect both to operations and to the interpretation of Bank policy and leadership in determining it" (Blough 1968:155). Ideally, the president needs to imprint a vision of development, both on the institution and the world, and to run a large international organization. Some have.

Since the Articles of Agreement say little about who can become a president and what qualities are needed, these issues have been contested every time a new president is selected. "The Executive Directors shall select a President who shall not be a governor or an executive director or an alternate for either" (Article V, Section 5). The reality, of course, has never been so simple. As part of the initial informal agreement between the United States and the United Kingdom, the president of the Bank would be from the largest shareholding country; that was the United States. In return, the Europeans would select one of their own to head the other Bretton Woods twin, the IMF. This arrangement has been by and large accepted by latecomers to the institution. For most part of its

Table 2.1 Presidents of the World Bank

Name	Tenure	Previous occupation	Theme
Eugene Meyer	June 1946–Dec. 1946	Banker, CEO	Groundwork
John Jay McCloy	March 1947–June 1949	Lawyer, businessman	Launched bank
Eugene R. Black	July 1949–Dec. 1962	Former ED, banker	Financial diplomacy
George D. Woods	Jan. 1963–March 1968	Banker	Transformation
Robert S. McNamara	April 1968–June 1981	Political appointee	Expansion
Alden W. Clausen	July 1981–June 1986	Banker	Latin debt
Barber Conable	July 1986–August 1991	Congressman	Reorganization
Lewis Preston	Sept. 1991–May 1995	Banker	Client oriented
James D. Wolfensohn	June 1995–June 2005	Banker, investor	Inclusive bank
Paul Wolfowitz	June 2005–June 2007	Political appointee	Anticorruption
Robert Zoellick	July 2007–	Political appointee	Inclusive, sustainable globalization

history, "the choice of an American, and usually an American banker, as World Bank president was not openly contested" (Kahler 2001:43). Indeed, until the 1990s, U.S. presidents often had difficulty convincing people to take the job. Since then, the process of selecting the Bank president has become controversial and occasionally politicized. Normally, the U.S. President would establish a search committee, chaired by the Treasury secretary to select the Bank president. In practice, the U.S. President decided the nominee, who does not need Senate confirmation. The American ED would formally nominate the candidate to the Board, which would then select him/her with little debate or opposition.

The selection of the Bank president can be contested within the American government. The Treasury and the State Department often disagree. President Truman, for example, was about to nominate Lewis W. Douglas as the Bank's first president, but his decision was "vetoed" by then Treasury secretary Henry Morgenthau, who argued that Douglas's connection with "big business and Wall Street, his tie-ins with international financiers, and his general point of view" (Mason and Asher 1973:41) made him the wrong person. In the process of selecting Preston's successor, the Clinton administration was divided into two camps with two visions. Clinton's nomination of Wolfensohn "was not the unanimous one of his senior advisers" (Kahler 2001:47; Mallaby 2004). The strong opposition to Wolfensohn raised by Treasury secretary Robert Rubin later made it difficult for them to work together.

Sometimes, the disagreement with the president's choice came from the EDs, or the public in general. President Lyndon Johnson's nomination of Robert McNamara caused concern because the four previous presidents of the Bank had been businessmen, lawyers, or bankers. All were impeccable establishment figures accepted by Wall Street and by the U.S. Treasury. As an architect of the unpopular Vietnam War, McNamara was seen as a political liability. In 2005, the Bush administration leaked that it might nominate Paul Wolfowitz, then deputy secretary of Defense, to replace Wolfensohn. Governments of Bank member states were stunned. Some thought him unqualified because of his lack of knowledge of development. Some opposed him as a conservative hardliner, brought in to neuter the Bank. Others insisted that Wolfowitz would never be able to manage the Bank's 10,000-strong bureaucracy. The sentiment among Bank staff mirrored that when McCloy was leaving the Bank (Kraske 1996:73):

> Well, Mr, McCloy, we like you fine, but what is going to happen when you leave the Bank? Who is going to be the next President of the Bank? Suppose you put some damn politician in there, what's going to happen then?

Despite strong opposition from many governments, outcries of NGOs, and the insistence of a group of EDs representing a total of 108 developing countries to meet Wolfowitz to "elicit his views on issues of special concern to developing countries" (Press release 2005), the Bush administration had its way and nominated Wolfowitz.

The departure of Wolfowitz two years later triggered another push to reform the selection process on two basic principles: transparency of process and the competence of prospective leaders regardless of national origin (Birdsall 2002; Bapna and Reisch 2005; Guha 2007). The Board prepared a profile of key qualities for nominees:

- A proven track record of leadership
- Experience managing large international organizations, a familiarity with the public sector, and a willingness to tackle governance reform
- A firm commitment to development
- A commitment to and appreciation for multilateral cooperation
- Political objectivity and an independent stance

This profile was the compromise in the face of calls for radical changes in selecting Bank presidents. Radical reform was proposed because, to many, the position should be open to international competition, so that candidates from developing countries could have an opportunity to compete. Some argue that an American citizen appointed by the American President can undermine the institution. Others do not see nationality as an issue so long as the president acts as an international civil servant. Wolfensohn put this idea in a precise way (2005):

> It is beyond my grade to decide who runs the Bank, who runs the Fund, who runs the international institutions...I might remind you that I was not always an American. I may look like an American, but I don't sound like an American, and I don't walk like an American, but I am an American. This is something that the global leaders need to deal with, and I think it should be an open process, and the Board should be involved.

The debate continues on "the traditional 'gentlemen's agreement' on the U.S. prerogative to name the new president" (Marshall 2008:77). If the European Union (EU) is seen as a single entity, it is the largest shareholder and could in theory demand a European as Bank president. As a former Bank VP commented, "The most amazing and—for a European—the most frustrating experience is to witness how the European countries never seem to be able to use their superiority in the number of votes" (Ritzen 2005:100). The Europeans may complain about the U.S. candidates, as they did in 2005; they have been unwilling to challenge the Americans partly because they cannot agree among themselves and partly because of the trade-off with the IMF. The EU and the United States have "imposed costs, not only in restricting the pool of candidates, but also in undermining the legitimacy and timeliness of the selection process" (Kahler 2001:4).

Senior Management

Initially formal lines of authority were clear.

> The President is the chief of executive office of the Bank. Under him, the Vice President acts as general manager with responsibility for assuring the effective operation of the other offices and departments. It is the Vice President, too, who directs the formulation of policy recommendations for the President. (Annual Report 1947:21)

The presidents determine the size, structure, and responsibilities of the senior management team (MDs and VPs) and choose who serves at that level. When the Bank started, there were just 11 in the management team. As the Bank expanded in size, the presidents created the office of managing director (MD), charged with the responsibilities for the Bank's operations worldwide, for overseeing its administration, and for whatever other responsibility the presidents decide to delegate. In 2008, the senior management team had a total of 36 (including 9 for IFC and MIGA).

The management consists of three groups: those in charge of the region/countries, those running sectors, and those in corporate affairs. Some presidents depend on a single person to manage the daily routine, while others have a committee. One person quipped that the regional vice presidents (RVPs) are 'the only real VPs, the rest are VPs with training wheels.' Others think sector VPs do the real operations work, while RVPs just bring the countries together. How the president organizes the management team affects the incentive structures of the Bank staff.

Senior staff are drawn primarily from within the Bank. Most VPs have been in the Bank for their whole career. Presidents have occasionally brought in as VPs, people with experience in either national governments or other international organizations. On occasion, EDs have, after a suitable period of quarantine, become VPs. The argument is that new blood is needed if a president is to alter the direction or ethos of an organization. Yet, career staff predominate. During Wolfensohn's first term, all but one of the MDs had long experience in the Bank, although the most successful, Shengman Zhang, was a former Chinese ED.

In 2008, two of the three MDs and one of the six RVPs were brought to the Bank from outside. The other five RVPs in the team had all served the Bank for more than 20 years. Whether recruits from outside the Bank into senior positions are successful is questioned. Josef Ritzen, a former Dutch minister of education and a VP under Wolfensohn, seemed to think that attempts had failed.

> As far as I can keep track, they were all gone within four years, so that all the present operational Vice-Presidents are still old Bank hands with at least twenty years experience on the Bank group. This is top staff, consisting of highly motivated professionals, but it does lack the infusion of new blood. In other words: rejuvenation through interchange with the outside world has not been successful in the Bank. (2005: 108)

Shengman, the MD under Wolfensohn, agreed, "The Bank seldom brought people from outside to the senior positions, except at a time when radical reforms were to be introduced. Even then, the survival rate of these outsiders at senior level is less than 25%" (Zhang 2006:249). Whether the practice of bringing outsiders for senior positions will work remains an open question, but the practice will change the incentive structure and expectations for the Bank staff. "The Bank of the past was a career institution, where people worked for many years and left very reluctantly" (Marshall 2008:82). 'Old Bank hands' with a career commitment and with superannuation and psychic ties are still likely to outstay temporary appointees who see the Bank as but one step in a diverse career.

"Diversity has long been an issue and a challenge" (Marshall 2008:82). The Bank did not have its first female VP until the 1980s. The first female MD and the first female VP in operations came only in 1997. Diversity was also a problem in terms of nationality. Senior positions were initially occupied primarily by Americans, British, a few Europeans, and people from the English-speaking subcontinent. Recognized as an issue since McNamara, there had been little serious effort to change the situation partly because of the emphasis on meritocracy and partly because of the processes of internal promotion. Thus, when the first female non-European VP in operations had difficulties working with people in the region, especially CDs, it was difficult to see if it was a lack of acceptance, a clash of cultures, personality, or management style. Nationality normally is not a consideration for senior positions; yet, it can be a factor when a specific position is in question.

The countries of origin of the 2008 senior management team of IBRD/IDA were as follows:

Managing Directors—El Salvador, New Zealand, Nigeria
Chief Financial Officer—Italy
Senior Vice President, Chief Economist—China
Senior Vice President, General Council—France
Senior Vice President, External Affairs—Jordan

(*Regional VPs*)

Vice President, Latin American and the Caribbean—the United States
Vice President, Middle East and North Africa—Italy
Vice President, East Asia and the Pacific—the United States
Vice President, Europe and Central Asia—Japan
Vice President, Africa—Nigeria
Vice President, South Asia—Chile

(*Network VPs*)

Vice President and Network Head, Human Development—Botswana
Vice President and Network Head, Operations Policy and Country
   Services—the United States
Vice President and Network Head, PREM—the United States
Vice President and Network Head, Sustainable Development—the
   United States

(*Other VPs*)

Vice President and Treasurer—the United States
Vice President and Corporate Secretary—Bulgaria
Controller, Strategy and Resource Management—Bangladesh
Vice President, Human Resources—Turkey

Professional diversity has been an issue too. Traditionally, macroeconomists have found it easier to climb the ladder within the Bank than sector specialists. Some no longer see their original training as sufficient:
'There was a time when I had a doctorate in economics, but over the
years I have become a full-time manager.'

The Staff

Both supporters and opponents of the Bank acknowledge that its real
asset is its staff. "Highly educated (large numbers with PhDs and other
advanced degrees), with a broad range of experience, multinational (representing some 120 nations), multidisciplinary, motivated, determined,
optimistic, self-confident, and sometimes arrogant are descriptive terms
that come readily to mind" (Marshall 2008:80). The Bank initially
adopted two principles for recruitment: "First, that appointees shall have
a high order of competence; and second, that the staff be recruited with
due regard to geographical representation" (Annual Report 1946:7).
Qualifications and competence have always been given greater weight
than geographical representation. Careful selection would, in the long
run, pay large dividends in the form of efficient and sound operations.

   The staff is just first rate. It is unusual for international organizations to keep people in this high calibre. The cynical view is: we
   get around diversity by hiring people from 10 graduate schools.
   There is little pressure to hire outside from the merit dimension.

The senior officer may have overstated the narrowness of the graduate
education. It is true, however, over 20 percent of the staff have PhDs

and the share goes up to 25 percent among the Bank's economists. Even if some of them did not come from Harvard, Yale, Princeton, Stanford, Oxford, or the LSE, they have often had some short-term training at Harvard or other ivy-league universities (Figure 2.1, Table 2.2).

As the size of the Bank expanded, the principles of recruitment did not change. The Bank began with only a staff of 26, with 12 EDs and 38 member countries (less than one person per country!!). In the

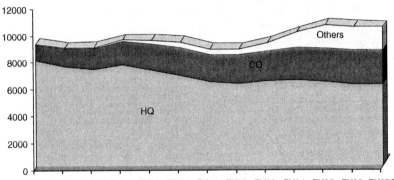

Figure 2.1 IBRD Staff by HQ and CO Location, FY95–FY07Q3

Note: CO—country office; HQ—headquarters.

Source: Human Resources (HR), World Bank, "Strategic Staffing Update Paper," June 2007.

Table 2.2 Grading System

Grade	Representative job titles	Staff at grade level %
GA	Office Assistant	0.1
GB	Team Assistant, Information Technician	1.1
GC	Program Assistant, Information Assistant	12.0
GD	Senior Program Assistant, Information Specialist, Budget Assistant	9.4
GE	Analyst	10.1
GF	Professional	18.2
GG	Senior Professional	29.2
GH	Manager, Lead Professional	16.5
GI	Director, Senior Advisor	2.8
GJ	Vice President	0.4
GK	Managing Director, Executive Vice President	0.1

Source: World Bank, *The World Bank Annual Report 2007.* Washington, D.C.: The World Bank, 2008:9.

following six months, the Bank recruited 150 people; within a year, the total number of employees at the Bank reached 300. The fastest growth was in the tenure of McNamara: from 1,600 in 1968 to 5,700 in 1981.

By the end of March 2007, the Bank employed 10,337 active salaried members: 9,308 regular staff and over 1,000 consultants on various terms. Once a relatively homogeneous cadre of engineers and financial analysts based solely in Washington, D.C., they have developed into a multidisciplinary community that includes economists, public policy experts, engineers, environment and social policy experts, and other social scientists, including political scientists; they are spread across the world. About 30 percent are in the field.

Traditionally, the staff had made the Bank a career with a promotional path (see table 2.2). This changed significantly in the past decade, after the adoption of the Strategic Compact in 1997.

Between 1998 and 2003, "close to half of the Bank's operational staff at GE+ at June 1997 left, replaced by new staff with new skill sets" (HR 2004:1). Many new recruits are mid-career professionals employed to fill a skills void; they joined the Bank because the Bank's programs expanded significantly in terms of coverage. In addition, the Bank has always employed a number of ex-academics who left universities in early or mid-career. 'I left Harvard and entered the Bank, no regrets,' explained one regional chief economist. 'This is where actions take place.' Another said, 'The Bank had leverage to run surveys which I could not have access to as an academic.' A third recalled, 'After I received my tenure, life at the university became too comfortable. I took my sabbatical for a year here and then extended for another; 25 years later, I am still here doing exciting things, which I would never have the opportunity to do as an academic.' Another added, 'I left Harvard because my ex-students went to do all the exciting and real things with the collapse of the Soviet Union.'

Professionals from other fields have joined the Bank with a commitment to development and the desire to get their hands dirty. Some are engineers and some are lawyers. One explains:

In August 1991, I was in Budapest advising on privatization when the news about Yeltsin in Moscow came. Everything was silent in Budapest. It was actually quite dramatic. A couple of days later after I came back to DC, I got a call from the Bank, saying that the Soviet Union was falling apart and the Bank was going to need a lot of people and it would really like me to come in. It was like landing the man on the moon for the first time, going to

Central Asia and the former Soviet Union. I just decided it was a piece of life I was not going to pass up, even with less than half of my pay.

These mid-career recruits often are happy to contribute in their areas of expertise and leave management to 'those with political nous.'

Another sign of diversity is the range of professions. Economists and engineers were joined by an increasing number of social scientists—political scientists, sociologists, and lawyers—and people with special training such as environmental engineering or environmental economics.

Diversity in nationality, gender, and race is a key issue in terms of both recruitment and promotion. The Bank tried in the past decade to increase the number of its staff as well as those in management positions from Part II countries (i.e., all except the top 26 rich countries). Contrary to criticisms that the Bank had no staff from developing countries (Woods 2006:190), the Bank staff came from 164 countries at the time when the critique was made (Table 2.3).

Most Bank staff welcome diversity and see it important to work with people who have local knowledge and appreciation of local conditions. Internationally recruited staff (IRS) are often said to mimic the countries they are from: some are relaxed; others tend to be quarrelsome. Some are quiet, others devious. Some are headstrong, others emotional.

Diversity has raised a few concerns too. Some fear overemphasis on diversity might undermine the merit system and the incentive structure. Others wonder whether the effort of diversification is more artificial than real. After all, half of the Bank staff received some of their education from only 20 or so universities (HR 2004:47). This is particularly the case for those from developing countries, who are often the social and political elite in their own countries and get their education in American or European universities. For example, one former VP of the Bank was a Tanzanian national. The son of a diplomat, he was educated at Harrow School and received a PhD in engineering from Oxford and an MBA from Harvard Business School. Many argue that it is not their background but their education and socialization that make them accept the basic tenets of the Bank. As Ralph Miliband put it, "The social provenance, and the education... of top civil servants makes them part of a specific milieu whose ideas, prejudices and outlook they are most likely to share, and which is bound to influence, in fact to define, their view of the 'national interest'"—in this case, the interest of the Bank (1973:111).

Table 2.3   Diversity Indicators, IBRD Net Staff, FY02-FY07Q3

Indicator	Reference	FY02	FY03	FY04	FY05	FY06	FY07Q3	Benchmark
Part II	Managers	34.4%	37.3%	39.9%	41.7%	42.2%	42.3%	43–48.5%
Gender	GF-GG staff	39.9%	39.9%	40.0%	40.9%	41.3%	41.6%	45%
(Female)	Managers	24.7%	27.1%	26.7%	26.6%	28.4%	28.1%	30%–35%
Race (SSA/ CR)	HQ-Appointed GF+	8.2%	7.9%	8.2%	8.6%	8.4%	8.7%	10%

Note: SSA: Sub-Saharan Africa; CR: Caribbean Region.

Source: Human Resources, World Bank, "Strategic Staffing Update Paper," June 2007, p. 14.

To respond to these concerns, a Bank Human Resources paper, "Evolving from Diversity to Inclusion in the World Bank Group," notes that "diversity is not only about the indicators we monitor—nationality, gender, race—but about different backgrounds, perspectives, styles, personalities" (HR 2004:45). It emphasizes a shift from *diversity* to *inclusion*, "characterized by an enabling environment that positions an organization to attract and retain diverse staff, by ensuring that all groups—regardless of characteristics such as gender, age, race, source of degree or any other diversity dimension—have fair chances for favorable career outcomes" (HR 2004:45).

Young Professionals

In the 1950s and the early 1960s, the Bank was able to recruit experienced mid-career professionals. As its programs expanded and national economies thrived, it became difficult to find sufficient number of qualified mid-career professionals willing to relocate to Washington, D.C. The Bank in 1963 created the Junior Professional Recruitment Program to bring "outstanding young university graduates into the Bank for intensive in-service training, working in at least two departments and, in most cases, taking part in one or more field missions to member countries" (Annual Report 1964:17). Two years later, the program was renamed the Young Professional (YP) program. The YP program is one of the success stories of the Bank. Its recruits have formed the backbone of the Bank staff, especially in managerial positions. For example, five of the six current RVPs came out of the YP programs in the 1970s and the early 1980s.

The YP program seeks to attract a small group of highly qualified development professionals under the age of 32. On an average, 10 percent of the total annual recruits for IBRD come through it. Once recruited, these young graduates spend two years on assignments, organized around six-month rotations in various regions and sectors. They are encouraged not to specialize in one sector or one country. Many choose to work in the field. They are thrown straight into the fray and are trusted to get things right. There is supervision and assistance, but they are also given a lot of freedom and trust. This is the way the Bank, at its best, develops its staff. The YP program gives these young recruits a head start. Thereafter, they manage their careers by themselves, just like the rest of the staff. But, 'the Bank is not a "one-man" institution; loners do not do well.' Most former YPs we interviewed attributed their successes at the Bank to their experience during the rotation and the mentors who supported them thereafter. 'With active mentoring,' explains one senior official, 'we can fully utilize the talent and make strategic deployment when we need it.'

The program has changed significantly since its inception. For example, a female graduate from Fletcher School of Law and Diplomacy was encouraged by a Bank recruiter to apply for a position in the YP program in 1970; her initial application was returned with the request that 'next time include your typing speed.' Fortunately, the recruiter followed up his initial suggestion and rang the dean at her university before applications closed. She was listed for interview. The discouragement continued. The human resources representative told her there was an upward optional quota of one woman and was more concerned to ask how long she would stay. An Indian director responsible for helping select YPs told her that he did not agree with employing women, but, as the interview had been scheduled for an hour, she had to stay. After she reported for her first assignment, the director called out, 'Send him in.' When she was sent to the Latin American desk, she was told by a director, 'Sorry, the region is not ready for women yet.' After several such encounters, she went to the Bank president. McNamara said, 'I can get you appointed, but I cannot watch over you and protect you.' He then called the director of human resources, ripped into him, and said, 'You are meant to avoid such problems.' Of course practices have changed and hiring qualified females is no longer a problem.

Two key features remain. First, the YP program remains very competitive. Each year, about 10,000 applicants meet the minimum requirements, which include academic record, professional/country experience, and commitment to development. About 1,500 are short-listed, and only 35 are eventually chosen. Second, despite all the efforts to make the institution inclusive, a survey of the recently recruited YPs shows a high proportion have PhDs—65 percent among those recruited in 1996, 2001, and 2006. Their universities remain concentrated (74 percent from universities in the United States or the United Kingdom). In 2004–2005, 83 were recruited as YPs. Of them, 39 came from American universities; 11 of these were from Harvard, 4 from MIT, and all except one or two were from the traditional leading universities, such as Berkeley, Stanford, and Tufts. There were 22 from British universities—Six from the University of London, four each from Cambridge and Nottingham, three each from LSE and Sussex. The rest came mostly from well-known European universities. In 2006, we found to our delight one YP from Griffith, our own Australian university; that was rare indeed (HR 2007b:10).

These YPs come from both developed and developing countries, but overwhelmingly attended Part I institutions for their highest degree; the United States accounted for 49 percent, the United Kingdom 25 percent, and France 7 percent. For example, in 1999, 2001, and 2006, the total number of YPs was 99—59 of them were from Part I countries and 35 were from Part II countries, but 94 of them received their education in Part I countries (HR 2007b:10). The range of selections may be getting slightly more diffuse, but the competitiveness remains.

Selected FY2007 YP Statistics (HR 2007)

Degree Type

- 26 out of 35 incoming YPs have a PhD, with one having 2 PhDs
- 2 YPs have 4 graduate degrees, 7 have 3

Degree Institution

- The United States (20) and the United Kingdom (9) institutions
- High dispersion
  - 29 different institutions for 35 YPs
  - No more than 2 from any university (Cambridge, Columbia, Cornell, Oxford, Harvard, LSE, Pantheon-Sorbonne)

Academic & Experience Background

- 24 YP have multi-country academic experience
- 10 YPs have attended a Part II university
- 14 YPs have prior WBG experience

They came from a variety of disciplinary fields, but economists remain the largest group. Among the YPs of 1996, 2001, and 2006, 47 percent were economists. Other professions included accounting and finance (4 percent), business (15 percent), engineering (7 percent), environment (2 percent), health (7 percent), IT (1 percent), social sciences (15 percent), urban (3 percent) (HR 2007b:8). Many at the Bank have welcomed the diversity in professions but are concerned that YPs trained in other fields might not be as ready for managerial positions as macroeconomists.

This chapter provides a brief introduction to the Bank, its changing mandates, and its players. The initial mandates and the formal structure of the Bank can provide a framework for analysis. They can identify what observers think the different actors ought to do and the formal relationship players may have. They do not tell us what happens, whether the EDs have the will or capacity to determine what the staff of the Bank do, whether or how widely presidents can exercise their undoubted authority. Neither do they explain whether, how, or why RVPs and staff are able to influence the decisions of the Bank. That is the purpose of the next five chapters.

CHAPTER THREE

Politics and Management

All organizations face a question of control. There is no shortage of arguments that the Bank is run exactly as the Articles of Agreement state: "The Executive Directors shall be responsible for the conduct of the general operations of the Bank, and for this purpose, shall exercise all the powers delegated by the Board of Governors" (Article V, Section 4[a]). The question becomes the degree of control that the states can, or should, exercise through their EDs. If the Board is meant to control decision making, how do the 24 EDs exercise their authority? If the Bank is a presidential institution, does the formal presidential authority equate power with control? We argue there is a danger in taking formal descriptions literally. Studying domestic politics, few would argue that the British monarch or its representative in a constitutional monarchy, such as Australia or Canada, determines national policies, even though the Queen or the Governor General gives the royal assent to all legislation and appoints the prime minister. Nor would anyone argue that the president in a presidential system, like the United States, or a hybrid system, like France, makes all the decisions either. So why should the Bank operate precisely on the line of the formal constitution?

The issue of control is more about relationship than the formally defined authority. What is the relationship between the EDs and the president, between the president and the Bank bureaucracy? What are the levers available, and how have they been utilized? These relationship beg for examination because of "the special difficulties of the international civil servants [derived] in part from the institutional loneliness"—the president serves as both the prime minister and the chief bureaucrat, while each of the vice president units is a ministry without ministers (Claude 1971:192). This chapter explores these relationships—EDs and presidents and presidents and the senior management—by examining the formal rules and, more importantly, the norms, the culture, and changing relationships over time.

Executive Directors and Presidents

In theory, the ultimate political control of the Bank rests in the hands of the Board of Governors. In practice, their meetings are "a huge jamboree," and authority is delegated to the Board of Directors (Ritzen 2005:91). The Articles of Agreement give EDs unique roles; they are expected to represent and protect the interests of their countries and convey their governments' policies to the Bank. According to the Code of Conduct for the Board, EDs must "respect the international character of the duty of the President, officers, and staff of the Organizations," and "it is their duty, together with the Alternative Executive Directors, to devote all their time and attention to the business of the Bank and the Corporation, respectively, that the interests of those Organizations require" (Code 2003:3). Most EDs accept that 'our primary duty is to the Bank.'

Representing the Interests of Member States

Countries naturally push their national interests through their representatives in IOs. How they do so varies significantly from the United Nations, International Monetary Fund, World Trade Organization, and the World Bank. One key feature of the EDs is their 'internationality.' They are Bank employees even though they are sent by their governments. EDs act in conformity with *prior* instruction (or advice), combined with the (informal) *ex post facto* consent of the member states to the Board's major policies. The consent relationship varies across countries and from EDs to EDs. The American ED, for example, has close contacts with the White House and the Treasury. The Chinese ED tends to get specific instructions from the Ministry of Finance. Those representing multiple countries "operate with quite a free mandate" (Ritzen 2005:98). For all EDs, representing single or multiple countries, 'we do not have to act on behalf of our country all the time,' said one ED; 'we also have obligations to the Bank.'

To assert that these EDs are on a short leash from their government, able to bring a clear vision of their government's wishes to the Bank's deliberations, oversimplifies. Even for EDs representing a single country, government is never a single entity. Demands on American EDs, for example, can come from the President, Treasury, State Department, or Congress. Their interests are seldom aligned. It is therefore not unusual for EDs to clash with Congress or even the President or Treasury or State Department officials and make decisions on the basis of their own judgment. Jan Piercy, the American ED from 1994 to 2001, was known for her own ideas, initiatives, and outspokenness, both at the Board and with the Clinton administration. The Chinese EDs, according to many senior officials at the Bank, tend to be interested in many things in addition to what concerns China. The competing domestic demands and wide range of interests of governments create opportunities for EDs, including those representing single countries, to work with the management and the staff for the benefit of the institution.

For EDs representing groups of countries, balancing the interests of their own government, the countries they represent, and the Bank is a way of life. What EDs do in the event of disagreement between the members whom they represent is left entirely to their discretion.

In the group to which the Netherlands belongs, for example, the ED has always been Dutch, and the Alternative EDs rotate among the other 11 countries in the group. The Dutch EDs are from either the Department of Finance or the Department of International Development and tend to serve five or six years. They are assisted by five or six people drawn by rotation from the countries they represent; these assistants can be quite high officials in their own government. With a large group of countries as the constituency, 'you are not only thinking of your country or the countries you represent, you also think of the Bank itself. There has to be some unity in your approach,' recalled a former Dutch ED. 'We do not write the Bank program for the country; we do not run the government, of course, and in that sense, we are *postillion d'amour*.' Our role is something like a 'go-between' or 'intermediary.'

Voting

Bank critics constantly point to the weighted voting system to justify their position that the Bank is dominated by the United States and other large shareholding countries. The formal rules state each ED casts his/her votes weighted according to the subscription each country or group of countries has contributed. The formal rules also demand that important matters, such as an increase in the number of EDs, shall be decided by an 80 percent majority of the total voting power. Since the United States holds 16.4 percent of the total votes, this can be seen as a veto in these cases. Consequently, in principle, it is argued, the weighted voting system guarantees that the battle over the direction of the Bank and major policies takes place in the Board, and large shareholding countries control the institution.

Formal rules often do not explain the actual operation of the organization. 'We simply do not vote,' said one ED. If anyone at the Board says, '"I demand a vote," it is almost like making an allegation,' says another. According to Shengman,

> In the 10 years when I worked at the Bank in various capacities, I only remember twice when the votes were taken. One was in 1996 when the management proposed smoking ban in the building, some EDs, especially those from developing countries opposed it, accusing this as the "American anti-smoking hegemony" and arguing that the Bank was an international organisation and should not be subject to the US laws. We debated this issue for a long time and some EDs were never this excited when any loan and project proposals were debated. At the end, Wolfensohn decided to put this matter to a vote and the anti-smoking side won with a slight majority. The second time it was in 2000 when the management proposed to increase the administrative fee for borrowing. Without any prospect of ending the debate while a new fiscal year was coming, the president called for a vote. (Zhang 2006:227–228)

From the beginning, the Board has operated as a collaborative institution, rather than a competitive one, partly because many EDs are fully aware of the diversity of interests within states or in the group of states they are required to represent. Differences are mediated through formal and informal communication and exchanges. Most of the time, influence has to be exercised through other channels and in other manners. The imposition of decisions through voting seldom achieves the desired objectives in international organizations.

Routine

Even though EDs seldom vote, their routine is heavy, and they are often swamped by details, as many, including the most critical, often note (George and Sabelli 1994:207–222). The EDs meet twice a week as a full Board. As an ED commented, one of the qualities the Bank president must have is to get "this dilatory mob" start at 10 a.m. and "keep our noses to the grindstone" (Drake 1981:5) for full days on Tuesdays and Thursdays. Six Board committees meet two to three hours every other day. In addition to project approval, the Board receives a flow of issue papers, action programs, and policy proposals. The practice of flooding the Board with loads of documents started with McNamara, who wanted to keep the EDs busy and to provide them with a sense of participation "while he was running the Bank" (Kraske 1996:205). "Documents to the Board averaged less than 300 annually in the 1950s...rose to 510 in the 1960s and jumped to 1,140 in the 1970s" (Kapur et al 1997:1183). Nowadays, each ED every week has to go through thousands of pages of documents to prepare for Board meetings. As one ED recalled, 'Yesterday, I had to go through 1,300 pages of documents coming to the Board; 550 documents on 12 different substantive topics and 12 under stream-line guidelines.' EDs are well aware that the initiatives come from the management, and they can only react. They also understand why the president and the management decide to do so: they 'did not want 24 directions—by deluge.'

The heavy schedule of the Board is managed by the Bank secretary, later renamed corporate secretary. The presidents chair the Board meetings, but they have "no vote except a deciding vote in case of an equal division" (Article V, Section 5[a]). By tradition, the presidents set the agenda for the meetings of the Board, with the assistance of the Bank secretary, who is described by some EDs as the president's "control mechanism," but they cannot go about business without its help. The secretary has always held a high position in the Bank hierarchy in order to liaison between the president and the Board, and the secretaries have all had long serving experience. In its first half century, the Bank had only three secretaries. The rationale of Wolfensohn's decision to ask Shengman to be vice president and the secretary followed McNamara's logic: a former ED would be in better position to build bridges between the president and the EDs. Through the secretary, the presidents decide what projects and programs will be submitted for the Board's approval or what kind of policy papers will be given to it for discussion; they determine how things can be done on a daily basis, mediate the different interests among EDs, and ensure their endorsement of management's decisions (Zhang 2006:226–230).

Actions and Reactions

EDs do not take initiatives, even though some EDs might like to think they set the directions for the Bank operations. In practice, they are reactive and responsive. It is a long-established tradition that the president and the management initiate and present the projects, programs, and policies to the Board for the EDs to consider. The Bank's second president, McCloy, stated that "the confidence of investors in the Bank's financial soundness depended on the Bank's arm's-length relationship with governments and with political bodies in general" (Kraske 1996:66). That provided the justification for the absolute priority for the management's initiatives. It was agreed that the Board would *only* consider papers brought to it by the management. The Board is like "an opera" where the president is "the author of the script, the conductor and the prima donna, replacing now and then a failing fiddle or a hesitating violin, and jumping at times among the public to ask for a better performance" (de Groote 1981:8).

The reactive role of EDs is apparent even on the most important business of the Board—approving the programs and projects. According to the Articles of Agreements, all loans (for projects or programs) must be approved by the Board. In the late 1990s, only about 15 percent of the projects went to the Board; since then, even fewer projects have gone there for discussion. It is largely a formality; in a two-hour Board meeting, for example, the EDs can approve ten project or program loans, with amounts ranging from a couple of million to several hundred million dollars. The power of approval is limited. First, a project goes to the Board only once for approval, while the staff handle it through the whole process—from project identification, analysis, appraisal, and negotiation before it comes for approval and thereafter its implementation and completion to the ex post evaluation. Second, the technical complexity and information asymmetry make EDs reluctant to tackle projects: 'Projects can be immensely complicated, and it is very difficult to penetrate into where the real difficulties in a project might lie ultimately,' explained a former ED. 'Projects are very difficult because you can always be hoodwinked by staff who perhaps do not tell you everything,' said another.

Since 'the management makes the judgment on projects,' some EDs insisted, 'the Board should focus on country strategies, policies, and effectiveness.' Others agreed. One ED said,

Policies, on the other hand, are more interesting and can always be discussed by the type of people who are at the Board. It is a good thing in that sense that we have moved away from project approval. There is, of course, the cost involved that you are not quite sure whether the budget flows are really going in the directions of the priority program that is being presented by the government. This is at the core of the big argument between the adjustment loan people and the project loan people.

That has its own problems. A Country Assistance Strategy (CAS), for example, which sets the direction every three years for the Bank program in a given country, is the favored subject of EDs. "Today detailed and frequent discussions of each country's strategies and policies are the board's central fare, requiring fancy footwork to tread carefully around the boundaries of topics with a clearly political character" (Marshall 2008:76). Yet, by the time CAS is presented to the Board, it is more or less a final version, and the country team has already received the endorsement from the government and consulted the concerned EDs, both from shareholding and stake-holding countries.

EDs appreciate the consultation beforehand, while fully aware of their consultative rather than decision-making role:

> There is a wide range of communication with the staff. The staff is very good at communicating with us, and they like to know what they will face. It is one way to lobby/influence the EDs and another way to get their preparation work done.

At the Board meeting when CAS is introduced, the normal procedure is for the ED representing the country to give an introductory statement. As a CD said, 'There is often a mix of relevance and irrelevance from EDs, but there are no surprises. Then I would thank the EDs and the staff and promise to report the meeting back to the government.' The Board, explains another ED, 'of course usually goes along with the management because the document has been prepared with prior communication with major offices.' There are occasional 'loose cannons' in the Board, and if they raise critical questions, the EDs concerned often join Bank staff to defend the document. 'You have the dual responsibility to the Bank and the country you represent, and you have to be very careful not to speak often at all,' explained one ED.

> You do not speak up unless there is something really not correct in your view. Let's say if there were accusations of corruption at some level or other, which is very sensitive, of course. You could

say that you have found that there is another side to this and that there is really no firm evidence that anything had gone badly wrong. Corruption is a serious issue, but you do not want a meeting on the CAS to end up with a feeling that 'gosh, what a terrible mess this country is in, and the money is all going into the wrong direction.' You want to make sure that the money goes to the right direction without evoking bad feelings of the government.

On controversial issues, EDs are cautious about criticizing a CAS because of the potential of 'retaliation' by their colleagues. The fact that EDs are "divided on dozens of other issues outside the boardroom" (Razafindrabe 1981:2) was one of the reasons that McNamara could "go to the Board meeting, asking everyone's opinion, emphasizing the need for consensus, then telling the EDs his own rather different views, inquiring whether anyone had any objections, and then before anyone had the temerity to do so, he had concluded and moved on to the next subject" (Qureshi 1981:11).

This continues to be the practice:

> "Mr Chairperson, from our chair we want to say that we are mildly positive with a number of serious criticisms." It is almost a liturgy, a Board meeting with most of the 24 Board members responding on a topic, mostly without any sign that they have heard what previous speakers have said and with the almost certain reply, that "Staff thanks the Board and will take the comments and considerations into account." (Ritzen 2005:98)

The Board also considers, discusses, and reviews the policy papers prepared by the anchor or the research sections and reports and studies from the OED. These documents do not need its approval, but EDs sometimes spend hours on each without contributing much. For example, on some occasions, the Board meeting starts at 10 A.M. and sometimes ends at 6 P.M. when the whole agenda was to consider and discuss one OED report. This process is often seen as second-guessing, micromanagement, and/or "a waste of talent and money, without contribution to a democratic form of representation" (Ritzen 2005:98). It engages EDs without shifting the direction of the Bank's work

Presidents, management, and staff want endorsement from the EDs to legitimize their activities. Senior officials appreciate what EDs are supposed to do, what they are doing, and where they come from. They are conscious that EDs sometimes need to discuss issues from political point of views. 'What we try to do is to explain our positions, policy papers, and issues by providing excellent technical and economic analyses. Our explanations may not be immediately to their liking, but I think EDs appreciate and respect this.' After all, most of them are civil servants in their own governments, and this is the way they serve ministers at home.

Most Bank staff, especially senior ones, appreciate that the EDs 'are conduits to their governments.' Their participation is necessary for the president to succeed. As former MD Shengman Zhang acutely pointed out to his boss, Wolfensohn, "The Board may not help you accomplish anything, but it can make it impossible for you to achieve anything" (2006:27). Even though 'the Board never gives instructions,' commented another senior officer, 'it is important for us to keep very close ties with many EDs outside the boardroom—we interact with them, brief them on a regular basis, and make sure some things would not end up at the Board meetings and would be settled in a bilateral way.' A sector manager made it even more explicit: 'When we finished all the steps of the project cycle before we sent it to the Board for approval, we would put out feelers, meet EDs, test the temperature; indeed, we maintain regular exchanges with the advisers of the EDs throughout the process.' This is partly to avoid unnecessary direct confrontations at the Board meetings and partly to legitimize what they do.

Enlisting the support of the ED is a common practice, especially when projects have high political risks or are controversial. 'If projects are stuck at the minister's desk, we will go to the ED, asking for help,' said a senior official. 'When an important project is stalled at the minister's desk,' said one ED, 'I will call the government and give them a push.' The support is mutual. When the management decided to revive the Bank's business in large infrastructure projects in early 2000, opposition from NGOs and suspicions from some donor countries were high. Some staff carefully communicated with EDs to get their support. For example, after almost ten years, the Bank decided to resume the Nam Theun Hydro Project in Laos in the late 1990s. The project was designed not only to provide electricity to local people, but, more importantly, to generate income for a country with limited revenue sources. The sector and country staff invited the EDs concerned to the field to see the project and observe how the environmental and social assessments were done. To recruit their support, the team also held numerous workshops, seminars, brown-bag lunches, and other formal sessions to show the EDs that this was the sort of the development initiative the Bank should take.

Senior Bank staff also consciously seek help from the EDs in their region. As one former VP illustrated,

> When I first went to the region, I had no experience or much knowledge of the region. I spent a lot of time talking to the three EDs representing the countries in the region. Later when the new president came and had a different agenda with which I did not agree, the good relationship with the EDs helped a lot.

Sometimes the relationships can be tense. Wolfensohn's violent outbursts often upset EDs (Mallaby 2005). When Wolfowitz decided to suspend a project in Cambodia, the Australian ED warned him, 'Tell us before you take any actions.' When Wolfowitz stormed that 'he ran the Bank,' EDs retorted, 'No, you don't; we do.' That occasion was unique because the action had been self-inflicted. On a day-to-day basis the Board depends on the ideas brought to it by the president and the management. Such a dynamic relationship is often missed in accounts on what the Bank does or does not do.

In sum, the EDs are an integral part of the Bank. They have limited capacity to second-guess the Bank staff; they do not reject projects put before them, and they often play a reactive rather than proactive role in the Bank operations. Most of them want to make a contribution. Bank staff understand that. Indeed, the higher level the officials are, the more appreciation they have of the value of regular contact and close relationships with EDs to anticipate potential problems. There is, however, no indication that EDs could ever develop the capacity to be more than reactive or that they want to, or could, pursue the heroic controlling role desired for them by institutional redesigners and international relations theorists.

Presidents and Management

Presidents tower over the Bank, and determine its international reputation. "The World Bank is very much a presidential institution, with the president exercising substantial authority by mandate (as chair of the board, and with significant power to appoint staff), and by setting a tone; the president is expected to provide strong leadership within the Bank and in the development community more broadly" (Marshall 2008:77). In terms of formal authority, presidents can have a tremendous impact on its operations and other activities, "going beyond the impact of a CEO of any organisation that works in a market" (Ritzen 2005:109). In its history, several presidents managed to "dominate the Bank, its staff, its board of directors, and almost any other audience that needed to be controlled in the pursuit of his mission" (Kraske 1996:204). It is wrong, however, to assume that the Bank of the 1950s, the 1970s, or the 1990s was just Eugene Black, Robert McNamara, or James Wolfensohn writ large. The key was whether the presidents were 'able and willing to provide leadership.'

If, as Robert Cox pointed out, "the quality of executive leadership may prove to be the most critical single determination of the growth in scope and authority of international organization" (1969:205), then presidents depend on their ability to (a) develop a vision of the Bank's role in development; (b) make decisions; (c) trust and delegate; (d) persuade; (e) work with the Board, donor governments, client countries, and staff from the senior management team to the professionals; and (f) establish a reputation and prestige in the public arena and within the Bank. How they interpret the leadership role may be the key to success. The staff expect the president to lead; they also need to be trusted and persuaded, rather than ordered. Presidents need advice and support too, especially from those with long experience, knowledge, and networks, to run the organization.

Presidents are outsiders brought in to run the Bank. There is no guidebook for presidents (or for writers who seek to assess the performance and activities of presidents). Their position provides potential, but their ability to lead varies. We will explore here their visions, their relations with senior management, their management capacity, and their reputation and professionalism, "defined as personal influence of [the Bank's] actions" (Neustadt 1990:ix).

Presidents' Visions

Few presidents came to the position with clear visions about development or the Bank. For many, the appointment came suddenly, as a surprise or a means of departure from a previous position with a degree of dignity. For these leaders any strategies will be developed on the job, as they arrive without an agenda. McNamara initiated his development drive after a year or two at the Bank, having assessed what he wanted to do. He spent the next decade putting his stamp on the Bank's directions. Clausen and Conable had no clear agenda when they took the position and never developed one. Their appointments were sudden; they arrived without preparation. Their lack of experience in development, in international organizations or even in working with politicians made them 'weak' presidents who could rarely take the lead. For example, at the peak of the Latin debt crisis in the 1980s when the flow of private capital dried up, Clausen realized that it was the responsibility of the Bank to keep capital available to the middle-income developing countries, which had been its traditional clients, and to the poorest countries, which had also been affected. Because of his advocacy of an active role of the Bank, the Reagan administration refused to reappoint him for a second term.

Conable, a conservative Republican congressman, had to admit that he had not realized the extent to which multilateral development bank lending was more effective than bilateral aid programs, and therefore, it was in the interest of the United States to support the institution (Rowen 1987a). He is seen as coming to the Bank to do what Secretary of Treasury James Baker asked him to—forcing the Latin debtor countries to restructure their economies at the peak of the debt crisis, while he also repeatedly told the public and Congress that "the Bank should be a force of development rather than an agency for managing Third World debt" (Rowen 1986). Preston is often considered weak not because of his ability or what he did during his tenure, but rather because he believed in responding to changes rather than initiating them.

Wolfensohn was the exception. "He arrived with unprecedented enthusiasm for the job: he may have been the only president who actively sought the position over many years after a varied career; and his extraordinary personal skills in many domains—finance, culture, sport—won him the enduring title of 'renaissance president'" (Marshall 2008:49). The departing president McNamara had in 1981 recommended Wolfensohn to the American government as his successor. Wolfensohn campaigned hard for the job ten years later when Preston was appointed and again after he died. He had thought of the role in advance and had a vision about international development (fighting against global poverty) and the Bank as an institution (building a humane and cohesive institution). He was full of ideas, some effective, others less so. These ideas, whether on corruption, HIV/AIDS, comprehensive development framework, or the knowledge bank, showed his passion. He was determined to carry his ideas through no matter how difficult. With a vision, he was able to grab opportunities. His ego, temper, and impatience loomed large in media reports, but they could not dilute his contribution to the Bank and international development.

Wolfowitz was a surprise appointment. He came to the Bank with heavy baggage, but not much vision. Some questioned his 'experience in development,' some were concerned about his 'personality,' and others wondered if he would adopt 'a unilateralist American approach' to redirect the Bank away from the priorities set by his predecessor. To quieten his critiques, Wolfowitz initially adopted a conciliatory tone and cast himself as an international civil servant with a genuine passion for development: "I really do believe deeply in the mission of the Bank [and] it's a unifying mission, and frankly that's going to be fun" (Bowley and Sciolino 2005). With no say in the selection, the Bank staff 'gave him the benefit of doubt.' After all, Wolfowitz had served as the U.S. ambassador in Indonesia in the 1980s. He adopted the big theme promoted by Wolfensohn—anticorruption and good governance. Whatever his real vision about the Bank might be, he was unable to convey it to the world or the Bank staff with his hypocrisy—telling the developing countries to "do as I say, not as I do" by "bypassing procedures and rules" (Ball and Alden 2006).

Katherine Marshall, a veteran of the Bank, summarized the problems (2008:57):

> Wolfowitz came to the Bank with a difficult legacy, because of his prominent role in launching and prosecuting the war in Iraq that began in 2003. He faced three special challenges as a result. He needed first to demonstrate that he had made the shift from a US official to an international civil servant, by changes in style, approach, and stance setting himself apart from the policies of the US administration. Second, he needed to find ways to build both trust and understanding within a notoriously difficult international bureaucracy, establishing alliances and finding ways to understand the institution. And third, he needed to establish at least the first indications of his strategic approach to leading development issues. He failed on all three counts.

Robert Zoellick, former U.S. special trade representative, was well known in diplomatic circles, had wanted the job, and came to it with a number of ideas. When he took over the presidency in July 2007, he adopted six strategic themes for "an inclusive and sustainable globalization." The themes include (1) overcoming poverty and spurring sustainable growth, (2) addressing the special problems of post-conflict states and avoiding breakdown of the state, (3) engaging with middle-income countries, (4) playing an active role in fostering regional and global public goods, (5) advancing development and opportunities in the Arab world, and (6) building on this unique and special institution of knowledge and learning (Zoellick 2007).

Visions give direction and the capacity to stamp a personality and style on the Bank. Few presidents develop a credible vision; even fewer manage the Bank in such a way it can be realized.

Managing the Bank

Managing the Bank requires the president to have a high professional reputation. Public standing leads to the so-called law of anticipated reactions on both sides. Those who work with the president, whether the EDs, management, or the staff, do what they think they must to satisfy requests while they test him out. They in turn expect the president to respect the institutional norms. Doubts existed when both McNamara, as the secretary of Defense, and Wolfowitz, as the deputy secretary of defense, were appointed. McNamara managed to build his reputation as 'one of us' in the international development community and one of the best presidents of the Bank. Wolfowitz was never able to shake off his tarnished reputation as a neocon partly because of his disrespect for the institution and its norms in managing the Bank.

Presidents must work with their senior management: the MDs, the VPs, and the country and sector directors. Their relations define the success or failure of the president as the chief executive officer of the Bank. When they arrive, there is always a cohort of officials in situ—experienced, well informed, and well networked. Suspicion about these long-serving officials is often the main reason for the incoming president to change the management team. Some have done it aggressively, while others are cautious. As a condition, the trio McCloy, Black, and Garner came to the Bank together. McCloy and Black then depended on Garner as a VP to run the Bank, while McCloy convinced the private investors to support the institution, and Black acted as a development diplomat to ensure the expansion of the Bank programs. Black's distaste for administration meant that "he left the responsibility of running the shop to Garner" (Kraske 1996:93).

From the 1960s, insiders acted as deputies because of their knowledge of the Bank and their extensive networks. Burke Knapp served in the latter part of Black's tenure and continued under Woods and McNamara. Absorbed and consumed by his commitment to getting IDA under way and his role in promoting development in India, Woods delegated the task of running the Bank to Knapp. McNamara set the agenda and the direction for the Bank; he also trusted and "respected the experience of Burke Knapp and Peter Cargill, his senior vice presidents" (Kraske 1996:170). Ernest Stern gained increasing influence in the later part of McNamara tenure, as he admitted at the farewell for the president: "I am no longer the same average employee that greeted you 13 years ago" (Stern 1981:15). He then occupied a special position as lieutenant for the following 15 years.

The chief operations officers, whether called vice presidents, senior vice presidents, or later managing directors, can oversee the daily routines. When the president is 'weak,' unable or unwilling to make crucial decisions, these deputies fill up the gap. Stern might not have liked some of the decisions McNamara made, such as the creation of an evaluation department (which according to him looked over his shoulder all the time) or the introduction of the nutrition program ("whoever heard of a Bank lending for health," gasped Stern), but he supported the president because McNamara was the boss (Stern 1981). With Clausen and Conable, who failed to exercise leadership, the staff understood it was their deputies, Ernest Stern and Moeen Qureshi, who ran the Bank. Clausen brought in three key players, the general council, the secretary, and the chief economist, hoping to create what he called "a feeling of brotherhood" and a collegial environment in the management team. The three made limited contributions outside their own immediate concerns, while the management committee created by Clausen "was dominated by the senior vice presidents of finance and operation, who often disagreed" (Kraske 1996:240).

Conable, without management or development experience, chose to switch the two senior vice presidents, Stern and Qureshi, in operations and in finance, hoping to break their grip. He failed: the two deputies ran the Bank and continued to under Preston. Stern was eventually appointed acting president when Preston was hospitalized in February 1995.

Deputies might run the Bank, but they could not set the direction with the same legitimacy as the president. This is the distinction between management and leadership: "Managers do things right; leaders do the right thing" (Bennis and Nanus 1985:21). When the president cannot provide the leadership, the Bank is vulnerable to internal bickering and external attack.

Thus, Wolfensohn was determined to run the institution himself. He had been warned that the bureaucracy at the Bank would "swallow him and within months dictate what he was going to do." He got rid of Stern immediately and insisted that two MDs (Kaji and Koch-Weser) be in charge of operation—"No, no, no," Wolfensohn insisted, "we could not have one as that would allow the person to amass too much power" (Zhang 2006:104). He removed the power of the 'regional barons' who held sway when he first arrived and wanted to run the institution himself. Many in the management moved on; there was only so much space in the sun, and Wolfensohn monopolized it. Toward the end of his first term, U.S. Treasury secretary Paul "O'Neill found it incomprehensible that Wolfensohn lacked a second in command, preferring instead to delegate haphazardly to a chaotic caste of favourites" (Mallaby 2004:291). By then, Wolfensohn's own experience had told him that he needed a deputy to run the institution while he concentrated on setting directions. Eventually, he chose Shengman Zhang, a bureaucrat par excellence, 'who had been asked to run this or that and ran them extremely well and then his portfolio just kept expanding,' commented several senior Bank officials. In 2001 as the long-serving MD Sven Sandstrom retired, Shengman was asked to be the MD in charge of operations in all six regions and the networks. When reminded of his original preference for multiple MDs, Wolfensohn commented, "That was then; you are you and I want you in charge" (Zhang 2006:103–104).

Even though his "ability to inspire trust had always exceeded his ability to trust others" (Mallaby 2004:157), Wolfensohn trusted Shengman to run the Bank. According to Shengman, like Eugene Black, Wolfensohn was neither patient nor interested in administration. Both had a grand vision for the Bank, but did not like to run the shop. Black delegated the responsibility to Garner and Wolfensohn to Shengman. The two deputies were similar: "Garner, a man with a predilection for organization and operation, willingly and effectively played the role of the faithful manager and disciplinarian, allowing Black to rule the Bank as the understanding father figure" (Kraske 1996:93). 'Shengman was a great manager, the man who made the trains run on time, and a stabilizer and a disciplinarian for Wolfensohn, who needed somebody to make him focus and get decisions made in the right way, reasonably rapidly,' stated one former ED. Both presidents depended on their deputies "like an army upon its marshall" (Kraske 1996:93).

To manage the daily routine of the Bank, the deputies need the trust of the president, who in turn needs the respect of the deputies. The working relations between the president and his deputy are summarized by Shengman (Zhang 2006:112–113):

- Never embarrass your boss in public even if he has made a mistake because any slight disagreement between the top management can be misinterpreted and the subject of gossip in a large bureaucracy.
- For him as well as for the interest of the institution, in private, one needs to be firm and frank in dealing with the boss to prevent

unnecessary mistakes. Indeed, this is part of my responsibility in the position. Even if what I told him might hurt, he would appreciate it afterwards. As the deputy, you cannot always worry about your own interests or be afraid of losing your position.

- Respect your boss, you can gain his trust. This is the key for a good and cooperative relationship.
- At crucial times, you need to be able to make authoritative decisions. On important issues or when you are not sure, always consult him before making the decisions.
- Inform him as much as you can about daily routine, no matter where he is.
- Leave all the opportunities for publicity to the boss. There can be only one boss, one leader in any organization. There is no position for a competitor.
- Being the deputy means a lot of hard work, including making difficult decisions and solving difficult problems.

Wolfensohn could be volatile and impatient, with a "phenomenal temper," as he admitted himself toward the end of his Bank career: "I probably could have been nicer at some times" (2005). His ego was resented, but his commitment was seldom questioned. His senior officers bent at times and fought back at others. They too had their pride and professionalism. The working relationship was not always easy. Mallaby reported the experience of Gautam Kaji, one of the three MDs. One day Wolfensohn lost his temper and demanded the whole management team submit an undated resignation letter. Kaji did not hesitate and dictated a letter: "You wanted a letter; here it is, date it whenever you feel like it" (Mallaby 2004:156). Shengman had a similar experience with his boss, who yelled at and cursed his deputy when he felt that he had been embarrassed at the Board meeting (Zhang 2006:110–111).

One evening at 7:00, I was in my office going through files. The phone rang and somebody was shouting at the other end: "I am very unhappy with you." 15 minutes later, the phone rang again. He was still cursing, "You were so careless and so unprofessional. This afternoon when I reported to the Board, I was embarrassed because of you." By the time he rushed into my office, still steaming, I had already cooled down, telling him: "If you cannot trust me, I do not have to have this job." Then he demanded calling the person in charge. I told him that it was past 8:00 pm and people in the HR had already gone home. "You think everybody is like you and me," I said. "We will have to wait until tomorrow. If we made the mistake, I would take the full responsibility. If the allegation is true, I will resign." Sometime later, Wolfensohn apologized, "Sorry. I should not have lost my temper the other day. You did a good job. I am glad that you did not resign." After this, I drew a conclusion: to work for this kind of boss, one must do three things: first, you must do a good job; second, when the storm comes, you should not be afraid; and third, be ready to resign any time.

Whether the senior management is welded into a team or operates as fiefdoms depends on the president. In his second term, Wolfensohn was more confident in his job. He and his deputy, Shengman, tried to build a senior management team. They understood that the VPs were their first-line generals and needed independence, but there were corporate priorities and broader issues that should be incorporated into the regional and sectoral programs. A weekly meeting of the senior management was necessary to integrate the work in each region/sector with that of the Bank as a whole. It prevented VPs from becoming little barons. Recalled one VP,

> I think Wolfensohn did bring people together, perhaps not always without a little pressure from people who said it was an important thing to do so. We had a weekly meeting and we would have every month senior management days together and once a year we would have a two or three days of senior management retreat at which there was a combination of presentations of important issues and a general discussion with the president about the state of events and issues. In sum, there was a team-building exercise and efforts to prevent VPs from developing into chiefdoms.

There was regular communication between the president and his VPs. E-mail messages were sent to the president at night, anticipating events or issues.

> Vice presidents had a personal e-mail account for Wolfensohn that was separate from his World Bank account. We would send things to him but tried to be selective, not to overload the circuits. We needed to make sure that he would not be caught off guard; he would be informed of the issues that might come out the next day, such as that he might get a phone call on corruption

in one of our countries because there had been an article in the newspaper that day, or Condoleezza Rice might show up at the West Bank and Gaza.

VPs also kept MDs informed. The president and his deputy would call if there were things to be done right away. Open communication between the president and the management team created a congenial working environment. At the end of his era, according to Wolfensohn and Shengman, the Bank operated as a "cohesive organisation" that "cares, and that is conscious of the fact that it is not just money that drives the institution—it is knowledge, it is experience, it is caring" (Wolfensohn 2005).

Wolfowitz wanted none of this. His stint at the Bank showed how not to run the management as a team. Within months of Wolfowitz taking office, any sense of collegiality between VPs and the president disappeared. He got rid of Shengman and other senior members of the management and put two assistants brought in by him on generous open-ended contracts despite the political nature of their appointment. They were given grades GJ, a super-senior grade level that was only exceeded by the MDs, senior VPs of IFC and MIGA, and the president himself. Even though they could not be included in the senior management team, Wolfowitz worked almost exclusively through them. They seemed to be the only people he trusted. He and his assistants regarded running the Bank like running the Pentagon:

> They came to the Bank as if there had been a politically contentious election, and they were the new administration coming in. Therefore, they could remove everybody who was an appointee of the prior administration and thereby the whole administration. At this famous senior management meeting, Robyn Cleveland (Wolfowitz's most abrasive offsider) came in and asked the assembled group of senior managers, "How many of you are political appointees?" After a long pause, somebody said, "Only you!"

Regular senior management meetings were cancelled. Communication was shut down. E-mail messages providing information and advice received no response. Requests for decisions were left unanswered. There was a sense of void: 'He never responded to anything we, as VPs, sent him, and he did not seem to be interested in anything that we told him, nor did he ever ask for our advice.' Unlike his predecessor, Wolfowitz never 'confronted' his senior people. 'He went straight to the people several levels below, leaving the VPs and sometimes even CDs in the dark, many senior managers recalled. 'Wolfowitz was a man with an incredible amount of distrust.' Worse still, 'Wolfowitz played on the feelings of competition among senior managers.' Very quickly, 'Wolfowitz was systematically destroying the culture at the Bank—you are part of the institution, not only an individual; you work with your peers, your managers, and your colleagues that support you—and I will forever hold that against him.'

The difference between Wolfensohn and Wolfowitz in terms of management was their capacity to motivate. However difficult the staff found Wolfensohn as an individual, however frustrating his vanity and insecurities, no one doubted his commitment, his industry, and his preparedness to make difficult decisions and take the responsibility that went with them. By contrast, and to widespread surprise, Wolfowitz refused to make difficult decisions, and on those sensitive issues, he preferred his VPs to do so as long as they were to his liking and from which he could distance himself if necessary. Neither was he prepared to explain his decisions or lack of them. In essence, during a short two-year period, Wolfowitz was never able to *manage* the Bank.

Selecting the Management Team

The Bank is a presidential institution partly because the president is responsible for the appointment and dismissal of the officers, who serve at the pleasure of the president. Often, even among senior officials, the selection of VPs was a mystery; these jobs were never advertised. For 'king-makers,' such as Knapp or Stern, 'the Bank was their life; you tended to expect they got where they were.' Even then 'VP selection is a black box.' For almost ten years after the 1987 reorganization, some believed a 'mafia system' dominated the selection process—'relational meritocracy' with each layer of officials bringing personal armies with them. This changed in the late 1990s, but a grooming system was not in place until Wolfensohn's second term.

Then a committee of VPs met every month for succession planning. The committee would put together a list that these VPs considered to be highflyers with potential for promotion, initially for CD positions and possibly later for VPs. The committee would give this list to the MD and the president if and when they had to make strategic postings. These highflyers were observed closely. 'Shengman spent a lot of time going out and visiting a lot of countries' according to a VP, 'not because he really wanted to visit the countries, but because he really wanted to see how the directors were doing.' They were able to fill the vacancies in senior management with people 'who were very devoted to the Bank's mission, people who could produce good results and perhaps people who fundamentally did not want to be a VP because they wanted neither rank or title.'

When Wolfensohn decided to change a VP, for example, the selection committee, chaired by the MD, decided who the candidates were and who would be selected. Once the committee finished deliberations, Shengman would take the recommendation to the president, who often "asked what my view was and often my view would be the same as the result of the committee, because I chaired the committee." Sometimes the government of a candidate or senior officials at the Bank would try to intervene in the process, but seldom successfully:

> Once when we were trying to select a director for the African region, one of the candidates on the short list was the special adviser of the president of her country. She was well qualified for the position and could have easily been selected. Then, the committee received a phone call from Wolfensohn, saying this African president would like his person to be selected. The committee members became nervous and suspicious right away, and she did not get the appointment. (Zhang 2006:252)

Wolfensohn could be lobbied by the Bank officials too.

> In 2003, the Bank had to select a Vice President for the Middle-East and North Africa. After going through the search and review processes, we decided on two candidates. To be cautious, I went to the field to see how they worked. One was young, while the other older. Each had his own specialties and advantages. Balancing everything, I thought the older one was more suitable for the job, while the departing VP wanted the younger one to succeed him. At the end the selection committee agreed with me. That departing VP went to see the President, asking for help. Wolfensohn then called me. I explained to him the process, and later to the departing VP too. The day before the announcement, Wolfensohn came to my office, asking me to reconsider the decision, because the departing VP had gone to him again, trying to sell his idea. I told the President, "Let's ask this VP to come to my office now." He came. In front of both of them, I explained my decision and then said, "The committee has made a decision. We are not going

to change it even if the President disagrees. Of course, he can veto
it." (Zhang 2006:113)

The nomination stood.

Candidates for VP positions were aware that VPs serve at the pleasure
of the president. Chemistry between the president and senior managers
is important for the smooth operation of the institution. When it does
not exist, the president often changes his team without too much fuss:
'Historically, the Bank has had a tradition of strong vice presidents, and
when there were major disagreements, they would simply say, "Okay,
pick your own team; I am gone".' Since the VPs are almost at the top
of the hierarchical ladder within the Bank, the outgoing VPs can get
a lateral transfer to another VP position, can rarely get a promotion to
a senior VP or MD position, or can 'step down' to a director position.
Often they choose to leave.

When asked how often a president would 'force out'—a synonym of
'fire'—VPs, a senior official explained,

> It happened in a couple of occasions, and the most famous case
> was with Ernie Stern, who used to be really important at the Bank
> for a couple of presidents, and he was asked to go because he was
> too powerful. There were other cases, but it does not happen to
> VPs frequently. The MDs maybe because they are too close to the
> president, but not VPs. We have been here a long time, seen ev-
> erything, and known how the institution works.

When VPs have to be removed, by tradition, they are treated with
respect:

> Wolfensohn made a decision to change our VP, who was very
> well liked by the staff and who did not want to leave the position.
> Wolfensohn paid respect to the staff and to the VP by coming
> over to *our* office, in *our* conference room and telling us directly
> what he was doing and why. He told us that he needed our VP
> in another position, and it was a promotion. He also told us that
> he did not want us to walk away that day mad. There was a lot of
> respect paid by him. We did not like the decision, but we did not
> feel that he had disrespected either the departing VP or us.

When senior managers, MDs, or VPs, are under siege by the president,
there is little that others, EDs or their peers, can do except offering moral

support. "From the start, Wolfowitz and his team made clear that he wanted eventually to reduce the number of vice-president units, and replaced some of those whose jobs were not limited" (Ball and Alden 2006). Senior managers understand it is the president's prerogative to choose his team; it was the process that alienated so many. Shengman reputedly told Wolfowitz when he became the president: 'My commitment and responsibility is to this institution; presidents come and presidents go; my job is to make this institution work and to provide whatever advice you want. You have my services.' Wolfowitz replied immediately, 'Absolutely, Shengman, I could not possibly run this institution without you.' Then he basically froze Shengman out of everything. The same technique was used with other respected senior managers—freezing them out from decision making to force them to resign.

Wolfowitz was never an institutional person, never wanted to play the institution game. The committee of VPs under Wolfensohn to plan the deployment of highflyers was abolished right away. Instead, Wolfowitz would choose people at will. For example, he encountered a water expert in India, not a manager, two levels below the director level. He made him CD for a large and important developing country in another region without going through any due process. When VPs sought approval for the appointment of country or sector directors or even country representatives, Wolfowitz could reject the recommendations even though the candidates had been vetted and had gone through interviews and panel selections. He never tried to explain his reasons, but it become clear that he did not trust the VPs he had inherited.

When some senior managers were to be forced out and EDs raised questions about it, Wolfowitz replied that he did not want to engage in discussion, that it was his decision and that was an end to it. His apparent capriciousness undermined his authority, and his way of politicizing the institution was considered by many senior managers as the worst possible sin. 'This is a very technocratic organization, and when someone who is very good, very competent, very energetic, very devoted, and highly respected was pushed out just because he was honest and because he told the president the truth, it sent a chill through the institution.' In addition, Wolfowitz and his assistants never showed respect to these senior managers. One VP, for example, asked whether he could leave at the end of the fiscal year; the reply was negative, and he had to go right away. Disrespect for the staff was considered as disrespect for the institution. Dismissing senior officials were not unusual; many presidents had gradually shuffled their senior ranks. What was new was the rancor.

Legitimacy and Reputation

The standing and legitimacy of presidents is an essential leadership resource, internally and externally. Despite claims that the Bank is an instrument of the American government, the institution was created as an international organization; people at the Bank do not represent their countries of origin. Political impartiality is seen as a crucial requirement for a president by those who emphasize the Bank as a bank and those who emphasize the international nature of the institution. All presidents have their own political views, and 'most of us understand that the Bank has some political overtones.' Yet, if a president cannot separate his personal political views from what the Bank does, the legitimacy of the president and the Bank as an institution comes to question.

For instance, in the Middle East, the Bank has always had to tiptoe through minefields. It has been criticized for doing too little or too much for the Palestinians, for its close or distant relationship with the OPEC, and for its work in Iran and Iraq (Kapur et al 1996:977–981; Kraske 1996:182–183). Wolfensohn showed special interest in the region, especially the Bank's role in assisting the Palestinians. After the second intifada in 2001, Wolfensohn took an unusual step of making public his views on the economic havoc caused by the Israeli-Palestinian war. He criticized the Israeli decision to close the borders that prevented 180,000 Palestinians from working in Israel and instructed the Bank staff to work out a way to resolve the impasse. They approached it as a development issue, presenting security in economic terms. The Bank sought to be politically impartial in negotiating with the Israelis on opening the border and providing assistance to the Palestinians.

When a sense of legitimacy is lost, the Bank loses leverage internally and externally. When Preston was unable to cope with the campaigns against the Bank in the mid-1990s, many inside felt the Bank was drifting. When Wolfowitz's problems became publicly known, they created a range of obstacles for the staff. Why, the clients argued, should we be required to crack down on nepotism in the civil service when the president of the Bank does it himself? The staff broke into open and public revolt. There were public petitions, from CDs and the governance staff, both asking that the issue be resolved quickly as their jobs were becoming difficult. By the time Wolfowitz left, his position had become untenable because he could not deal with client countries on an equitable basis nor staff whom he was supposed to lead. Reputations matter.

In sum, the picture of the president is one of a powerful official, but a position where the influence needs to be husbanded and used wisely. The powers are to command and to reorganize, but not to hire and fire except at the senior levels and then only with difficulty. Presidents must mobilize and motivate. When reputation and legitimacy are lacking, as happens in the gap between a departing and an incoming president, the Bank 'goes into automatic pilot.' When a strong president leads, the Bank is run as a presidential institution. When presidents do not, strong VPs or even CDs can keep the Bank on the 'auto pilot.'

Vice Presidents

VPs, especially RVPs, are the vital players in the smooth operation of the Bank. They are 'accountability managers,' said one CD. 'They can bring some coherence to a complex institution,' said another. Even when there is a strong president, like Wolfensohn, directions from the president's office are mostly broad and need to be translated into specific programs. VPs welcomed the strategic directions provided by Zoellick, but also admitted that little detail followed. They had to make it happen. As one RVP frankly pointed out,

> I have been a VP for three and half years, and nobody has told me what to do. It is a little scary. Zoellick has come in and given a structure and told people in general but no one has sat down with me and said, "I would like you to double the lending, open an office in this country, or do this or that." Shengman used to provide some of that, and I think the president now thinks his MDs are doing this, but they are not. It works now because most RVPs are very experienced people in the Bank. I do not know what they want, but this is what they get; they are getting a well-managed group, and I am going to do the lending.

In early 2004, the management established the Bank-wide organizational Effectiveness Task Force to "consider ways to improve the effectiveness and efficiency of the Bank's operational complex in managing the result" (Zhang 2005). The task force recommended a region-driven process of strategic planning, budgeting, and team-based delivery programs. It proposed that "top-down strategic decisions come first" (Task Force 2005:16). The strategies and policy directions would be set at the corporate level by the president and the management team collectively, and then each RVP unit would translate the expenditure directions and performance targets to country units and sector units. This top-down approach would only work when the management was able and willing to set the direction for the Bank in general and in regions in specifics. When there was no direction given to RVPs, they would have to 'pick up all these little clues the president sent out and then make their own decisions.'

Because of the top-down approach, VPs are granted a lot of freedom to run their region or sector. The position is high enough for them to become 'barons' easily if there is no sense of team generated by the president. They must work with the president, their peers, and the country/sector directors. When the president shows an interest in a country, a region, or a sector/subject, it can empower or debilitate the VPs; the RVP needs to make sure the relevant CD is well informed about what the president wants. Some countries will never hit the radar. Some regions will receive little attention. VPs will fill the vacuum. If the president has no views or priorities, the VP will take the lead, assuming that, until told otherwise, their priorities will be those of the region and the Bank.

Wolfensohn was never shy in telling people what he wanted in terms of the general directions or projects or programs in a specific region or country and indeed often pushed very hard at those agendas; Wolfowitz was just the opposite by giving no directions. 'He showed no interest in my region and did not care what I was doing there, but he meddled a lot in Africa and in the Middle-East.' This made life extremely hard for the VPs in the regions in which he was interested. When the president makes a mistake or upsets the client countries, it is often up to the VPs to do the damage control. Under Wolfowitz, senior Bank officials had to spend a lot of time in damage control by explaining the Bank's positions to the staff as well as the client countries. Unlike his two predecessors, Zoellick was never too aggressive or too passive. At the management meeting he held every morning,

> Zoellick would gently nudge people in the direction he wanted to go. For example, he would say, "I want a response to the food crisis; let's go out and do something." You respond to the food crisis. This is fine in dealing with specific emerging issues by this sort of driving the ship by telling the crew what to do, but it is not a long-term strategic planning. No one sits down with the VPs to work out, say, a three-year or even a year plan that would outline what the general direction of the Bank program in a region

would be. This is nice, and it gives us a lot of discretion to share the regional programs. It is extremely difficult for those coming from outside.

In practice, VPs tend to be insiders, have served at the Bank for a couple of decades, and carry the institutional memory. When an incoming president takes up his position, he must rely on experience. The advice provided by the experience and institutional memory may or may not be welcomed. Wolfensohn was horrified on his first trip to West Africa to discover that the Bank was required to provide defensive lending—giving loans to countries to ensure that they did not default on their previous loans. When he exploded in outrage, his VP for Africa, Kim Jaycox told him not to be naïve: "That's the way it works. You may not like it, but that's the way it works," he [Jaycox] screamed. "We can't forgive the debt, so how do we get out of it" (Mallaby 2004:104–105)?

Since VPs are located in the HQ and most of their CDs are in the field, they have to spend time talking to the CDs on the phone at any time during the day or night. 'We as VPs are in a crucial and strategic position,' they argued. 'We connect the management team with the staff, and we are the one who have to set strategies for countries and sectors, decide what projects and programs to deliver, and then monitor the delivery.' It was described as herding cats. Most RVPs travel the regions, talking to the field staff and client government agencies and finding out their needs and capacity to absorb the assistance. Some RVPs spend as much as 40 percent of the year on the road.

Putting together a range of data on VPs and their responsibilities, we can come up with a routine of a composite RVP when in Washington, D.C. It could include

- getting to the office at 6:30 or 7:00 in the morning to clear all the e-mail messages from the country directors, EDs, the government officials of the client countries, staff, and sometimes even NGOs;
- meeting with the operations director, special adviser, and the secretary early each day, perhaps to discuss the "top ten" things of the day (actually often more than ten); 70 percent of the time one of the ten things would involve who would visit which country in the region—the president, MDs, EDs, or VPs; and
- attending, 8.30 a.m., under Zoellick, the president's daily meeting with all VPs (in the absence of a VP, the operations director would step in).

From 9 a.m. on, there would meetings with sector staff doing projects in the region, with CDs or country managers who were in the HQ, with human resources people on the regional strategic assignments, with bilateral donors, and with NGOs. In some regions, government officials from donor as well as client countries can demand meetings and briefings. RVPs also spend time with EDs, especially those representing the countries in the region, outside the Board meetings to exchange information and build trust. Sometimes they have lunch with other VPs. 'It is hard for you, as a VP, to understand what other VPs are doing in other places' unless special efforts are made. It is easy to be enclosed in silos. When the president does not take the lead, some VPs informally meet to exchange information, discuss common concerns, and plan for strategic deployments.

The Staff and Their Organizational Culture

In one sense, the Bank is an institution where 'ideas are freely and fiercely debated.' 'Yes-men do not climb high in this hierarchical institution,' neither would they be respected by their colleagues (Zhang 2006:244). In another sense, "speaking truth to power" is as serious an issue for the Bank staff as for domestic civil servants. Staff are delegated considerable trust and discretion, but they are under constant criticism and scrutiny by their peers and supervisors, described once as "slash and burn" to reflect the cut and parry of internal criticism (Marshall 2008:82).

Trust and Discretion

"The World Bank, for all its flaws, was the product of the best minds in development," commented Mallaby (2004:171). The best way to allow these minds their maximum potential, the management recognizes, is to follow the principle of "trust them, rely on them and mobilise them" (Zhang 2006:80). The Bank could not be run hierarchically even though it has a hierarchical structure. Its operation remains quite flat, with constant interaction between the staff and senior management.

Compared with other international organizations, the Bank offers broad scope for its staff to take initiatives. People with new ideas can share and discuss them with their colleagues and supervisors and are expected to "sell" their ideas to the directors or VPs. Their ideas can be picked up by the president or the management and then become formal policies. Many at the Bank comment, 'We are encouraged to come up with ideas and have the freedom to sell our dreams.' Good managers, from the president to the VPs or the directors, know how to channel their energy and the intellectual curiosity of their staff. 'The president handed me a check of $500 million and said, fix it and come up with some ideas.' This is even true with the staff at the lower level of the bureaucratic ladder: 'This is your envelope and your budget; try to find the best way to do it.' Idiosyncrasy is not seen as a problem. This description contradicts the popular image of a common set of policies pushed from the president to the management to the Bank staff, from the research to operations and where opposition is not tolerated.

'When I graduated from the YP program,' one director recalled, 'I was assigned to MENA and I had a great boss, who asked me to be the team manager for a $150 million project in Tunisia. "We will train you," he said, and this was how I learned.' A senior official remembered the days when they wanted China to join the Bank: "In 1979, there were indications that China was exploring the possibilities of "joining" the Bretton Woods institutions. Those of us in the Bank working then on Vietnam were finding excuses to make stopovers in Beijing" (Lim 2005:101). Another director in East Asian added,

> Then China offered us 60 visas, and it wanted "money" people and wanted to know how the Bank worked. We went to China for a month and conducted it like a normal Bank mission. We discussed many concepts that had not been used or known in China. This happened even before McNamara knew it, and it eventually led to the invitation from the Chinese government for McNamara to visit China in April 1980.

In a large and complex institution like the Bank, delegation, formal or informal, of authority signifies the trust the management has in its staff. It is not merely a matter of management style. Shengman used to joke about how "I worked my way up, not to come up to work" (Zhang 2006:223); he delegated responsibilities to VPs so that he could handle the issues he thought strategic for the Bank. As one former VP explained, 'We were supposed to meet once a week. If there was nothing to alarm him, I would just go in and crack a joke and leave in 3 minutes. He let us manage the regional programs and everything coming with them.' Paradoxically, many senior people argued that 'Shengman is an effective operator and a hands-on manager.' Many we interviewed regarded these as the criteria for a good boss—one who delegates but can also be a hands-on manager. One CD described his time at a sensitive place:

> He (the VP) let me alone, which is what I like in a boss. He was very supportive, but he let me run the show, even though it was quite a sensitive post and so inevitably attracted various kinds of flack, particularly when you spoke very much in public, and I did a lot of that. He came to my country a number of times, but he did basically what you would want from a boss: first of all, he was somebody I could go to with something I needed doing; he would be very thoughtful and quite often disagreed with me, which was usually the reason I was uncertain about how I should handle it. He did not otherwise interfere unless he was really worried that I was doing something that was not smart, and a couple of times his advice was really good on this.

Several VPs are known to delegate as well as for being hands-on management. One of them described his relationship with the RVP when he was a CD some years earlier: 'My VP had a certain amount of trust and respect for what I was doing, so he gave me a lot of freedom and there were situations in which I would need to ask him for his views when things were difficult.' This repeated message highlighted one key feature of the Bank culture: trust/discretion and responsibility/accountability come together.

Wolfowitz, according to everyone we interviewed, did not trust anyone except his two 'attack dogs.' He would send them to the field to find out what the people were doing without informing either the RVP or the CDs: 'I knew his assistant told this person in one of my countries what to do when bypassing me,' recalled one CD. 'I then picked up the phone and called him. I told him I did not care what they told him, but he should keep me informed in what he was doing in the field.' Lack of trust created further suspicion and animosity. When trust is lacking, confidence in management collapses.

Institutional Memory

The institutional memory is lodged with the staff. They know what was done in the past, what worked, and what did not. An incoming president, always new to the Bank, relies on experience. VPs, new to a region or a sector, may know little of the countries in the region or the different aspects of the network. They rely on long-serving staff for information and knowledge. The Board has even higher dependence on the staff when EDs rotate every two years or so. That is the continuing nature of bureaucracy: aware of the past, conscious of the present, and hopeful for the future. Institutional memory relates to both knowledge and connections. The international staff will move regularly; internal rules require that postings are for three to five years and, very occasionally, seven. Most senior staff have long memories and experience; they will have worked across more than one region and in more than one area of responsibility. They bring knowledge of what was done elsewhere, knowledge that is one of the Bank's principal comparative advantages.

A second reservoir of institutional memory stores connections in client governments, on who is most inclined to work with the Bank. Often locally employed staff will act the conduits of memory and serve as a vital connecting link (see Chapter 5).

Of course institutional continuity and memory can create problems too. Bitter experience produces cynicism and skepticism, an unwillingness to consider new methods, and a conservatism that sees new proposals as a challenge to past competence and credibility. Standard operating procedures can outlast their usefulness; there were complaints that a 'loan mentality' continued after the emphases had moved to more flexible approaches. Presidents may seek to introduce new blood to shake up the attitudes, but they will have to deal with a phalanx of staff who will explain why new methods will not work. The long service of locally recruited staff can occasionally make it difficult for some CDs.

Further, institutional memory may be easily hollowed out. If the 1970s were the years of the engineers who developed roads, dams, and electricity networks, the 1980s was the decade of the economists. By the end of the 1990s, many of the engineers had gone. In about five years (1998–2003), the infrastructure network suffered serious declines in staff (30 percent) as well as skills (HR 2004). When the Bank wanted to revive lending in infrastructure, it found that much of its institutional memory had been lost. High turnover led to a loss of experience. A review noted that 30 percent of the task team leaders had less that three years experience in the Bank (Task Force 2005:8).

Institutional memory and established procedures, whether beneficial or constraining, must always be taken into account in assessing opportunities for staff. Tradition is invariably contested, but still provides a firm basis from which to start a debate.

Frank and Fearless

'Speaking truth to power' is a difficult issue for all civil servants, domestic or international. In the earlier years, the Bank staff, still relatively small, had a collegial environment. As the institution expanded, it gained the characteristics of all bureaucracies. While the Bank staff have 'tremendous freedom' to argue the case with their supervisors and colleagues, they are expected to follow the rules, procedures, and norms. Open opposition to Bank policies outside its walls is not welcomed. They joined an institution, argued a VP. When criticism of the Bank, or rather the IMF and the Bank (critics often do not distinguish between them), over structural adjustment programs in the 1980s and the 1990s attracted public attention, some Bank staff shared the views. How to deal with internal opposition was the question. In 2001, for example, two Bank staff were sent on leave without pay, charged with publishing opinion pieces without permission. As a consequence, the Staff Association held an extensive discussion on the issue of internal opposition or, as some put it, of 'mixing truth and power' and 'thought policy.' Such public cases are still exceptional.

There is always the issue of truth and power. The operation staff, at whatever level, have multiple 'masters'—they are accountable to their supervisors as well as the client countries. The question is, to what extent should the Bank staff, especially RVPs or CDs, take the interests of their client countries as seriously as those of the Bank president or the management, especially when the president's beliefs clash with what VPs/CDs see as the interests of the region/country? When there is trust between the president and the senior management or between the VPs and the directors, 'speaking truth to power' does not seem to be a problem.

For many, who their bosses are determines how they react. 'Our VP is very open and transparent,' people in one region commented. 'She is strategic in thinking and wants to know what we can contribute, and we can always argue with her so long as it is for the benefit of the institution and our client countries.' 'By the way,' another veteran of the Bank asked us, 'did you ask him (RVP) about his argument with a CD? The CD was so courageous in dealing with the RVP, telling him the truth without putting glosses on it for the glory of the Bank or whatever.' Fortunately this RVP was a reasonable person and indeed appreciated the directness of the CD. There were other more nervous accounts. Not all managers are reasonable or take criticism graciously. "'You could never say anything different to (Ernest) Stern or even McNamara if you wanted to keep your job at the Bank,' said one. 'Only those without spine got into the senior position under Wolfensohn,' said another. Perspectives varied.

Bank staff are protected by an open-ended contract system and the Staff Association. They can work until retirement, which is mandatory at 62. They cannot be fired unless they have committed some offence. The system is designed to protect good staff from political pressures and from unfair management. It does have its downsides. It is hard for the Bank to remove even the few who are incompetent. This clearly shapes the incentive structure for people to speak truth to power.

Initially, some presidents had "difficulty accepting the Bank's Staff Association as a representative body" (Kraske 1996:241). Now most agree the management needs staff support for smooth operation and, to forestall problems, should work closely with it. Before the 1997 reorganization, for instance, Shengman met the staff association almost every weekend to secure its support (Zhang 2006:63). In the ten years under Wolfensohn, the Staff Association gained 'a seat at the table'; an environment of mutual trust emerged. At times its support was welcomed. When Wolfensohn expressed his determination to eradicate corruption within the Bank, the Staff Association threw its support behind him, declaring that they were proud of the staff's high standards and that any instance of corruption was a cancer that undermined the health of the institution (Chronology 7–15–98; 1–16–98). It bargained with the management over salary benefits and working conditions and sought to protect staff rights and employment. After coming to the Bank, Wolfowitz broke off effective relations with the Staff Association. It became a leading critic and Wolfowitz's chief nemesis, particularly over the salary rises and promotions for his partner and his advisers.

However, the factors that discourage the staff from speaking up are sometimes more indirect, even insidious. For many the Bank is a career. They can spend 20 or 30 years there and do not want to jeopardize their prospects by speaking out too vociferously. Few individual cases are sufficiently important to persist after the first ideas are rejected. Further, 'G-4 visas [allowing Bank staff to live in the United States] are a big trap, and people fear being tossed out, so they shut up.' Their children have gone to school in the United States, their spouse may have a job there, and they have built a life over the years. If they lose Bank employment, their G-4 visa status requires them to leave the country within two months. Those that have been there 15 years or more may apply for residence, but that takes time. Leaving the Bank disrupts their life.

Does that make them timid? Some worry that people from some developing countries might be too willing to become 'yes' men. 'It does not matter that much whether I would be here in Washington, D.C., Paris at OECD, or London for the British Department of International Development (DFID),' one put it bluntly. 'It makes a world of difference if somebody has to go back to some poverty-stricken war-torn country. How can we expect them to speak to power the way we would do?' The statement may represent the view of only some. It is symptomatic of the concerns that the formal rules may protect staff, but other factors may make them less willing to push their case.

In sum, it is difficult to identify a single Bank with uniform behavior. A former senior Bank official provided a succinct description of the organizational culture of the Bank:

> Bank staff tend to complain, and exuberant, unqualified support for any person or policy is rare...[yet] the World Bank staff is made up of many remarkable people—professional, dedicated, diverse, demanding of themselves and others, hardworking, and above all to the mission of working for "a world free of poverty" (Marshall 2008:83).

Conclusions

The Bank's formal structure conceals a more complex reality. EDs do not dominate; they influence and can sometimes push the Bank toward new initiatives. Presidents have great power if they have the vision, the management skills, and the reputation to mobilize and motivate the staff. RVPs have the discretion to shape their regional strategies. The discretion granted to them depends in part on the president's interest and priorities, in part on their own bureaucratic skills. Initiatives can come from anywhere, from the management and from the staff. We cannot assume that the obvious hierarchy always works like one. That will depend on the way that the staff seize opportunities to shape the agenda. How the organization of the Bank provides those opportunities is the subject of the next four chapters.

We end with an illustration of how innovative staff members can work with a president to give shape and content to a vague idea, an illustration of the belief in the Bank, if you are creative and persistent, you can make it happen. Sam Carlson, lead education specialist, now back in the Bank, tells the story:

> *To improve education in poor countries, my wife, Linda McGinnis (who was also Bank staff), and I came up with an idea to link schools in*

developing countries with those in developed countries through the Internet, a kind of virtual exchange. We presented the idea to our boss at World Bank Institute (WBI). Two months earlier, President Wolfensohn had come up with a similar idea to connect a school in Wyoming to schools in Uganda. This was in 1996 when the Bank was under siege by NGOs, and Congress was threatening to cut funding for IDA. It was important for the Bank to come up with new ideas to help people in developed countries to identify with people in developing countries. Wolfensohn had asked for a briefing on his idea of linking schools between developing and developed countries, but nothing had been done. So he gave responsibility for developing his idea to WBI where, quite coincidentally, we had just proposed to our management this virtual exchange program. So, this became a 'global idea'—the World Links for Development program took off. It was exciting because we had to transform this idea into a reality with no road map, inventing and improvising to make it work. There was no conventional wisdom or research on the issue, and no manager had a view on it. We just knew Wolfensohn supported the idea. Within two years, we connected several hundred schools in 20 developing countries, in Africa, Latin America, and Asia. In fact, with support from the World Bank and trust funds from Canada, Finland, and Japan, we established the first school connectivity in Uganda, Senegal, Zimbabwe, Mauritania, Rwanda, and several other countries. This even included broadband, satellite-based school connectivity for remote Ugandan schools located far from any phone line, where our recurring problem was monkeys who kept urinating on the satellite hardware, eroding the wiring (cages around the satellite dishes finally stopped them).

In August 1998, we briefed Wolfensohn in Wyoming, who said our program was too small, not ambitious enough. How could we scale it up? We started talking to the private sector. This was at a time when dot-com start-ups and the IPO market were at their peak. We proposed to approach venture capitalists who would offer pre-IPO stock from start-up companies to World Links, which we could sell after the IPO and convert into dollars. This was being done successfully in Silicon Valley. In other words, this was not a conventional Bank project. So we proposed to Wolfensohn that we spin off the program from the Bank and create a nonprofit organization, World Links. Our funding and work exploded; although the doc-com market crashed, and our innovative idea did not pan out, we did raise a lot of support from corporate foundations and individuals, in addition to bilateral funding. For two years I remained as Bank staff in WBI, but also headed this nonprofit organization, World Links, as its executive director, which meant I had line responsibility within WBI as a G-level staff and reported to the board of directors of World Links. This became *increasingly untenable as the organization expanded, as if I were strad-dling two horses whose trajectories were diverging. I left the Bank in 2000 for three years through the Bank's Staff Exchange Program to run World Links full time.*

Over the next three years the organization expanded quickly to 35 countries, covering 3,000 schools, a network of 22,000 teachers, and over one million kids. World Links was selected by the World Economic Forum as the number one program in the world, bridging the global digital divide, which increased our support from the private sector and enabled us to recruit high-value board members.

The World Bank is an institution where people can take initiatives. Do not take 'no' for an answer, at least not the first time. You ask why not and then persist if you believe in the cause.

CHAPTER FOUR

Regions and Sectors

As an international development institution, the Bank has to find the right mix of skills to develop the complex array of assistance it provides to its clients. It needs country experts, mainly economists and loan officers, who are expected to understand the macro-political and economic systems in a country, and sector specialists in many fields: agriculture, water, transport, energy, health. Both sets of expertise are needed; yet there is inherent tension between the two. Each group has its distinct epistemic culture and way of looking at the Bank's responsibilities. Some see country experts as the key to making things happen; others believe sector specialists are the movers and shakers. The persistent and continuing tension "between a geographic approach, which focuses on a country and large region, and a sectoral approach, which concentrates on arenas such as education, urban development, and energy" (Marshall 2008:71) has led to four major rounds of reorganization (1952, 1972, 1987, and 1997) in the Bank's history.

Each of the four major reorganizations tried to "establish the framework for closer working relations between the 'country experts' and the 'sector specialists'" (Annual Report 1973:7), and each produced winners and losers and shaped the institutional incentives for the Bank staff. As the result of the reorganizations, the balance between the two has swung like a pendulum, but tension continues. The most recent reorganization of 1997 once again tried to adjust the balance between the areas and sectors so that the Bank could "become more flexible in responding to client needs, more focused on professional excellence, and more efficient in its management of resources—both human and financial" (Strategic Compact). Together with decentralization (discussed in Chapter 5), the 1997 reorganization has significantly shifted the weight to country experts. The tension between the two has been particularly challenging for the management throughout the Bank history.

Country vs. Sector: The Inbuilt Dilemma

In its first couple of years, the Bank focused on two tasks: "Supporting postwar reconstruction and persuading the investment community that the organization's bonds were a worthwhile investment" (Galambos and Milobsky 1995:161). Since borrowing countries were themselves able to identify and prepare complete proposals, the loan department was "responsible for discussions with potential borrowers and for handling all loan applications, including analysis of the application, investigation of conditions within the application country, and negotiation of the terms of loan agreement" (Annual Report 1947:21). Loan officers and lawyers were soon joined by economists, hired to help member countries assess their total economic resources and capacity and establish priorities in their development programs. Since the Bank was operated much like a loan window, merely transferring funds from donor to recipient countries, the management did not need sector specialists. When conflicts over a specific borrowing emerged, an ad hoc committee resolved the differences.

The 1952 reorganization separated regional and technical operations. Loan officers were grouped into three regional departments, responsible for a geographical grouping of the Bank's member countries. A separate Technical Operations Department (TOD) was to undertake project assessments and advise borrowers on potential problems. The Bank "had to add to its staff of specialists particularly concerned with the assessment and execution of projects" because developing countries had neither leaders in business or government able to plan investments, nor technicians and managers able to design or deliver development projects (Annual Report 1954–1955:33–36). TOD quickly recruited specialists in electric power, transportation (i.e., rail, roads, and ports), communication, and agriculture (irrigation, land clearing, grain storage, etc.) to advise on economics, engineering, organization, and other factors bearing on the eventual success of projects. TOD often had to ensure the project was well designed, the engineering plans competently drawn, cost estimates complete and realistic, funds available to cover expenditures not financed by the Bank's loan. It also ensured the borrower had made adequate arrangements, not only for building the project, but for operating it once construction was completed.

Even though TOD's proposals were assessed by loan officers assigned to regional departments, it was clear sector specialists were in the driver's seat. In the following two decades (1952–1972), the sector specialists "ruled the roost with an iron hand" (Kapur et al 1997:41).

"Unfriendly rivalry" was endemic, and the relationship between area departments and the TOD was "the Bank's most difficult and pervasive organizational problem" (Mason and Asher 1973:76). At the core of this tension were the different perceptions of the Bank's role in providing assistance to developing countries. Some emphasized that no projects were freestanding; lending projects had to be evaluated within the broader economic environment of the borrowing country. In loan discussions, those with detailed knowledge of the prospective borrower asked about the project's impact on the general economic and fiscal policies, the flow of private capital, and the institutional measures necessary to support it. They "were especially sensitive to the needs of the recipient member countries and often became convinced that maintaining good relations in the area of their responsibility outweighed other considerations" (Galambos and Milobsky 1995:168). They saw their role as "diplomats." Their sector critics often regarded them as *accelerators* in lending processes, disregarding the minimum requirements for accepting the Bank's assistance and overemphasizing the political elements of proposals, especially when they developed special links with the clients. For example, the RVP for Latin America, who was "openly sympathetic to the post-Peron government's economic policies," made it possible for Argentina to secure borrowing from the Bank on rural development that was opposed by many EDs (Ayres 1983:110). It remains true. In China, after 1989 the CD helped the country draft a letter to the Board to withdraw all six projects awaiting approval in order to avoid embarrassment; he then used an earthquake as an opportunity to bring China back to the Bank list. With Kemal Dervis as the CD in the Balkan region, the Bank played an important role in bringing about peace and reconstruction programs to Bosnia, which was not even a Bank member (Mallaby 2004:116–144).

Country experts tend to work with borrowing countries on a close and continuing basis; their perceptions of the country's needs and the Bank's role in the country tend to be formed in this context. Their 'sympathetic' approach to client countries was criticized by both those who argue that the Bank provides assistance to countries that cannot absorb the aid or have serious corruption problems and those who claim that the political views of the Bank's country experts often block assistance that is badly needed by poor countries.

In contrast, sector specialists claim they have to act as *brakes* because they treat projects as "an 'island of sanity' in a sea of irrational policies" (Ayres 1983:43). They argue there are certain technical standards a project must meet. A hydro project, for example, must be technically sound and bring potential benefits to the people. They were "less influenced than were the area experts by the recipient countries; TOD's experts—many of whom were engineers—blended a claim for 'independence,' that is, for technical objectivity, with 'zeal for the correct technical solution' at the project level" (Galambos and Milobsky 1995:169).

The difficulty, their critics say, is that they often paid little attention to land use, cropping patterns, distances to market, anticipated prices, and especially the macroeconomic condition of the country or institutional aspects of the project—whether the utility companies had the capacity to collect payments or the country to afford the loans or sustain the projects. Sector people were also criticized for pushing loans because of their narrow focus on technical feasibility and neglect of political conditions such as corruption.

These are not only "personal beliefs" (Burki 2005:124). They are also institutionally derived from their education and training and endorsed by their position in the Bank. As the Bank expanded, especially after the creation of IDA, the old ways of mediating the tension was no longer adequate with the country experts and sector specialists sitting in one room discussing each project. At the same time, "neither TOD nor the area departments would probably have developed as effectively as they did if one or the other had been completely subordinated" (Galambos and Milobsky 1995:174). The reorganization in 1972 merged the seven area departments and the eight projects departments into five regional offices, each with responsibility for planning and supervising the execution of the development programs within the countries. Each regional office had control over the sector specialists, financial analysts, economists, and loan officers required to carry out its responsibilities.

Whatever the formal rhetoric about closer working relations between country experts and sector specialists, the reorganization really strengthened the position of economists and financial analysts. Sector specialists, especially "the engineers, had lost substantial ground when the project organization (formerly TOD) was eliminated and they were spread among the regional offices" (Galambos and Milobsky 1995:181). With most specialists decentralized to regions, the "general precepts in the international marketplace of ideas" were translated into actions within "country-specific contexts" (Ayres 1984:21). Modifications and adjustments were made according to the political, economic, and social needs of the borrowing countries. Projects work became more specific. The downside was that with no central department supporting them, they could not exert the same dominance over operations as they had in the 1950s and 1960s.

After the 1972 reorganization each RVP had directors for country programs and directors for projects. Sector departments were in parallel with the country departments. In theory, country economists should work side by side with the sector specialists under each RVP. In practice, there was continuous tension between country program departments and project departments. The country program departments sent out missions to the field to gain firsthand knowledge of the needs of the countries, while the projects department often insisted on its own way in designing and supervising projects (Gill and Pugatch 2005).

The 1987 reorganization is often considered as the most dramatic, not because of its substance, but because of the way it was conducted. Whatever the formal pronouncements, it was designed to (a) streamline and reduce the people on the payroll, (b) put its pampered staff in their place, and (c) create an internal market for the staff (Kapur et al 1997:1201). It reduced six regions to four, strengthened the RVPs and created 19 large country departments that covered a cluster of countries, each supported by a technical team of sector specialists, financial analysts, economists, loan officers, and engineers. It "brought under one department all the necessary elements of a country program— economic analysis, dialogue, strategy formulation, and project preparation and implementation capabilities" (Lim 2005:91). For those, only a few, in charge of only one or two countries, the arrangement was ideal. It allowed the technical specialists to concentrate on learning about the country and serving their 'only' client. This arrangement gave directors of country programs capabilities unprecedented in the Bank. As former CDs recalled, 'We had all the power.'

In regions where CDs were put in charge of eight to nine countries, the real power and authority were in the hands of RVPs. Each RVP was in charge of several subregional offices and a technical department. In Africa, for example, there were six subregional divisions (Occidental and Central Africa, Eastern Africa, South-Central Africa and Indian Ocean, Western Africa, Sahelia, and Southern Africa) and one technical division. There were three country departments in East Asia and Pacific and three in South Asia, but the two regions shared one technical department. The technical department provided services for the region(s) alone. Little interchange occurred between technical departments across regions. Although CDs with multiple countries had both country experts and technical specialists under their management, in practice, they could not have enough knowledge of both clients and sectors, and they had to rely on division chiefs of each sector.

Reorganization of 1997

Upon coming to the Bank, Wolfensohn proposed another reorganization as part of his ambitious $400 million (the price tag was revised in 2001 to $576 million in FY 1999–2000), 30-month reform initiative—the *Strategic Compact: Renewing the Bank's Effectiveness to Fight Poverty*. In the mid-1990s, the Bank was under siege from both right and left, from critics who asserted the Bank was "staffed by a dangerous breed of technocrats, whose overweening confidence in prescribing policies for the poor was matched only by their manifest incompetence" (Mallaby 2004:59). The effectiveness of its projects had declined steadily.

Whatever the external causes of reorganizations, they are always driven by interests within. Fifty years after its creation, the Bank had become "a sprawling, messy empire of loosely linked programs, spread across nearly a hundred countries and a dozen different types of projects" (Mallaby 2004:148). Independent fiefdoms reigned, information exchange was limited, and resources could not be shared (Zhang 2006:77). Wolfensohn was determined to shake up the old "clan system"—"a chief hired a favoured protégé, and protégé hired another protégé, and nobody said anything nasty about anyone" (Mallaby 2004:158)—and get rid of the regional barons, who carried both the institutional memory and institutional weight.

Sector staff complained that they were losing their technical edge because even the large country offices were too small for them to pool all the necessary resources. They needed larger groups to exchange ideas, improve their skills, and utilize their expertise. Meanwhile, CDs, especially those with multiple countries, had difficulty appreciating what countries needed because sector people pushed for their own projects as a means of survival (Sud 2005). Finally, like all his predecessors, Wolfensohn wanted a Bank organized in his way and with his trusted (if any) people in charge. Determined to make the institution "less bureaucratic and more outward-looking and loosen it up so that people could express their views and not feel that they were in boxes" (Wolfensohn 2005), Wolfensohn pushed through his ambitious Strategic Compact, which contained four objectives:

- Refuel current business activity to protect the level and quality of the Bank services
- Refocus the development agenda
- Retool the Bank's knowledge base to build a knowledge bank
- Revamp institutional capabilities.

The last objective was to be achieved by shifting accountabilities and resources to the field and introducing a matrix management system.

A matrix management system seeks to create an 'internal market.' It had become popular in the corporate world in the 1980s and followed the trend of public management reforms that introduced market systems and networks of coordination to replace hierarchical controls (Pollitt and Bouckaert 2000). Some functions (like finance, personnel, or information technology) exist to serve others across the institution. Others, such as agriculture, infrastructure, and transport, serve customers, in this case the client countries. They all have different demands and political systems. In traditional project management, the focus was on a single objective: to build a road or a dam or a school. A project team was formed for this objective and disbanded upon its completion. With the matrix system, sector specialists would be pooled in one network, but receive their assignments from the regions/countries. It was a way to institutionalize lateral communications to enable an organization to address many projects simultaneously. The matrix system allowed Wolfensohn to break down the barriers between regional independent fiefdoms.

The organizational structure of the matrix system looks simple. Horizontally, there are six regions: Latin America and Caribbean (LAC), Middle East and Northern Africa (MENA), Europe and Central Asia (ECA), East Asia and Pacific (EAP), South Asia (SA), and Africa. Vertically, four thematic networks were created as hubs for sector specialists: Human Development (HD); Environmentally & Socially Sustainable Development (ESSD); Finance, Private Sector and Infrastructure (FPSI); and Poverty Reduction and Economic Management (PREM). Each region and each network is headed by a VP. The networks are located in a grid system with the six regions.

Each sector network had a number of regional offices, headed by regional sector directors (RSDs) and assisted by regional sector managers (RSMs) with specific responsibilities.

Table 4.1 Matrix Structure 2005

	Africa VP	EAP VP	S. Asia VP	LAC VP	MENA VP	ECA VP
Number of Countries	47	20+[1]	8	32	19	30
Number of CDs	14 CDs	6 CDs	6 CDs	6 CDs	5 CDs	8 CDs
HD VP	RSD	RSD	RSD	RSD	RSD	RSD
Education	RSM	RSM	RSM	RSM	SM	RSM
Health	RSM	RSM	RSM	RSM	SM	RSM
Social protection	RSM	RSM	RSM	RSM	SM	RSM
ESSD VP	RSD	RSD	RSD	RSD	RSD	RSD
Environment	RSM	RSM	RSM	RSM	RSM	RSM
Rural Dev.	RSM	RSM	RSM	RSM	RSM	RSM
Social Dev.	RSM	RSM	RSM	RSM	RSM	RSM
PREM VP	RSD	RSD	RSD	RSD	RSD	RSD
Economic policy	RSM	RSM	RSM	RSM	RSM	RSM
Gender and Dev.	RSM	RSM	RSM	RSM	RSM	RSM
Poverty Reduction	RSM	RSM	RSM	RSM	RSM	RSM
Public Sector & Gov.	RSM	RSM	RSM	RSM	RSM	RSM
FPSD VP	RSD	RSD	RSD	RSD	RSD	RSD
Finance	RSM	RSM	RSM	RSM	RSM	RSM
Private sec. & Energy	RSM	RSM	RSM	RSM	RSM	RSM
Transport	RSM	RSM	RSM	RSM	RSM	RSM
Urban, water, sanitation	RSM	RSM	RSM	RSM	RSM	RSM

Note: 1. Pacific islands are counted as one.

SD—sector director, SM—sector manager, RSD—regional sector director, RSM—regional sector manager

Within each network, there are several themes that are headed by sector managers (SMs). About 80 percent of the Bank staff are located in one of the horizontal grids (sector specialists), and almost all of them are located in the HQ. Most people on the vertical grid (country experts), however, have gradually been relocated to the field. Those on the vertical line of the matrix system, though much smaller in number, are supposed to purchase services from those on the horizontal line of the grid (sector specialists), who 'sell' their services to the country teams. This arrangement was designed to create an internal market and also to allow sector people to fertilize their 'best practices' across regions and countries.

Matrix System at Work

It was difficult to get Board support for the expensive reorganization; it was even harder to make the matrix system work. Few people had any idea how to create an internal market or sell services to internal customers. In addition, tension between technical expertise and country priorities remains. There are two simplified categories of work the Bank undertakes in all client countries: upstream engagement—knowledge management and learning (diagnostic)—and financing, preparation, supervision, and implementation of new operations (lending).

The country team is responsible for developing strategies and packaging the assistance the countries need. Each country develops a three-year CAS, now called country partnership strategy in some cases. CASs list challenges the country is facing, the government's priorities, and the assistance the country needs from the Bank. The Bank has instruments (services) from which the country team can select to provide assistance, such as normal IBRD lending, IDA concession lending, trust funds (funds entrusted to the Bank by donor countries), analytical and advisory activities (AAA), and technical assistance (TA). In developing a CAS, the country team tries to "provide a long enough framework to deal with tough developmental issues that a country typically faces" (Nankani 2005:69); it has to decide what the country's priorities are and what instruments the Bank can utilize. "This is where selectivity comes in: selectivity was driven not only by our understanding of what we thought the major levers for growth and poverty reduction would be, but also by the nature of our policy dialogue with our [government] counterparts and, indeed, the policy debates more generally" (Nankani 2005:69).

Networks can have quite different priorities and may or may not have the experts countries need. CDs control the budget and purchase services from the networks, which provide people and expertise. If a CD decides the country needs some analytical work on secondary education, the sector in the region may decide the work is not worth the effort or not a priority in terms of allocating people. CDs sometimes have to compete for sector experts. Alternatively sector specialists provided to the CD may know what works, but not anything about local conditions. Moreover, the Bank has its corporate agenda; the network has to ensure that is fulfilled and the global best practices disseminated across regions. "The creative tension of matching one to the other was designed to produce creative synergy and respond to changing country realities" (Marshall 2008:71).

Within the matrix system, the two different lines of authority in theory should combine to make a balanced decision, as no one side has sole decision-making power. This was the essence of reorganization in 1997—overlapping responsibilities were designed to break down the traditional, vertical, hierarchical command-and-control organizational structure, combat parochialism, and build flexibility into the Bank's responses. However, proliferating channels of communication and accountabilities under the dual reporting system not only created confusion, but also made the matrix system difficult to manage, a problem identified in the *Harvard Business Review* when the matrix management system was first widely adopted in the corporate world (Bartlett and Ghoshal 1990).

"The matrix system is more management intensive" (HR 2004:iv). The Bank president or MDs have to balance corporate strategies, sector interests, and region/country demands. They are not necessarily always consistent. When Wolfensohn placed governance on the agenda, the PREM's governance unit had to ensure these ideas were implemented through its analytical work, lending, and other programs (Chapter 8). The governance people had to compete for resources within PREM and with other networks. After the management adopted the infrastructure action plan in 2001, the network did not have enough people with the skill and willingness to return to power, dam, or road projects to meet demands from countries.

Merging technical expertise and country priorities is the key to success. For example, within the environment sector, there were thematic teams on environment, health, climate change, global environment policy and economics, natural resource management, carbon finance business, and biodiversity. Country teams have to work with a wide range of players—central and subregional governments, donor countries, and civil societies—and need to be selective in determining what services they can purchase from the sector and ensure sector experts brought in can work with these players. It is not always easy.

By 2001, it became clear that the country teams dominated the matrix system. This was partly due to its initial design. CDs have the local information, authority, and the budget to purchase the services the countries need. In a 2001 review on reorganization, the task force explained,

During the Compact the Bank transformed many parts of its organization architecture, with some encouraging results but some unintended consequences and disconnects. The organizational *structure* of the Bank significantly changed toward strong country directors—and a more client-focused and country-based organization supported by global sectoral and thematic networks. (World Bank 2001:29)

The country-focused matrix was consolidated when Shengman was appointed as MD in charge of all sectors and regions. His strong belief in the importance of the country/region offices contributed to greater emphasis on them in the matrix system.

In the Bank's history, countries/regions have always been considered as the core departments at the Bank. They are of the most importance. Only those who are the best can become the regional vice president or country directors. Those who are in charge of regions and countries have the most authority and therefore these positions are the most sought-after. (Zhang 2006:86)

Given that the turf battles temporarily tilted toward regions and the prominent position of country offices, the survival and expansion of the sectors rested on the ability of SDs to think and plan strategically. They are primarily managers; the best also strategically plan for programs and expertise needed in the region. 'As SDs, we need to ensure sector managers see the synergies in the region,' claimed one SD. Many issues do not fall neatly under thematic groups. For example, in the HD network sit education, health, and social protection. 'Child development would fall into three thematic groups, and sector managers need to work together and come up with some good packages for the country teams.'

SDs and SMs should be able to predict demands and recruit the skills ready for the requests of the CDs. 'We always need to plan ahead and see what we can offer to the countries in the region, what comparative advantages we as the Bank have, and what kind of new programs we can sell to CDs,' said one SD. This is also one of the greatest advantages the Bank has: 'If you have imagination and have new and good ideas, you can achieve a lot.' Sectors with strategic directors tend to expand, and their programs thrive; where SDs are less imaginative, the programs can shrink quickly. 'One only needs to sell services when the sector has a bad manager and the SD is incompetent,' explained one SD. 'Otherwise, countries demand our services and experts.' In one region, for example, in the past five to six years, the programs and the size of HD have expanded significantly, but those of PREM have shrunk considerably. During the same period, PREM in another region thrived. As its SD explained,[1]

> Structures do not matter that much; people do. Operations is not just about the substance, programs, or projects, AAA or lending, or what should be done. It is how to use the process to build close partnerships with countries and how to build broader consensus and then let things germinate. If we let sector people concoct projects, it tends to be supply-driven, and questions of relevance will rise. If we let CDs control the whole programs and projects, we cannot guarantee the quality. My role was to bring the two sides together and plan ahead and plan strategically.

Planning is particularly important for SDs because "Bank-wide client service activities are at present fragmented into about 5,000 tasks (active in fiscal year 2004), led by close to 1,700 task team leaders (TTLs) chosen from about 2,000 GE+ operation staff" (Task Force 2005:8). Given that 30 percent of TTLs had less than three years of Bank experience, SMs spent a large proportion of their time and energy supervising TTLs. Planning is left to SDs.

Same Structure, Different Operation

While the idea behind the matrix structure might be simple—creating an internal market where country teams could purchase services (knowledge and expertise) from the networks—it was complicated in execution and even more difficult to keep the two lines of authority balanced. 'For two years, it was a mess—CDs had money, no people; SDs had people, no money,' commented a regional operational adviser. The initial confusion led everybody to ask, how would country offices purchase services from the networks, how would networks charge country offices, who would decide what to buy and what to sell, how would the staff (country experts and sector specialists) be managed, and how could the countries' demands and sector supplies be balanced.

---

[1] The difference of the performance for PREM in the two regions might not only be the consequence that the PREM SD in one region was acting, while the other carried two hats of SD and chief economist; it may also be the different qualities of the two: one was a technical person in his entire career, while the other was a YP and a very good macroeconomist.

The management did what the Bank was good at—gave its staff great leeway and left them to make it work. After the management decided the main organizational structure, "each region and network was allowed to design its organization relatively autonomously and in a spirit of deliberate experimentation" (World Bank 2001:6). This contributed to many different ways of balancing sectors and countries across regions. The matrix system everywhere shares three features: (1) sector people in general are located in HQ, while most country teams are in the field; (2) dual lines of command lead to shared authority and responsibility for program outcomes; and (3) managers have to live effectively with two bosses. When sector specialists located in a hub are pooled for work assignments in a country where the country team knows the conditions, they are in theory accountable directly to the boss in charge of technical aspects and indirectly to the boss in the place where a project is undertaken. This system overlies the traditional hierarchy with some forms of lateral authority, influence, and communication.

In practice the dual lines of communication and accountability can operate quite differently. As "initial implementation proceeded on a region-by-region and network-by-network basis and without a transition plan to show how the various initiatives would eventually be brought together," this created "significant difference between regions in the size of country units, the interface between country and sector directors, the configuration of technical units, country team practices, resource management practices, and task team practices" (World Bank 2001:31). The great variation can also be explained by the history, operational culture, and leadership provided by not only VPs but also SDs and CDs of each region, as the following section on three regions, EAP, SA, and LAC, illustrates.

The three regions have had different degrees of decentralization. Until 2008, LAC, due to its geographic location (the same time zones as HQ), was less decentralized in the sense that many worked in HQ. EAP and SA were the most decentralized of all the six regions. In LAC, therefore CDs and SDs could work closely. As one SD stated,

I am accountable to both RVP and network VP. I attend meetings of both regarding decision making. Yet, if the meetings with two VPs are in conflict, I go to the one called by RVP because as the SD, I need to plan ahead and know who our competitors are in the region and in the countries in the region to protect our budget and ensure our programs will not be squeezed out.

To ensure close collaboration, SDs assign a sector leader (coordinator) to the country offices, colocated with the CD whether in HQ or in the field. These sector leaders in the country office become 'double agents' in the sense that they are expected to represent the interests of both the sector and the country, but on different occasions. They work with CDs as a team in providing a collective understanding of needs of the client countries, identifying the programs and projects, and bringing the 'best practices' to the country through their lateral communication within the thematic groups. 'There is a collective ownership,' stated a former CD. These sector coordinators attend the management meetings organized by the CD to express and defend the sector's interests, while attending management meetings organized by the SD or the SM to defend the country interests. The matrix system therefore provides a framework, not a straitjacket, for the two sides to work together.

Merging the two sides is important in LAC as the relevance of the Bank in middle-income countries is increasingly in question. 'We need to know what the countries want and what we can offer that other donors and private sectors cannot, and we need to be creative,' stated an SD in the region. 'CDs are our first clients.' When crime and violence were identified by several country teams in the region as major issues, sector staff needed to develop new ideas in a way to meet the demands.

> We do not do prisons, but we can do slum upgrading as part of infrastructure and urban renewal. The way we design parks, roads, lighting can all affect the environment where crimes might take place. For example, when we help build a park or renovate buildings, we want to make sure there are no blind corners where drugs could be traded. We would put lights there. In several of our countries, people were worried that crime rates might affect their tourist industry. We would include building recreation centers, reintegrating ex-combatants, or providing counseling services into our urban renewal projects. To do all these, often CDs, SDs, and anchor people work together, exploring all the instruments available.

The benefits of the system used in LAC, with sector coordinators integrated in country teams, were acknowledged by the Bank management as well as RVP offices. A review of public sector reform notes that "in (large) country offices, where the specialists sit in proximity, and...with country management teams representing all the areas, there tends to be better coordination" (IEG 2008:65). Other regions have tried to learn.

ECA is known to have more explicit, 'naked' CDs—CDs who did not have sector people supporting them in country offices. Yet many, who have worked in ECA, neither feel they are naked, nor see naked CDs as a problem. 'I could get all the help I wanted and when I wanted from sectors,' recalled a former CD. Another argued,

> Being on the spot enables the country director to identify demand and needs as they arise and to organize responses to them. At the same time, being on the spot enables the country director to call a halt to foundering programs or projects where the client has withdrawn support. Program teams are often reluctant to cut their losses for fear that doing so will be interpreted as failure. (Kavalsky 2005:42)

The advantage of a naked CD is the ability to call off the unsatisfactory projects/programs.

Recently, the RVP unit in ECA is trying to build a closer relationship between the country and sector teams by adopting similar practices to LAC, albeit with some modifications; 'plagiarism is not a problem in our line of duty; we need to repackage the good experience to fit the condition in this region.' Since there are many countries in ECA, the regional management team is considering sector hubs in Europe to achieve coordination between sector and country teams. It also acknowledges that

> no system is trouble free, and there will always been tension between sectors and country teams. It is important to improve the quality of dialogue and keep CDs focused on corporate priorities as well as country priorities. With a hub set up in Europe, sector people would be closer to the clients and be more sensitive to the needs and demands of the client countries and the country teams. Meanwhile, we need to keep rotating these people so that we can keep connected with international experience and global knowledge. We do not want to become another regional bank.

In EAP, matrix management always works in favor of country teams. All six CDs are in the field, while SDs are in HQ. They meet formally twice a year during the spring and fall conference. Being in the field and with less direct communication with SDs, CDs in EAP drive the agenda. They may seek to choose the sector people and often get who they ask for. These sector staff work closely and comfortably with CDs and their operational advisers.

In SA, however, 'Country programs are driven by sectors,' even though their CDs are in the field too. This was to a large extent a product of an initial bitter power struggle between the strong CDs and the RVP after the matrix system was adopted. The RVP used sectors in fighting this battle.

To understand the differences, we can look at three large countries in the two regions: China and Indonesia in EAP and India in SA. Even though CDs have similar responsibilities—"managing the Bank's lending portfolio, providing policy advice, and guiding Bank-government relations" (Gill and Pugatch 2005:2)—the nature of these responsibilities varies greatly from country to country, depending on their size and program. All three countries have relatively large country offices. About 110 people work in Beijing's office, 150 in Jakarta, and 250 in India. In all three countries, about 20 percent of the staff are internationally recruited, and 70 percent are professionals. In EAP, sector people in the field, including sector coordinators who are either lead (I) or senior (H) specialists, working with CDs as a team, have no hesitation to state that they work for the CDs even though they 'belong' to the network and their 'bosses' (SMs or SDs) are in Washington, D.C. Indeed, many of these sector coordinators (whether international or local staff) gain a high degree of country knowledge, skills for "making things happen," and the ability to partner with other donors and stakeholders in the country (Task Force 2005:6).

In both Beijing and Jakarta offices there seems to be a harmonious relationship. Sector staff comment on the team work and leadership provided by the CDs. On the organizational chart in the region, sector people are accountable through solid lines both to the CD and the SDs in HQ, rather than a secondary reporting relationship as in other regions (see Figure 4.1). This cooperative relationship between the country experts and sector specialists may have its roots in history. After the 1987 reorganization, China hosted one of the largest country offices in the Bank, with more than 100 professional staff members, of whom about 40 were macro- and sectoral economists. The large number of professionals under one roof allowed the Bank not only to provide timely analytical work, but also to influence policy making in China (Burki 2005:134). Indonesia historically also hosted a large office with extensive expertise. Close coordination between the CD

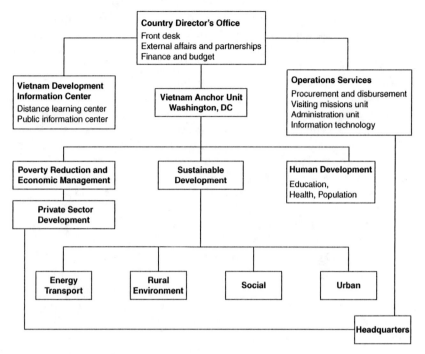

Figure 4.1 Organization chart of the World Bank Country Office, Hanoi

and sector people was the key to attracting a large amount of trust finds. As one SD explained, 'Attracting trust funds from donor countries relied on an "unholy alliance between SD and CD".' Coordination also allowed the staff in the country office, both country and sector, to develop innovative programs by using trust funds and other resources, such as 'justice for the poor.' So long as the ideas were good, CD or SD would commit resources. In Cambodia, the government wanted to have a public expenditure review done, and the country team had limited financial resources at hand, while few sector specialists wanted to work there because there were limited rewards—the project would be too small to have much impact. The SD then instructed the SM to construct a team and commit some slush funds to the project. 'Such cross-subsidies are necessary from time to time to support the country team,' explained the SD.

This relationship is also mirrored in the evaluation process. When introducing the matrix system, the Bank adopted a new system known as 360-degree evaluation. That is, even though their professional promotion is approved by the sector board, sector staff are evaluated by their two bosses (country and sector), their subordinates, and their clients. Sector people in EAP discuss their evaluation with the CD and ask both the CD and their SM or SD to sign off.

Whatever the formal lines of accountability, CDs in EAP determine what activities have priority. That is primarily a matter of presence. Since they are there all the time, they direct daily activities. When a government asks for assistance or a response, the CD takes the lead. CDs will appreciate what avenues are being pursued and what is possible at the time. In EAP, one experienced operator asserted, 'I don't give a damn who the SD is; I care who the CDs are, especially the big CDs.' Another senior local staffer agreed, 'If the CD says do it, I do it.'

Such a working relationship is in a direct contrast to the one in SA where the CD is only one of a dozen people who signs the evaluation review for a sector member. SMs write references, and they may or may not seek the CD's input. Sector people in the field office see themselves accountable to the SMs or SDs in HQ, who are responsible for their promotion and assignment. In SA CDs commented that even though they saw the sector people everyday, they did not have much influence on their careers. This includes locally recruited sector people who also reported directly to HQ:

> If you do not like the way they work, there is no way to get rid of them. I am only one of the many people who sign their perfor-mance evaluation. We have to work with what we have, not what we like. We need to engage, support, and let them know what expectations are, but we can only do it gradually.

The frustration could be clearly detected in SA. 'As a CD, I am sup-posed to drive the program,' commented another CD. 'I cannot choose the staff; SDs do, and they decide who I am going to get and how many I am going to get.' Some CDs in SA felt they were more 'naked' than those in ECA. 'If there were three education projects going on in India led by three TTLs, reporting to three different SMs, where was coher-ence?' asked one former CD. The situation in Bangladesh was worse: 'Power was all over the place,' a former CD said; the CD had little say over the selection of sector team members, especially when it was dif-ficult to attract good people to the country.

In India, there are 18 lead specialists, but the SDs/SMs are all in HQ. The balance of power between the CD and the sector staff tilts to the sector in SA because of the general perception that CDs rotate, while sector people, especially locally recruited people, stay. When new CDs come, it takes time for locals to become comfortable with them. The same should also be the case in EAP, yet the culture and the history of the Bank in the region have helped establish different norms of practices. People accept whoever their CD is. It is the position rather than an individual they relate to.

In SA, sector people answer to the CDs only in an indirect way, even though they see them every day. Sector staff say, 'While we support the CD, we keep daily contact with the sector manager, who depends on our feedback to build a work program and the priorities of the program.' 'We talk to the CD and support the CD, but the CD is only our client, who funds part of our program.' Some state that the CD is 'a peer adviser to the tasks; we are independent from the CD, and we report to the HQ directly.' One of the consequences of this direct line to sectors is that 'economists are concerned about the economic situation, but not so much about education or health, in their decision making, and vice versa.' Country programs, however, need the support of multidisciplinary teams. This multidisciplinary concern is satisfied in LAC by placing a sector representative in the country team and by the general cooperative working principle in EAP.

The different relationship can be explained partly by history and partly by the leadership provided by the RVPs. In SA in 1997, the RVP, facing several strong CDs, decided to strengthen the power of sectors. One way was through budgets. In EAP, CDs have a contingency budget. They keep it and use it appropriately. In SA, there was no contingency budget for CDs, who had to allocate their budget to the sectors; SMs could then juggle funds between projects, depending how they turned out. In effect in SA the SDs and SMs, not the CDs, had the contingency budget. Of courses, sector people still had to deliver the projects for the CD. Some people admitted, 'Looking across East and South Asia, it is difficult to appreciate it is the same Bank people are working for.'

Development

The Operations Policy and Country Services (OPCS) was initially created as a network to serve the Bank as whole; more recently it was listed as a separate unit reporting to the president directly. OPCS remains a 'plumber' job—'problems come to you; you do not have to look for them, as other RVPs do,' explained a former VP of OPCS. It is the interface of the Board, senior management, and the operations complex, responsible for all or any sector and country services. In 2003, the Bank split FPSI and created two separate networks: Infrastructure and Private Sector Development. A year later, it added another: Financial Sector.

Toward the end of the Wofensohn's tenure, the management organized a task force to review the performance of the reorganization, especially decentralization and matrix system. In 2005, the Task Force recommended merging seven networks into four:

Table 4.2 Recommended Restructuring

Networks in 2005	Recommended Networks	Projected staff strength
PREM	Economic Policy, Finance, and	829
Economic Policy	Private Sector Management	
Public Sector	Economic Policy	
Management	FSE	
Poverty	PSD	
Gender	Poverty	
OPCS	Human Development	528
Financial Management	Health	
Procurement	Education	
	Social Protection	
HD	Sustainable Development and	1014
Health	Infrastructure	
Education	Environment	
Social Protection	Agriculture and	
ESSD	Rural development	
Environment	Water Supply and	
Agriculture & Rural	Sanitation	
Development	Energy	
Social Development	Transport	
	Urban Development	
	(Other global product groups	
	not defined as Sector Boards)	
INF	Governance, Institutions, and	550
Water Supply and	Capacity Enhancement	
Sanitation	Public Sector Management	
Energy	Financial Management	
Transport	Procurement	
Urban development	Social Development	
(and other global product	Gender	
groups not defined as		
Sector Boards)		
FSE	—	—
PSD	—	—

Source: Task Force, "Organizational Effectiveness: Final Report," February 15, 2005, 40.

Wolfowitz accepted the proposal to merge networks, but not the details of the recommendation. In 2007, seven networks were merged into three. Sustainable Development included the old ESSD and Infrastructure, while PREM and HD stayed separate. The merger placed more than half the sector specialists under one umbrella. Sustainable Development covered more than ten broad thematic groups: agriculture and rural development, information technology, economics and regulation, energy, environment, financial and private sector, oil, gas and mining, social development, transport, urban development, and water. These specialists represent quite different cultures: 'Those who do social development tend to involve in process, listening, and inclusive socialization, while engineers in other sectors have high discipline on targets, but are not fully socialized.' They also have different views on the world. Wolfowitz explained the reason for the merger as 'tearing down the turfs between departments.' For many at the Bank, it meant managing something unmanageable. The result, according to a network VP, was that 'I can try to persuade countries to take on these projects or programs, but my persuasion is only persuasion. It is the RVPs and CDs who set the regional and country programs.'

Despite a close working relationship between the country and sector staff in EAP, some structural issues remained, as in other regions. One was that, as an internal study indicates, since the adoption of the Strategic Compact, there had been a 15 percent reduction of regional sector specialists. This was partly because the system encouraged people to be leaders (such as SMs or TTLs) rather than team players. The problem was also caused by lack of mentoring. Senior people want to be in the country offices, rather than networks. More importantly, with CDs controlling the budget, there is great uncertainty for SDs. "Lack of predictability in resource envelopes of sector units... encourages sector managers to be risk averse and to limit strategic hiring" (Task Force 2005:8). A typical SM oversees 20 TTLs, about 100 projects, across as many as six to eight countries and has to write 400–500 management letters a year; oversight is often ineffective.

One objective of the matrix system was to spread the Bank's best practices around the world. Yet there has been "low cross-support between Regions (only 2 percent of recorded time of non-managerial sector staff is spent supporting activities of other Regions) and insufficient staff rotations across Regions, as well as between the Regions and the Network Anchor" (Task Force 2005:36). Furthermore, the system offers few incentives or resources for regional staff to contribute to the collective of the network. They provide services requested by CDs, but they have little accountability to offer knowledge and technical support to other regions, to ensure adequate response to global programs, or to support corporate needs. The same is true with CDs (Task Force 2005:27).

Conclusion

"The World Bank's sector work has deep traditions going back to its earliest years, but today its terminology and ethos are driven largely by a 1997 reorganization that aimed to emphasise technical excellence with global reach" (Marshall 2008:71). Since then the Bank staff have finally mastered the intricacies of the matrix system. The matrix system, however, has not settled the debate on the right mix of country focus and sector expertise. The tension remains partly because of the dual role of the Bank—as a diplomat and a financier—and partly because of the different emphasis placed on regional or network VPs by the top management. For now, at least, with the control of the purse, CDs and thereby country experts have more influence in deciding the packages of assistance and their implementation. Sector specialists are increasingly becoming regionalized—an officer working on social safeguard programs (e.g., pensions and other social security programs) in the EAP region tries to move around and do similar projects across countries in the region. This trend raises some serious concerns that the Bank might lose its advantage as a global development institution. Meanwhile, the variety of relationships contradicts the popular myth that the Bank has one set of policies pushed around the world.

CHAPTER FIVE

Centralization and Decentralization

The most common picture of the Bank is its impressive building in Washington, D.C., a block away from the White House and three blocks away from the U.S. Treasury. The edifice symbolizes its authority, while its location suggests its allegiance. Meanwhile, from its creation, the Bank has been trying to position itself as a global institution independent of its creators. It made a number of conscious decisions to provide more authority to those who worked closely with the borrowing countries. None, however, involved relocating the Bank staff to the field. In the 1980s and 1990s, balancing centralization in location and authority and meeting the demands of its member states became an increasing challenge when it was attacked by its shareholding and stake-holding countries. Decentralization of authority, functions, and staff to the field was seen as a solution to many of the Bank's ills. It became an important component of the 1997 reorganization. Over 75 percent of CDs and over 40 percent of the sector people are now working out of the field offices. The questions are (1) how decentralization has changed the incentive structure for the Bank staff, (2) to what extent decentralization has affected the operation of this global institution in terms of cross-country fertilization, and (3) how decentralization empowers the staff in the field at the expense of the management.

The Early Years

The Articles of Agreement state,

> The principal office of the Bank shall be located in the territory of the member holding the greatest number of shares. The Bank

may establish agencies or branch offices in the territories of any member of the Bank. The Bank may establish regional offices and determine the location of, and the areas to be covered by, each regional office. (Article V, Section 9 & 10)

Presidents decide where staff are located.

From its early years, the Bank realized the need for a presence in the countries where it had operations, either on a permanent basis or through missions. It created its first field office in 1947 in Paris when it made its first loan to France. To assess a loan application from Chile, the Bank sent out its first mission, also in 1947. In 1952, the management organized the operational activities on a geographical rather than on the functional basis. Three Area Departments of Operations were created: Asia and Middle East; Europe, Africa, and Australasia; and Western Hemisphere (Chronology 47). Creating region-based departments did not involve moving people to the field. The ideas, authority, and decisions were all generated and implemented in HQ. This centralized operation fitted the dominant ideas on development then— developing countries would follow a similar development process as developed ones.

As McNamara came to the Bank, development theories were changing. Bottom-up grassroots development was advocated, and more "missions" were dispatched "to conduct surveys, prepare economic reports, inspect projects and evaluate progress" (Mason and Asher 1973:73). Resident offices were gradually established. By 1971, there were 10 offices: 8 to individual countries and 2 as representatives to regional groups of countries. Africa was the main focus: permanent offices were created in Nairobi and Abidjan. The office in Indonesia covered the widest programs. As part of the "earliest experiment" with decentralization, the entire Nigeria Program Division "was transferred to Lagos," recalled Ed Lim. "As part of transfer, I moved with my family and lived in Lagos for three years" (Lim 2005:90).

> The experiment at decentralization failed. The Bank was simply not ready to delegate substantial responsibilities to the field, and after several years of continuous tension between the chief of mission in Lagos and programs director at headquarters, the Program Division was returned to headquarters. (Lim 2005:90)

Thereafter all the residencies were small, with only one or two staff; their functions were limited to economic reporting and project identification, but with no authority to make decisions. They were not seen as part of the career structure. "Out of sight and without authority, the field personnel are also often out of mind when higher-level, more responsible jobs become available at headquarters" (Mason and Asher 1973:73). Decisions were made in HQ, and work was done there too, partly because of the relatively small size of the institution, which "operated more like a medium-sized family corporation under the direction of a strong president than like a large corporation or government ministry managed in accordance with well-recognized principles of administration" (Mason and Asher 1973:738).

The culture of visiting missions dominated the Bank for another 20 years. Missions had a diplomatic (even evangelical) ring. Of course that procedure of constant visits, whatever their duration, had consequences. When time was short, preconceived ideas of what was possible often limited the available options. When on missions, supervision of the project was left to the government—sustainability of projects became a serious issue. As one official explained,

> In the 1970s, the Bank did a lot of big rural infrastructure development projects in West Africa; they all failed. Sustainability became an issue, and I was asked to see if there was another way we could do it.

Moving closer to the field was one of the suggestions. In the 1980s, the shift from lending for development projects to assistance to general economies demanded staff with more knowledge of macroeconomic and political conditions of the countries rather than the technical expertise. These were some of the ideas behind the 1987 reorganization—creating large country departments, supported by technical people, and sending a few representatives to the field. The way the reorganization was conducted undermined the initial thinking but the efforts continued when, in the early 1990s, Preston instituted more changes to the Bank's structure, designed to overcome some of the problems created by the 1987 reorganization. One measure was to increase the Bank presence in the field. Some talented Bank staff were sent to work as Res Reps in the field: Ed Lim in China, Chrik Poortman in Zimbabwe, Shigeo Katsu in Ivory Coast, etc. Working in the field provided them with opportunities to accumulate valuable experience with client countries. A VP argued,

> It was a great learning process—you read operational manuals; if you want something new, you need to know where the boundaries

are. You also need to be willing to take risks and know where you can push the boundaries, know who you can talk to and who the guardians of the law are. Then they will help you.

Ed Lim agreed. Even in China "we pushed the envelope of what was feasible alongside the Chinese reformists, but we were never far enough ahead to be irrelevant" (2005:105). These experiences became stepping stones to higher office.

Apart from the Res Reps in a few strategic countries, the responsibilities of others in the field remained trivial. They served as the eyes and ears of the Bank; their role was to build contacts, understand the wishes of the national leaders and the needs of the country, and facilitate the work of missions. If the president visited, they smoothed the path, sometimes successfully, as in Mali, or less so, in Côte D'Ivoire (Mallaby 2004:94–101). Occasionally they had to smooth ruffled feathers after a visit of the Bank president or managing director.

Despite these efforts, until the mid-1990s, the Bank remained a centralized institution: the action was in Washington, D.C., and the power was jealously guarded. Variations, however, were a different matter: they existed not only between large and small countries and across regions and countries, but also project to project. One Bank senior official explained, 'Even in those days, in preparing the projects and programs, you had to tailor them; there had never been one-size-fits-all.' This was the case even with the highly criticized structural adjustment programs: sector adjustment loans were generally seen as both less complex and less intrusive than structural adjustment loans; yet, large Latin American debtor countries often ended up with sector adjustment loans, while small and much less developed African countries took the overall structural adjustment loans (Helleiner 1986).

The Change in the 1990s

After 15 years with weak presidents unable to deal with external challenges, the Bank was under the siege when Jim Wolfensohn took the presidency. NGO-led campaigns against the Bretton Woods institutions had stalled lending and threatened its future. The Bank was portrayed as out of touch with its clients and shackled to a Washington perspective. Many of its staff became risk averse. The failure of structural adjustment programs had led to antipathy in many client countries. Meanwhile, some resident representatives had shown how an effective leader on the ground could interact with national leaders to build an understanding of what the Bank could offer. Jim Adams in Tanzania is often cited as an example. President Nyerere's antipathy to the Bank was deep seated. Adams worked assiduously to rebuild bridges to the country.

Revitalizing the institution became the first priority for Wolfensohn. To do so, he pushed through a radical reorganization under the auspices of the Strategic Compact (Mallaby 2004). One key component of it was to decentralize the institution in terms of authority, responsibility, and personnel to the field offices. Moving staff, financial resources, and responsibility to the offices in the field, it was argued, would allow greater speed, flexibility, and borrower participation in designing country assistance strategies, preparing and supervising projects, and carrying out research. The reorganization created more CD positions and many were moved to the field. Since then, *country ownership* has become a Bank mantra, with greater emphasis on the clients as drivers of initiatives and processes.

Country Directors (CDs)

As the result of reorganization of 1987 and especially 1997, CDs gained more prominence and influence in Bank operation. They were the vehicles for decentralization and country ownership, pushed forward during Wolfensohn's tenure. One immediate result of decentralization was an increase in the number of CDs, from 19 after the 1987 reorganization to 51 in 1999. The idea was then to establish a direct link between the Bank and the client countries through CDs and their country teams. Since then, the number has shrunk as the responsibilities and authorities were consolidated at a regional level. Some of these CDs head single-country offices, while others represent multiple countries. Decentralization in terms of moving country units to the field was embraced by the Bank staff quickly. By 1999, 23 out of 51 CDs had been relocated to the field. By 2005, 32 of 46 CDs were based in the field, and in 2008, 32 of 41.

Overall, almost 80 percent of CDs were in the field at the end of 2008 (Table 5.1). In Africa, a continent of small countries, only Nigeria had its own CD and, 9 out of 11 CDs serviced more than three countries. In EAP, three CDs head a single country (Indonesia, Vietnam, Philippines), while China and Mongolia are combined. All its CDs are in the field. In SA, there are five CDs in the field, and all run single-country offices. The sixth CD is based in Washington, D.C.,

Table 5.1   Country Directors: 2008

	No. of CDs by region	No. of CDs in field	Single-country CDs	Two-country CDs	Three-or more country CDs
Africa	11	10	1	1	9
EAP	6	6	3	1	2
SA	6	5	5	—	1
ECA	7	4[a]	1	1	5
MENA	5	2	1	—	4
LAC	6	4	1	1	4
	41	32 (78%)	12	4	25

Note: 4[a]—4 CDs are in the field, and another one was moving to the field at the end of 2008.

and covers Afghanistan, Bhutan, and the Maldives. In LAC, only Brazil has its own CD, and four of its CDs are in the field. In ECA, one CD heads a single country (Russia), and one is responsible for two countries (Turkey and Cyprus). In MENA, there is one single-country CD (West Bank and Gaza). MENA has more CDs in HQ mainly because of the difficulties of setting up an office in a particular country without offending the others.

CDs are important players in the Bank's operation, whether in HQ or the field. They are the managers of the Bank's portfolio in global economic hotspots; they represent the Bank in the field and represent the countries where they work in Washington, D.C. They are the 'front-line' generals in the Bank's operations. They may have different managerial styles, and their capacity might vary. They are still the crème of the crème. Almost all CDs come to the job with previous knowledge of development; most have worked at the Bank for a long time.

Normally, RVPs select CDs. Good chemistry between them is important for the smooth operation in the region, particularly when CDs are located in the field and RVPs in HQ. The president and MDs get involved in the process only when strategic appointments have to be made, such as the CDs for Brazil, China, India, or those which need special attention. In these cases, the president and MDs are provided with a short list of candidates with a ranking for final decision. For example, after the Asian financial crisis, the Bank's program in Indonesia collapsed, and its reputation was ruined. The Bank needed a heavyweight CD, who not only had credibility, but also access to the president. Mark Baird, then VP for Strategy and Resource Management, 'stood down' to become the CD for Indonesia. After leading the Bank team at Rio Summit in 1992, Andrew Steer built his reputation in the Bank on the environment. He was already a director when the management decided it wanted a person with high caliber in Vietnam. He was 'headhunted' for the job and built a team there before moving on to Indonesia. Besides long experience in the Bank, most CDs are trained as economists. Many started as YPs. In 2008, for example, LAC replaced all its six CDs; four out of six new appointees joined the Bank as YPs. In EAP, five of the six CDs were YPs. The YPs' experience in different regions/countries and especially as macroeconomists, has prepared them for the CD's job. In addition to technical and managerial excellence, specific considerations may be part of the selection process where appropriate: experience working in post-conflict regions, ability to work with the major donors. Even the nationality of the candidate may come into the picture in rare cases.

Many CDs see decentralization as positive: 'CDs are the best job in the Bank, and the best CD job is the one in the field,' one CD proudly declared. Decentralization takes them closer to the action. In the field they do not feel they are mere ciphers. They witness changes on a daily basis and involve government counterparts directly in the debate on the formulation of projects or programs (Gill and Pugatch 2005). 'When you are in the field,' one CD explained, 'you have a lot of independence, and it is so much easier to get the balance between the institution and the client.' Another CD confirmed, 'When you are on the ground, you can have very different perspectives to when you work on missions when you tend to have preconceived ideas.' A CD, who later became a VP, encapsulated his experience away from the field: "I had withdrawal symptoms" (Gill and Pugath 2005:66). Another describes his experience working in Africa, Central America, and SA: 'This is what I do, and this is where I do it.' The general feeling is that there is 'no comparison' between HQ and field jobs. 'The field is better. You can feel your mission; you are close to clients and can see the impact; meanwhile, we are not caught up in bureaucracy and meetings, nor suffer from the bureaucratic aggravation.'

Some CDs like to be away from HQ so much that they seek one field position after another: 'In all 21 years while I have been working in the Bank, I have spent all my years, except 6, in the field, and, for most years, I have been separated from my immediate supervisor by at least one ocean.' Of course, being away in the field has its downside: CDs remain tied into the Bank's career structure. An initial three-year term can be extended; after five years, they will have to move on. The pyramid structure of the Bank makes it difficult to rise beyond director level, and there are not many VP positions to which they can aspire. A few see the CD position as their last job, and some retire when alternative options do not develop. There is some rotation between countries and regions. Smaller offices act as training grounds for larger. Yet, reentry to the Bank, though guaranteed, may be difficult, and lateral movement may not always be available. Since 1997, there have been both managed and competitive rotations for directors. Lateral transfer depends very much on timing. 'After a hardship appointment, many want compensation,' commented one CD. There may not be jobs available. 'You just have to apply.' A couple of CDs had to wait for a year or so after finishing their terms because there were no available CD positions. Some found it difficult to get another proper assignment because they had lost touch with their networks. One CD, after a post with high profile, floated around HQ for some time:

> I worried that they might make me redundant; I took this job, which is a sort of oubliette in the Bank sense. It was disheartening because they had told me how great a job I did, and the president and the managing director promised that there would not be a problem for me to get a good job once I was done there. Of course, things changed and a new president came, and there was no institutional commitment. I took this one, and now I am growing to like it.

CDs, like the rest of the staff, have their preferences. 'I had a choice to be the CD for either China or Indonesia,' one explained. 'I decided to come to Indonesia because there is not much the Bank can offer to China.' A CD for China commented, 'After this post, nothing seems to be too interesting.' Upon his arrival, a CD for Indonesia told the government, 'It is great privilege to be here and assist the country.' A CD for a smaller country explained how difficult it was to move laterally to another more interesting and larger country. Two CDs did not take their families to the field because both hoped it just was a stepping stone. This did not escape the attention of the client countries. How CDs see their position shapes the way they do their job.

Responsibilities

CDs have common responsibilities: communicating with the government, identifying what assistance the country needs and what the Bank can offer, negotiating with the government on the assistance packages, and managing the country office. As the manager of the country's portfolio, CDs need to take strategic leadership in working out CASs, nowadays often called country partnership strategies. If the country is no longer eligible for IDA, does the country need IBRD loans? In what field? What advantage can the Bank offer? In addition to loans, CDs have many instruments they can offer—AAA, TA, trust funds, funds and assistance from other multilateral institutions, or even private investment or forms of assistance. Packaging different products to meet the country's need is important, and creativity is what CDs need. Being in the field allows CDs to work closely with the government to identify needs that may not have been recognized by the government.

Managing Country Offices: With decentralization, managing the country unit becomes important. Even though CDs have only a few people directly accountable to them, the number of people working out of the country office can be large. Several issues complicate management. First, SDs and SMs are located in HQ, while the projects are designed and carried out in the field. Second, there is the challenge of managing both internationally recruited staff (IRS) and locally recruited staff (LRS).

First, each region organizes support for CDs in slightly different ways. There is no single Bank template. At a minimum, the CDs are supported by a country management unit that includes an operations officer, one or two assistants, and the country economist—and sometimes a governance adviser. While the country economist and governance adviser (if there is one) are key players in working out the CAS, they are nominally accountable to the SD in PREM. CASs are developed in the country office; projects and programs are designed, prepared, implemented, and supervised by people working out of the country office, if not on a permanent basis, at least on missions. With the matrix system, CDs may decide what and SDs may decide how; managing the relationship between *what* and *how* is not always easy.

In LAC and a few countries in EAP, sector coordinators provide not only technical expertise, but also links between CDs and SDs; it is therefore easier for the CDs to plan the program and monitor progress. For many CDs, especially in smaller countries, however, such direct support is not available. They depend on sector staff on missions and find it frustrating. 'I have known the sector people, local as well as international, working in my country, better than the sector manager in my country; yet, assessment of performance is done by a sector manager, who is not only in HQ, but also overstretched,' said one CD. 'There is little quality control they can provide.' For smaller countries or countries with smaller projects, CDs have difficulty getting support from SDs or SMs for the projects or products they want. 'We like to have this person to work on this project,' said another CD, 'but it is not up to me to decide.' 'I can say what item is vital for my country program, but the sector manager may disagree,' commented another CD. 'For example, I would say we need to start secondary education with an AAA before we decide whether any IDA loan is necessary; it can be very difficult if the SD does not agree with me and that happens.' Managing the country program for many smaller and less preferred countries means that the CDs concerned spend time and energy chasing resources.

A second complicating factor is the balance between IRS and LRS. CDs sit at the apex of local offices, where the total staff may rise to well over 100. Of those, only a small proportion (10 to 20 percent) will be IRS. Seldom are they assigned to their country of origin. Many international staff, on deployment to the field, are a breed apart. They like working in the field and want to stay there. It gives them a better sense of the country they seek to help. They regard a position in HQ 'disempowering': too many meetings, too many assessments of the work that other people are doing; not enough access to the clients, who represent the essential work of the Bank; and too easy to be bogged down by bureaucratic in-fighting. International staff are rotated every 3, 5 or 7 years, except for a rare few who have 'refused' to be relocated. The Bank's ultimate outlier, Scott Guggenheim ('there are outliers and outliers, and then there is Scott,' was one admiring colleague's quip) has been in Indonesia since the early 1990s. When he did get an assignment to work out of HQ, he based himself in Indonesia. His was a freewheeling style that focused on the local demands; he had no wish ever to work in Washington, D.C. The reaction of these officers in the field was not unusual. There was a belief that the Bank allowed greater scope for experimentation than was widely recognized, particularly in national offices away from Washington, D.C.

The 1997 reorganization introduced a 'one Bank, one staff' policy—that is, local staff and IRS should be treated the same in ranking and in performance assessment. The intent was to open up the opportunities for local staff. It has created a management challenge just as more responsibility is delegated to the country offices. International staff are supposed to bring the global best practices to the countries, and local staff provide local knowledge. The constant tension can be seen in many country offices; some CDs argue, 'the "one Bank, one staff" was a naïve idea' rather than practical policy because of the limitations of benefits and promotion.

The local professionals, whether engineers, economists, or procurement experts, can be as highly qualified as IRS, with doctorates from American or European universities. They choose to work in their own countries, where they have their families and friends. They are therefore paid 'local rates' that are adjusted for cost of living and local expenses, leaving them better off than their local counterparts but worse off than their internationally recruited colleagues. Their promotion prospects are limited too if they do not want to work in other countries, because promotion to higher levels of the Bank hierarchy requires international experience across regions. A few local staff have taken on projects in neighboring countries without being relocated. It remains questionable whether this experience will help them in their careers. One explained,

> I have been working on energy finance for five years, and have done some work with HQ staff across several countries—Afghanistan, Eritrea, and India—while I am a locally hired person in Bangladesh. This kind of work has helped me bring good lessons back to my country and help cross-fertilization in the region. Serving different clients, however, created some trouble with my managers regarding charges—whom to charge, on what, and at what costs. If all managers are open minded, there will not be problems. But this is not always the case.

In general, local staff serve in the office much longer than international staff. Some of them have worked for 20 years or more. They have connections with the national bureaucracies out of which many of them came and understand the intricate local politics. 'After all,' said one, 'we have to live with the consequences long after they [the CDs and IRS] have gone'. Many provide the institutional memory, a continuing source of insights and information about the country. They can offer the CD a depth of experience and a series of networks. Their experience, knowledge, and ability sometimes can also impede the Bank's work. The Bank is a global institution; if no global practices are spread because locals insist the local way of doing things is the best way, what would be the relevance of the Bank? It can be a real headache for CDs when local politics is highly polarized, and some local staff may become identified, even connected, to one side or the other. Some LRS bring their political biases to the office, and open confrontation can erupt during meetings.

In some small and poor countries, where few international staff want to work on a permanent basis, CDs depend on locals. But 'few LRS would fight HQ staff on a principle even if they do not believe HQ people are right' or think TTLs only get the job half done. 'We are as risk averse as civil servants,' one long-serving locally recruited economist bemoaned. 'We are well paid, and no universities in the country can match our job security, salary, trips, pension, and social status; it gives us a sense of importance, but we also become so insecure and are afraid of losing our job.' Integrating the IRS and LRS into a team can be a great challenge for many CDs.

Working with the Client Countries: Working with client countries involves interactions with the government on behalf of the Bank, interactions with the donors on behalf of the country, and interactions with the civil societies and the public. CDs and their teams represent the Bank to client countries. 'When I took the position as the CD, the MD went with me to see the country's new prime minister,' recalled one CD. 'The MD was telling the prime minister, "In the old days, it was my job to know how to help you. Now, he is here, representing the Bank".' CDs become the contact point between the Bank and the government, working with the staff of the Ministry of Finance. Location changes the dynamic and possibly the capacity to achieve outcomes. Rather than being visitors on a mission, the Bank staff are available for consultation in a timely manner. Face-to-face meetings are constant. Lines of accountability become more blurred; immediate access to national officials can be more pressing than links to Washington, D.C. The internal processes and meetings at main office fade into the background.

Even though formally CDs share similar responsibilities in providing assistance, their ability to do so depends on a wide range of factors. The size and location of the client countries can make a difference. In small and aid-dependent countries, the Bank looms large in the local economy, and CDs attract media attention. Their statements make the front pages of the local press, and they can hold the same prominence as ambassadors from their important allies. CDs and their teams may talk regularly at ministerial level and can ask to see the president or the prime minister in the expectation of an audience within the next day or so. Even if they try not to abuse that privilege by asking for access too often, it is an indication of their impact.

In large countries, such as Brazil, China, or India, the Bank is a minor player. The CDs are likely to talk to officials at the third or fourth level of the ministry of finance, see the minister rarely, and the president not at all. The Bank president may meet the minister, but not necessarily the president of the country. Large countries also tend to have a variety of representatives in Washington, D.C., anyway, especially Latin American countries, whose close geographic proximity means that their ministers and officials visit Washington, D.C., frequently. The Bank becomes just one of their contacts. Governments in these countries may ring the Bank president if they are annoyed.

Some CDs have prominence as much as a result of their own reputation as for the Bank's activities. This is one reason Bank presidents insist on making the final choice of CDs for large countries. For example, David Dollar may not have the access to the finance minister, but he frequently lectures in Chinese universities. An economist with standing in his own right, he has the ability to argue the Bank's case by talking about economic constructs to the intellectual community from which the government increasingly draws policy ideas. He does radio interviews that are heard across the country. He runs a blog that can act as a powerful instrument for disseminating opinions. In sum, CDs in the field "can have a direct effect on public opinion through a communication strategy and can judge firsthand how to position the Bank effectively in the country context" (Kavalsky 2005:42). Influence can be often exerted in both small and large countries by working through the local intellectuals, assisting in their research, and allowing them to speak and say as locals what Bank officials could not say.

Attitudes toward the Bank vary. Some countries welcome the staff; others treat them with suspicion. Ed Lim worked in China and India. He described the Bank's relationship with China as "a marriage made in heaven." There was no doubt that China ran the program, but it saw the Bank as a much-valued partner that made a difference in its transition from a command economy to a market economy. In contrast, the Bank's relationship with India "should be seen as an arranged marriage." India felt either entitled to support or that it did not need the Bank (Lim 2005:107, 108). The contrast was striking. The attitude of a country might not depend only on size. East Timor and Cambodia were chronically suspicious, whereas Vietnam was very supportive. The local attitude to the Bank as an institution matters.

Easy or difficult, the CDs' capacity to work with their counterparts is crucial for the success of the Bank. The process sets up a notion of dual accountability; Bank staff see their responsibility to the country as well as to their superiors.

China's minister of finance during most of the 1980s said to me when I took over the management of the China department: "I have been told that more than 100 professionals work for you in your department. I want to say to you that they also work for me—for the Chinese authorities. We should take joint responsibility for their work program." And he did—not himself directly, but through his vice minister. (Burki 2005:132)

One CD commented that now his real boss was the minister of finance, not the RVP. Heading one of the smaller offices in the region, he received little attention from the RVP. 'In Washington,' said another senior official, 'I work for an organization. Here I work for a client.' That dual accountability is regarded as fundamental in the field. When CDs deal on a daily basis with ministers of finance or senior officials and especially when the client governments insist that CDs and their teams are accountable to both HQ and them, traditional hierarchical lines of accountability are attenuated. The sense of accountability becomes more complex than a single line portrayed by PA analyses.

For the Bank staff, there is no comparison with a system that relied on missions. If there are no people on the ground, and the Bank work depends on missions, they may not always get access to the country. A former CD to Egypt, for example, wanted to visit the country. He was constantly told by his counterpart in the government, although he was most welcome, "the timing was not convenient for the government." It took some months and a growing sense of concern before anything could be arranged from outside (Sud 2005:249). Those on the spot have had much easier access, and they are far more aware of the need to adjust ideas to suit the local circumstances.

Whether in large or small countries, CDs can be important players in the local economy and sometimes politics if they can take a strategic leadership; understand what comparative advantages the Bank has, what the country needs, and how their teams can provide the necessary assistance; and build good relationships and trust with the client governments. There are potential dangers too. Staff could become too close to the country leaders: 'Muddling contact with friendship,' as one VP put it. As a result, "key policy issues will not be raised or will be raised too late because of the proximity of the country director to the policy makers" (Nankani 2005: 83).

CDs as Strategists: The Bank staff bring a smorgasbord of global goods, based on international experiences. They ask, where is the Bank's comparative advantage in this country? What can they bring that will distinguish the Bank from any other consultancy firms or other bilateral aid agencies? The larger and wealthier the country, the greater its human resources, the more the Bank staff will be partners in development, conscious of their limitations. The paradox is: 'In EAP, you have some of the best clients of the Bank, and they expect you to deliver some exceptionally good work,' explained one CD. 'There is some degree of complacency because the clients are generally so good that they pick up on a lot of mistakes that staff make.' Moreover, since these countries can raise funds readily in open markets, CDs will have to emphasis the knowledge and technical skills as their contribution. Initiatives often come from the client countries—the Bank is provided with a list of projects for discussion, and the staff will pick those where they can bring global knowledge to bear. CDs are aware that the Bank needs the country as much as, if not more than, the country needs the Bank.

In countries that are poorer, particularly in human resources, the staff have to be proactive in identifying areas where they can help. The process may be slow, starting with technical analysis or policy notes to raise interest. They may explain what the Bank can offer. Only then will the country agree to the assistance, whether a concessional loan from IDA, grants from donors, or TA. The government of poor and aid-dependent countries can be overwhelmed with what the Bank can offer. CDs and their teams can be in high demand. They might be required to do much of the government's work, selecting the projects/programs, and assisting in the development of the proposals. Where there is limited human expertise, the Bank's staff can become semi-insiders, crucial to the government's performance. On occasions, the Bank staff are asked to go on secondment to the government so that they can sit on the other side of the negotiation table for a couple of years. In these countries, challenges for Bank staff are greater also because "if you make mistakes, they tend to reverberate."

For most staff, the combination of knowledge and loans distinguishes the Bank from think tanks, consulting firms, or commercial banks. Pushing loans is often identified as one of the worst sins of the Bank, but it is not what is going on in the field. Rather than seeking to meet loan targets, most operations staff argue they commit to 'broad ideas of indicative progress.' 'What is the point of pushing loans if the country cannot absorb it,' said several CDs. Indeed, they are advised not to be pushy. 'Is there the sense out there of pressure to lend? I don't believe it,' said one senior official. 'We focus on results on the ground.' 'Volume is a perverse incentive,' said one SD.

CDs were once judged by the volume of Bank activity for clients. Yet, there have been no lending targets for the last 15 years, said a typical CD, who could not recall anyone who got a black mark for not lending enough. The Bank wants to lend, but the criteria are good projects, not targets. CDs are often asked by their VPs what they expect to achieve in the next years. Then they may be held to the commitments, but they do not believe that there is pressure to meet lending targets above those set in the CAS. The process is bottom up, with many of the initiatives coming from the field. Some officials worked with a country for three years without providing a single loan, but their tenure was still considered a success because they managed to keep open a dialogue on which the Bank could build when circumstances became more propitious. The process could be gradual.

A minister of finance may constantly seek advice, talk about options for developing proposals. The request for help often needs quick responses. In Bangladesh, for example, the political situation was delicate; the caretaker government was weak, and the chief adviser had only ten advisers.

> We were asked to give eight policy notes in six months—all on demand. We got a call from the government that wanted to know the economic impacts of the flood. We did a quick study and rough calculation. It became the first-page story of the newspaper because it carried the weight of the Bank's standing.

In those places where there is extensive donor activity, CDs and their teams can act as conduits to bring the demands and supplies together. An active CD on the spot can use the leverage of the Bank's funds and reputation to establish a powerful network of donors. In Indonesia, the tsunami brought a flood of relief funds, over $800 million, for the reconstruction of Aceh. The Bank acted as the donor coordinator, ensuring there was some common direction among donors, who did not have the capacity to deliver the projects themselves. A committee of representatives was designed to reduce the duplication. With donors' money, the staff, for example, were able to hire extra bodies to develop new initiatives, not only with the central government, but also with local governments, civil societies, and even farmers in villages. The activity brought the Bank into closer relations with the government. It won praises from some donors, even if it sometimes caused tension with others.

In Bosnia the CD worked with European donors, to determine what should be provided to rebuild infrastructure. He wanted to ensure the pledges of support were met and assistance provided in an evenhanded manner so that all sides could benefit from the 'peace dividend.' A competent and veteran member of staff was placed in Brussels to coordinate the efforts. A presence was important in dealing with donors as well as clients. That worked elsewhere too. "In Mozambique...the Bank was the acknowledged leader of the aid community, which included at least 20 bilateral and multilateral aid agencies in each country" (Pomerantz 2005:51).

Working with donors requires a different set of skills. One CD explained,

Donors often cause more headaches than the government. In government, I know who I deal with, where they come from, and why they are doing it. It may be frustrating to deal with them from time to time, but you are not wasting your time. This comes with the territory. The same cannot be said about donor community. I think all of us who have to spend a lot of time on donor coordination and donor management find that it is often not productive at all in working with donors who try to drag the coordination to their own direction.

A strategic role often depends on the CD's judgment of the root of the problem. After the Oslo Accord in 1993, the Bank opened engagement in the West Bank and Gaza, and there was a steady growth in the economy, especially in the second half of the 1990s. After 2000, however, the region has seen dramatic increases in unemployment and a decline in the economy. The Bank country team produced a couple of reports, identifying the root of the problem as the strict border control and crossing restrictions imposed by the Israelis after the breakout of the second intifada. If they were concerned about economic growth in West Bank and Gaza, they would have to talk to the Israeli government, presenting the case not from the point of view of economic development of Palestinians, but from that of security of Israelis. 'We were able to convince the Israelis that it was in their interest to negotiate with the Palestinians on border crossing, and it eventually led to the negotiation with us as a proxy between the Palestinians and the Israelis,' said the CD. It was one strategy that could be tried, even if it did not eventually work.

CDs need to find their own edge and right strategies to deal with development issues.

CD as diplomats: Countries have different cultures and political systems. Bank staff in the field have to adjust to local aspirations and idiosyncrasies. In Africa, relations were often laid back; in MENA, they were more formal. Moscow had different needs from Delhi, Turkey from Kosovo. While the Bank is a worldwide institution that prides itself on learning lessons internationally, staff have to be careful how they use examples. In ECA, countries in transition from communism want to know how their Western neighbors have done, but not what other developing countries are doing. The middle-income countries are willing to hear about the experience of Organization of Economic Cooperation and Development (OECD) countries, but not poor ones. In a region, political sensitivity is required too: the government in Sri Lanka may be willing to learn of changes in LAC or EAP, but not in India. In Morocco, staff do not talk about Tunis. These examples may seem trivial, but they are crucial to build trust. What they want to be, whom they aspire to emulate, are important factors in planning assistance. 'In the field, we are much more aware of these politically and culturally sensitive issues,' stated many Bank staff.

Bank staff are obliged by the Articles of Agreement not to get involved in politics. Yet, they need to understand those politics in order to appreciate where the support can be found, what might be achieved, and, above all, what the country can use effectively. The field staff are expected to understand quickly the political dynamics: 'Who are the players, where are the obstacles?' They need to develop intuition about 'what works.' Where will the champions of reform be?

Governments may be suspicious of the Bank; they may have a record of failing to meet the obligations that had previously been accepted. Some countries have stable governments, while in others, governments may be toppled without warning. CDs need to have the communication channel open with RVPs and even the president to protect the Bank as an institution, to ensure the safety of its staff, and to continue working with whoever is in power. It can never be easy:

> Suddenly ten ministers all decided to resign at the same time to protest against the corrupt president, and only three remained in the office. It was not our job to clean up the bad government. We cannot play politics, or we are dead in this country. What we can do, however, is to support those people and departments who are clean and continue working.

In another country, two prime ministers were jailed within a year. The military took over. In the caretaker government, the chief adviser, a de facto prime minister, was a former Bank staffer. 'What are we going to do? We do not like the military regime, but we cannot afford to pull out and leave the people in poverty;' explained Bank staff. 'Then we do not take the government head on; we unbundle it and work with those we think we can work with.'

During a crisis, CDs can be major or minor players. Client countries may need quick access to the Bank experts and funds (even though the Bank does not provide what its staff call 'ambulance services'). Decentralization allowed rapid action. One CD contrasted the minimal reaction to the Brazil crisis in 1995, when he was based in Washington, D.C., and the speedy response when financial crises hit the country in 1997 and 1999. In the latter case he could immediately have lunch with the minister of finance. The additional level of trust meant he was able to provide "jointly done analytical work, just-in-time policy advice, and financial support." Trust had grown because of the Bank's stance of "not pushing for reforms…for which there was no apparent ownership" (Nankani 2005:82). Basil Kavalsky was the CD, based in HQ, for Armenia, the Baltic States, Belarus, Georgia, Moldova, and Ukraine during 1993–1997 and later became the CD, based in Warsaw, for Poland and the Baltic states from 1997 to 2000. Comparing his experience in HQ and in the field, he emphasized the benefits of closeness, too.

> Decentralization forced the Bank to give far more responsibility to the country director, even though the pre-1997 system ostensibly integrated both the program and sector functions under the country director. Being on the spot enables the country director to identify demand and needs as they arise and to organize responses to them. (Kavalsky 2005: 42)

Availability encouraged utilization. 'They know we are here, so they will ring us up and ask advice' was a common refrain.

Representing the Country in HQ

Most client countries see the CDs as the representative of the Bank, their first point of call. CDs and the country teams therefore have a dual role themselves. 'During the day, I lobby my country on behalf of the Bank. At night, I lobby the Bank on behalf of my country,' explained a CD from a time zone that meant his video discussions with HQ had to be held in the evenings. For CDs in the field, there is a coordinator in HQ to keep the communication channel open with EDs, VPs, SDs, and other corporate bodies, such as the human resources division.

CDs are granted a great deal of autonomy, but exercising the autonomy effectively depends on good relationships with other players. CDs and their teams need to keep EDs informed and detect the potential objections or questions about any proposals, whether CAS or projects/programs, which have to go through the Board. EDs can however be useful in less official ways. CDs may test out ideas, get advice on the circumstances in a country, or, even as a last resort, ask EDs to make phone calls into the national bureaucracies to loosen some blockage. They are regarded as a potential asset to be activated where necessary.

Working with RVPs is the key for successful country programs. RVPs allocate the budget, developed over a series of months early in the year, and through discussions with country and sector directors. Budgeting is seen as a combination of 'art, science, and politics.' CDs are inevitably locked into the Bank's processes and must interact with their colleagues, through the matrix system. They must negotiate with SDs and will need to hold the latter to task if projects for which they are responsible are not progressing adequately.

Often the issue is not just about financial assistance. Many IDA countries do not have the capacities to absorb all the funds. Middle-income countries do not necessarily want loans. Meanwhile, RVPs represent the interest of the Bank and have the responsibility to get the corporate agenda incorporated into the country programs. How VPs share out the budget affects CDs' work in the field. When an RVP decided to increase the budget for several fragile states in a region, the CD in charge was able to have more staff and expand the country program. Meanwhile CDs for middle-income countries in the region had to redesign their strategies to keep the Bank relevant.

When the president or the VP visits the country, the CD and his/her team represent the country, inform them about what is going on, and make the country's demands heard. These visits may be frequent in some places, possibly up to six times a year if the country is temporarily significant to the Bank; they may rarely happen at all elsewhere. When the president shows particular interest in the country, the CD needs to ensure not only the president but also the VP is informed about local conditions. To many CDs, VPs are a useful resource to devise ways of doing what they want and ensure they are protected in Washington, D.C. Keeping the VP onside is important; there should be no surprises. 'Wolfensohn was very involved in the program in

West Bank and Gaza, and he visited the place regularly,' said a CD. The VP stepped aside to give room to the president, and meanwhile, 'he kept me fully informed of where Wolfensohn was coming from so that I could be alert.'

Direct links to the president, however, are not always to the advantage of the country or the CD. 'It is the sort of moth and candle syndrome,' said one CD. 'So I made sure that the VP knew exactly what was going on and could handle it in my stead.' Visits can leave problems behind too. After a senior Bank official promised the University of Rio de Janeiro Bank support to rehabilitate the university's museum, the CD recalled "how frustrating it was for me as a country director to be told by this Bank official, after the fact, that we would need to find a way to honor his promise" (Nankani 2005:72). This is the dual role played by CDs—representing the country while being part of the large Bank programs.

What CDs Do: The Diaries

A former CD, now a VP, said, '95 percent of decisions are now made at country level.' It is possible to get some feel of what CDs do by looking at their diaries. Three CDs gave us a three-week summary of their diaries. Their activities fit into four categories: internal Bank relations, both in-country and with HQ; talking to the country; talking to third parties; and providing information and education.

First, there are meetings with other Bank staff. Project planning meetings at the concept stage are chaired by the CDs, often undertaken with benefit of videoconference. Then there are the meetings with colleagues in the local office. CDs may not have direct supervisory responsibility for these staff, but they look to CDs for leadership. One had 30 minutes each week available as an open door, if staff wanted to talk. There can be briefings with visiting missions from Washington, D.C., or discussions on possible future actions, in areas as diverse as water supply, higher education, or the CAS. Sometimes CDs will meet with the lead specialists to discuss collaboration across the office or the response of the office to local criticism. Essentially these are all local activities.

CDs must also look upward. If an MD or RVP visits, they will travel with them across the country for a few days or accompany them to meet leadings officials. If a president comes, all the potential snags will be anticipated. Routes to be driven will be timed, venues checked, toilets located. Nothing will be left to chance. Some CDs have weekly phone calls to the RVP written into the diary; others talk with larger meetings by video link. In addition, every year there are two-day retreats for Bank staff to work with sector directors and managers, with sectoral presentations, draft action plans, and a wrap-up by the RVP.

Second, there are meetings with officials of the client country. In China, for example, they could include the Ministry of Finance, the National Development and Reform Commission (NDRC), or even the Olympic committee. Some meetings were significant—when a new loan was signed; others were routine. Where the Bank dealt with provincial/ state governments, there could be visits to those states to meet senior officials. Projects sites visited by the CDs may be hours away from the office. The process can be challenging and not always comfortable. Far from the image of limousines and five-star hotels that critics suggest, one official noted, 'the guest houses were not that easy. First you ask if the rooms have running water, then what hours it is on and only then if it is hot.' In the Baltic countries, when there was no heating, they had to take portable heaters and needed gloves to hold pens. In Africa, visits to projects were often made difficult because there might not be safe flights or even roads to the region. In the Congo all the airlines were blacklisted by the EU, and there were no roads.

The third activity is interaction with third parties. They can include meetings with other donor organizations, such as DFID, or groups of donors to discuss development of a carbon strategy. There were delegations or representatives from the IMF, UNESCO, Oxfam, or even corporations, such as Chevron. There might be social occasions for national days or meetings with ambassadors or heads of mission.

Fourth, depending on the local situation, there is the educational extension work: appearing on television, talking on the radio, giving interviews with the press, lecturing at universities, responding to criticism. CDs are public figures. The more significant the Bank is seen to be by the local community, the higher the profile (but not necessarily the better the reputation). Every CD speaks for the Bank in the community.

Diaries show how local the focus is. When a president or an MD visits, it is a big deal. RVPs come more often, but will be a centre of activity for the duration of the visit. CASs and loans need final noting or approval of the Board. Those apart, much of the activity is run without the Washington office as a dominant presence. CDs must relate to the demands, and the governments, of their region.

How it can work: One CD gave this written description of the careful wooing of a client.

In 1998, I paid a courtesy call (in my capacity as the World Bank's country director for the Philippines) to the newly appointed chief justice of the Philippines Supreme Court and asked him about his vision for what he wanted to accomplish. I was struck by his clear vision of a judiciary that is independent, effective and efficient, and worthy of public trust and confidence. I said to myself that here is a visionary leader and a champion of reforms that the World Bank would be honored to support. I offered our assistance. The chief justice was somewhat taken aback as his perception of the Bank was that it pushes conditionality and structural adjustment without due regard to the country situations. He cautiously asked what help the Bank can provide. I promised to send him a sample of documentation from other countries where the Bank was helping judicial reforms projects.

Next when I saw him, the chief justice said that they had read the documents that I sent him, and his team was interested in the Bank's help, but he and his colleagues were concerned about the judicial independence if they borrowed from the Bank. I told him that we are ready to help with technical assistance, and they do not have to take a loan, and there were varieties of ways in which we could help the Philippines to reform its legal system. The chief justice was surprised to hear this.

In the following months, we talked about the possibilities and mobilized grants from trust funds, combined with some of the Bank's administrative budget, to finance workshops, to bring people from others places to show what was done in other countries; and study trips. With this help, a judiciary reform program was developed by the Supreme Court team, and we stayed in a purely advisory role. Once the program was ready, we helped the chief justice to present it to the bilateral and other donors in the country (through local aid coordination groups as well as at the consultative group meeting) to raise as much grant financing as possible and promised to be a lender of the last resort. This approach of providing technical assistance and being a lender only if a funding gap remained was much appreciated by the Supreme Court and the government.

We stayed as supporters of the reform program and helped raise funds for it for more than three years. In the fourth year it became clear that more funds were needed than were available through grants alone, and the Bank was requested to provide a loan, which we did. The reform program is now in its seventh year, and the Supreme Court is using a blend of grants and loans to finance the second phase. At the end of the first loan, we organized an international conference on the matter. The Philippines government then took the second loan.

This story highlights several aspects of the day-to-day work CDs typically do, that is, being alert to reform champions in the country, who can provide leadership for key development priorities; providing information and promoting cross-country learning about reforms other countries are undertaking; using a variety of aid instruments to provide funding and TA to reforms agendas/champions; providing leadership in aid coordination; and working in partnerships with other donors. In short, help the country-owned reform agendas through a combination of money, knowledge and partnership.

Changing the dynamic: Locating more CDs and staff in national capitals has changed the way the Bank does its business. It has increased the levels of discretion and the freedom of CDs have. "In the field, the accountabilities seemed so much clearer, and the feedback loop was so much shorter. There was no comparison in terms of job satisfaction and effectiveness" (Kavalsky 2005:42). Decentralization has also changed the relationship between the field staff and those at HQ. There is a qualitative difference in having an RVP down the corridor and weekly meetings and being on the other side of the world, communicating by e-mail or videoconference and meeting three or four times a year. When the contacts with the officials in the client government happen on a regular, even daily, basis, CDs are ever more conscious of client demands and complaints.

Away from HQ, staff felt a sense of autonomy; there was less aggravation, fewer meetings, and less internal politics. They spent more time talking to clients about programs. RVPs endorsed the approach: 'If you have the confidence of the VP and room to maneuver, then CDs are crucial players.' They can have scope for creativity. Senior advisers laughed off the idea that there was any close control. RVPs normally do not understand the local conditions as well as the CD. 'The role of VPs,' a senior official said, is to 'help an autonomous CD to get his way in Washington; we don't need him in the region. The notion that we are dictated to from Washington is crazy; we require a massive engagement on the ground.' No wonder we were repeatedly told that 'the CD is the best job in the Bank, and the best CD jobs are in the field'!

Most RVPs recognize this reality. There is little impression of extensive orders from above to tell the CDs what they should do. The Bank, explained a VP, is a bottom-up organization. The local staff are the experts; they know what can be achieved. Only rarely will VPs, and presidents even less often, know enough of the political and economic conditions to override the local view. They make strategic decisions on directions for the Bank. Links between CDs and the presidents and senior management teams will depend in part on the significance to the Bank of a particular country. If it is regarded as important, if a senior official has a particular interest in what is achieved, or if there is a crisis, presidents and RVPs may both visit regularly and provide specific suggestions. Other countries, in some cases whole regions, may for a time be effectively over the horizon, with staff there left alone.

The other side of the same coin is that people in HQ, according to a senior adviser in a VP's office, can feel isolated because most action occurs in the field. Even RVPs can occasionally feel distant because information is inevitably 'asymmetrical.' The extreme case was the CD who reportedly welcomed his VP with the comment that the VP should 'keep out and let him do the job;' next time he wanted to give his approval for the visit and would agree only if there was a useful purpose for the VP to fulfill. Only CDs in their last rotation and of standing with the Bank could be as blunt.

A key issue is how the decentralization of functions, staff, and authority is balanced with global knowledge and the Bank as a global institution. In 2005, a management task force examined the impact of decentralization. It noted some issues that are important to development, such as HIV/AIDS, climate change, infectious diseases, or energy security, are global issues that transcend regions, countries, and even sectors and that require global efforts and global strategies. At the moment, these issues are still handled only at the region/country level. For example, in LAC climate change is a 'beam' within the SD network to pool all the resources there. In India, staff are working on developing a carbon trading scheme. Some RVPs champion regional flagship reports on water, governance, or education because many of these issues are otherwise only tackled at the country level. Decentralization may be seen as the best way to deal with national issues, but there remains a case on cross-national issues for a consistent Bank approach.

Decentralization has brought many Bank staff to the field, but distribution of human capacity varies greatly. Working in the field appeals to many Bank staff, but some locations are far more attractive than others. Plenty of people will take their families to live and work in New Delhi, Beijing, Jakarta, or Buenos Aires, where good international schools are available, society is relatively safe, work is interesting, and projects or programs tend to be large enough to add to their reputation. It is much harder to find those willing to live in Dhaka, Kinshasa, or Port Moresby.

OPCS conducted a survey in 2007 to find out what factors discouraged staff from applying for positions as CDs or country managers in fragile states, identified as Low Incomes Countries under Stress. It found the reasons were partly personal: separation from family, who could not move there; lack of access to medical services; or good education for their children. There were also institutional factors. These countries had less standing in the Bank's hierarchy, there was no chance to manage large programs or administer large loans, and often there was little 'cutting-edge' technical work needed. Reentry then became problematic. Many remained concerned that higher-level positions in these countries, whether country managers or higher technical people, would be 'the best dead-end jobs in the Bank,' to cite one remark on the joys and frustrations of being a resident country manager. To address the issue of attracting talented people to work in difficult places, the Bank would have to make these positions more attractive and recognize in promotion criteria the different skills staff had to exercise: client dialogue, donor coordination, managing politically sensitive reform (OPCS 2007).

Conclusion

Despite a public perception that the Bank is a Washington institution, decentralization in the past 10–15 years has strengthened the 'many faces' of the Bank, and CDs and their teams have gained a degree of autonomy that cannot readily be wound back. A key question that persists is, how to ensure that people in country offices will not go local? Hierarchy assumes a clear line of accountability. When CDs and their staff are in the field, they can feel they have joint lines of accountability, to their superiors and to their clients. The latter they see every day. A sense of dualism in accountability can be created. An overzealous commitment to the mores of a country can reduce everything to local solutions. Then it remains a serious question how the Bank as a multilateral institution can ensure that best global practices can be spread to its client countries.

Some have asked for *more* decentralization of responsibility, functions, and personnel to the field because even though actions take place in the field, project/program approval and appraisal still occurs in HQ. Others, however, have argued that decentralization has gone too far and reduced the effectiveness of the Bank as a global institution.

The contention will not be readily resolved. A former Bank official explained the mismatch between image and reality:

> The Bank...has a somewhat schizophrenic quality, with marked rhetorical focus on decentralization, a reality that most day-to-day decisions in practice are made by operational staff, and a mystique of centralized and often rigid decision making. (Marshall 2008:72)

CHAPTER SIX

Research in DEC and in Operations

The Bank is a bank because it offers financial assistance to developing countries. It is nonetheless more than a bank because it offers its client countries a bundle of services. While the management has emphasized that the Bank is a knowledge bank, its staff are aware their comparative advantage is the combination of knowledge, expertise, finance, and services. The Bank's intellectual role as a source of expertise and advice on development issues is widely accepted outside the Bank. Within the Bank, however, there are competing cultures about the generation, dissemination, and use of knowledge. To the operations staff, knowledge is a useful commodity to allow them to persuade and assist. To researchers, knowledge has its own value. These staff may not have quite the university belief in generating knowledge for its own sake, but within the constraints of the Bank's mission, they appreciate the weight of good ideas. We could add that knowledge as the basis for teaching and training, undertaken by the World Bank Institute (WBI), is a third culture beyond the scope of our chapter here. Outside the Bank, serious questions have been raised about the Knowledge Bank: if research people are also advocates of the Bank policies, can objective research be done? How can 'intellectual freedom' be balanced with the 'corporate agenda'?

The Bank management identified four objectives of research:

1. Supporting operation
2. Improving the Bank's policy advice to its member countries
3. Broadening the understanding of the development processes
4. Assisting in developing research capacity in the Bank's member countries.

Research is done throughout the Bank—by the research group in the Development Economics (DEC), research staff at the anchors, and operation people in regions and networks. The Bank prides itself on its research commitment. Many researchers are attracted to the Bank because, unlike other international organizations, the Bank 'is interested in research and has a strong culture of learning and clear procedures in conducting research,' a senior officer stated, comparing his experience at different organizations.

The first section of this chapter will provide a brief glimpse of this long history and the culture created and continued until today. The second section discusses the issues of who generates what knowledge at the Bank and what their priorities are. The third section explores knowledge dissemination. Balancing demand for and supply of research is a challenge. The last section highlights the constant tension in the project cycles—lending, learning, and knowledge creation. Even on the issue of research, the Bank has many faces.

History

Nowhere in the Articles of Agreement was research mentioned; yet, research has been an integral part of the Bank's economic work from the outset. In 1946 the Research Department was "responsible for economic, statistical and other research required in connection with the operations of the Bank." The department would cooperate with the research departments of the IMF and other UN agencies; "the research staff of the Bank [would be] confined to a small group of highly qualified economists and statisticians" (Annual Report 1946:8). It mainly served the management, the EDs, and the Bank's operations:

> The Research department is responsible for obtaining information and preparing studies and analyses for the use of management and the Executive Directors in their determination of economic and financial policy, for preparing specific studies of an economic and financial character as requested by other departments of the Bank, and for maintaining liaison on economic matters with other appropriate organizations. (Annual Report 1947:21)

The Research Department was renamed the Economic Department in 1948, and "the function of making studies of economic and financial conditions in the territories of members [was] transferred from the Loan Department to the Economic Department" (Annual Report 1948:31).

Once lending shifted from reconstruction to development, an immediate concern was the creditworthiness of the countries requesting the borrowing. Research focused on how the lending would fit into the broader development strategy of the country. "A number of the very able economists working in the Bank...were looking at the problems of developing countries and beginning to come up with remedial prescriptions" (Kraske 1996:98). Research allowed the Bank to understand the problems of the borrowing countries and their potential for development.

Research served operations: with the analyses provided by economists, general practitioners made decisions on the design of specific lending operations, the conditions attached to them, and whether and when to go forward. Eugene Black made sure that economists were expected to provide advice only. Indeed the Economic Department was abolished during the first reorganization of the Bank in 1952. "An Economic Staff was maintained to *advise* the management and operational departments on general economic, financial and investment problems of concern to the Bank, and to provide statistical services (Annual Report 1952–1953:42).

In 1960s, economists were given a larger role under George Woods, who argued, "You can't have a development agency unless it has as its fuselage the loans which are being made, but one wing has to be project work and the other wing has to be economics" (quoted from Kraske 1996:134). The Bank had to develop its capacity to initiate ideas. With decolonization on its way, scholarly studies on development mushroomed. Further, as the rich countries had "accepted a measure of responsibility for the progress of the poor," they had developed "institutions for granting aid to other countries, and these institutions are constantly evolving in the direction of greater professionalism and efficiency" (Woods 1965/1966:207–208). To keep the Bank relevant, "the Bank wishes to make its own knowledge and experience in the development field as widely available as possible" (Annual Report 1966/1967:17). Research, then, was not only designed to serve Bank operations, but to contribute to the broader debate over development.

In 1966, George Woods introduced the first of the staff numbered working papers:

The benefits of research are greater the further they are spread. Some of the work done within or for the Bank and its affiliated organizations may be useful to those who are engaged in the practice of sound economic development...[our research] will have unashamed pragmatic bias,...[yet] the papers may be a modest stimulate to further research, particularly in the troubled zone where theory meets real life. (Woods 1966)

Under McNamara, the Bank's research activities expanded in response to the growing diversification of its lending. In January 1971, the central economics staff were reorganized into three departments: the Economics Department, the Economic Program Department, and the Development Research Centre. The Economic Program Department was created to support and review Area Departments' country economic analyses and programs and to advise on the policy issues that emerged. The Development Research Centre (formerly the Basic Research Centre) was to undertake economic research closely linked to Bank Group activities and to coordinate with other research organizations outside the Bank. McNamara established a Research Committee to review the Bank's principal research activities and to improve the effectiveness of the use of the Bank resources. It was also to contribute to "the great discussion on how to advance the economic development of the underdeveloped world" (McNamara 1968:v).

There was little debate on the first part of the objective—serving and improving the Bank operations. Its remit to provide cutting-edge knowledge in development studies was, however, challenged by many in the academic community. As development issues were widely debated in the 1970s, the research at the Bank faced increasing criticism too. "The Bank, sensitive to some of the criticism of the academic community, undertook between 1977 and 1979 to set up Specialized Research Advisory Panels of outside experts to evaluate its research in six fields" (Ayres 1983:29). Some were positive, while others were not so.

Whatever the external opinions, the Bank's research was not highly respected internally, especially by its operational staff, who viewed the research staff "as misplaced academics who never built a dam or laid a road." In turn, the research staff considered the operational staff "as dam and road builders incapable of scaling the higher reaches of abstraction" (Ayres 1983:30).

Whether the research staff belong to the academic or operational community has always been debated. Determining their role decides the work they produce: theory building or problem solving. The issue became more problematic in the 1980s as the debt crisis dominated the Bank agenda. In December 1981, the Bank's new president, A.W. Clausen, announced a reorganization of economic analysis, research, and policy activities in the Bank. An economics and research vice presidency replaced development policy. Clausen appointed Anne Krueger, the first female VP, as its head. With the separation of research and policy, the Bank's research focused on macroeconomic stability rather than the traditional developmental issues. Economists' views overshadowed other research experts. "Direct concern with poverty and income distribution declined, and it was not uncommon to hear Reaganite denigrations of those concerned with the poor—terms such as 'bleeding hearts,' 'social planners,' and the 'flaunting of compassion' were used" (Stern and Ferreira 1997:535).

The 1987 reorganization consolidated the Bank's research and policy work and brought policy, planning, and research (PPP) under the umbrella of a new senior VP. The PPR vice presidency was organized to

- strengthen the Bank's capacity to provide intellectual leadership in the development field and to translate the results of research and other analytical work into tangible benefits for the Bank's client countries and
- enhance the Bank's capacity to manage strategic issues by linking the policy and research functions with strategic planning and budgeting activities (Annual Report 1987:24).

Several rounds of reorganization centralized and decentralized research activities and put research and policy together or in separate pools. The key challenge of each round of reorganization was how to create an effective working relationship between the research and the operations staff. Tension continued.

Disseminating the research findings is part of the Bank's activities. The Bank could help developing countries "not only because the Bank can be objective in its approach," but also because it "can frequently bring to bear the experience of other countries in dealing with similar problems" (Annual Report 1948:10–11). Knowledge dissemination assists developing countries by providing "the quality of the information and the range of available choices on which those decisions will have to be made" (McNamara 1978). For these reasons, McNamara introduced the first World Development Report (WDR) in 1978, which has since acted as a flagship, identifying the Bank's interests and proposed agenda.

Initially the Bank was one of the foremost lenders to poor countries. Since the 1990s, the Bank is only one of the many players that can supply financial assistance to developing countries. To revitalize the Bank, Wolfensohn introduced the concept of a knowledge bank.

The origin of the concept may have been fortuitous. About to make a speech, Wolfensohn thought that there was nothing new worth saying in the draft; he rang a senior officer demanding new ideas at the precise moment that the VP and a younger staff member were trying to think of a way to sell to their superiors the knowledge bank concept. They suddenly had the opportunity to promote their idea directly to the president who loved the concept, announced it immediately, and drove it thereafter (Mallaby 2004:159–160). It was a case of serendipity: a president in search of an idea and an idea in search of a promoter. They met at a mutually convenient spot, and the knowledge bank was born. It was a seductive image, but already had a firm foundation.

Knowledge Generation

It has been a long-held belief that the Bank needs to have an in-house research capacity: "Without an in-house capacity, integrating the results of research into the World Bank's everyday operations and making those results available to policy-makers in developing countries does not happen" (Squire 2000:109). The DEC is the hub of a larger group of researchers working on development and its problems, with a larger research budget, than any university. Research, however, is also done in anchors and in country offices. The fragmented structure of researchers, different kinds of research, and varied ways of conducting it are the main reasons for tensions between those who generate knowledge for its own value and those who do it for the purpose of its application.

Who Is Doing Research?

For many, DEC staff are full-time researchers; they absorb most of the research budget and have the greatest impact inside and outside the Bank. They have some explicit advantages:

> The in-house researcher has more knowledge about operational departments in fact, researchers at the World Bank spend about one-third of their time working directly with operational units. And the in-house researcher has a longer-term interest in the institution and will therefore be more committed to the institution's goals than, say, maximising publications. (Squire 2000:109)

These in-house researchers are headed by the chief economist. The chief economist 'guides the Bank's intellectual leadership and plays a key role in shaping the research agenda of the institution'. As economic advisers to the president, chief economists have always occupied a high position on the hierarchical ladder. In 1997, Wolfensohn appointed Joseph Stiglitz as the Bank's chief economist and upgraded the position to senior VP to help him build the Knowledge Bank. Most chief economists have gained international reputation before they came to the job. Some are household names: Anne Krueger, Larry Summers, or Nick Stern.

Chief economists are all from outside, even though their work and reputation are often well known within the Bank. The position is filled effectively by invitation. A search committee often starts with a long list of 50–60 reputable economists and then sends out invitations to apply. A short list is given to the president for the final decision. Even if invited, not every eminent economist wants the job. For example, between 2006 and 2007, seeking to replace François Bourguignon, the search committee eventually sent out some 50 invitations to those with the reputation, record, and expertise. Some declined. 'Not everyone wanted to work for Wolfowitz,' explained one member in the search committee. Finally, the short list was ready just when Wolfowitz got into trouble; he was in no position to call candidates for a discussion. The process had to be aborted until Zoellick became the president, because a working relationship between chief economists and presidents is essential. Zoellick eventually invited Professor Justin Lin of Beijing University to fill the post, the first appointment from outside the U.S.-EC network.

Chief economists of the Bank have all types of interests. Anne Krueger was known for her push for structural adjustment programs that divided the Bank before she left for the more congenial field at the IMF. Joseph Stiglitz was so publicly critical of the IMF that his position was regarded as untenable, and Wolfensohn had to let him go. Nick Stern was interested in improving service delivery and brought to the Bank his two-pillar framework, "focusing on the climate for investment in the private sector and for human capital" (Nankani 2005:72). They were reflected in the 2004 WDR on the delivery of services and the 2005 WDR on better investment climates. François Bourguignon, an expert in statistics and microeconomics, wanted to know why poverty persisted; hence, the 2006 WDR on equity. As economic advisers to presidents who often need fresh ideas, the chief economists' influence cannot be underestimated. In setting the research agenda at the

Bank, they can alter the focus of the Bank's programs and occasionally shift its directions.

Chief economists also manage the Bank's 'professional reservoir'—the DEC, which in 2008 had 88 researchers. Ninety percent of them are economists, over 90 percent have PhDs, and many are from Harvard, MIT, or LSE. A few have never worked in operations in their 20–30 years at the Bank; Alan Gelb since 1978 and Will Martin since 1988 are examples. Many spend a few years at DEC and then move onto operations, often at relatively senior levels. Few start from operations and then move to DEC because, as one former DEC director put it, 'it is difficult to keep up top research in operations.' But others disagree, and argue, 'After a spell of operations, you just do not want to go back to research; operations is addictive.' The different ways of looking at career paths reflect the fundamental tension between research for its own sake and operations with research components. DEC is small in size and budget by the Bank's standard, but tops others in the world. It absorbs more than two-thirds of the research resources. It has therefore good researchers, resources, and access to operations where crucial empirical evidence can be collected.

As the Bank expanded its programs, experts within DEC became thin in each area—half a dozen each in finance, poverty, and macroeconomics; one or two each in agriculture, environment, social protection, and education. It has become increasingly challenging for the chief economist and DEC director to balance research priorities and resource allocation. Thus the interests of the chief economist can have a significant impact on the direction of the Bank research. For example, after research on trade had gradually shifted to the World Trade Organization and UNCTAD, Nick Stern decided to bring it back and create a virtual trade department.

Operations staff also contribute to knowledge generation—whether in areas or in sectors. "Country directors," for example, "are constantly engaged in research, discussion, and formulation of *policies*, and they offer their own analysis of what policies matter for development" (Gill and Pugatch 2005:3). The Bank's chief economist works closely with six regional chief economists who have similar responsibilities as him, but on a smaller scale. They are economic advisers to RVPs, strategists for the regional programs, and managers of country economists. Their research is not designed to communicate with researchers outside the Bank, but rather to support operations. Like most staff at the Bank, they have a dual accountability—to RVPs with solid lines for their principal accountability and to the chief economist with dotted lines for secondary responsibilities. They meet the chief economist on a monthly basis to discuss the overall research agenda. Since sectors do not have chief economists, their anchors are responsible for whether and how much applied research is done. Anchor staff have become increasingly important in tackling the problems on the ground and providing understanding of development issues, especially because of problems "the Bank has long faced in ensuring a truly interdisciplinary focus, and integrating economic analysis with voluminous practical experience with projects and sectors" (Marshall 2008:73). Although 'governance' has been an important issue for the Bank, for example, only two or three people in DEC do research on governance; the work is predominantly undertaken in the anchor of PREM and WBI. Yet, 'there has been a long debate over the size of anchors and their mandates,' according to a senior official at DEC.

The combination of full-time researchers at DEC and people in operations doing research makes the Bank not quite a university and not quite a consulting firm, enjoying the benefits of both but engendering inevitable tensions.

What Is Researched?

Demands for research are driven by a number of motives—the desire to communicate with researchers outside the Bank, to provide policy advice to decision makers in the Bank as well as in client countries, and to assist operations, whether country or sector work. These demands do not always align. Competition for resources is one of the challenges the chief economist and the director of DEC face. "To set the Bank's research agenda, the Chief Economist meets with Operations and Network management each year" (DECRS 2007:8). The Bank is sometimes criticized for restricting its researchers from following their "intellectual inspirations" (Banerjee et al 2006); there are always designated priorities, and research is expected to be relevant to the Bank's mission. However, the institution operates internally as a marketplace of competing ideas, and there are spirited debates over the latest thinking on development. Those advocating new ideas have to rise above the clamor of the crowd and gain acceptance for their work. It is, according to some researchers at DEC, not a matter of restricting research topics, but competing to justify the novelty and relevance of their research. If people want to pursue cutting-edge research, they bid for resources through an internal competitive application process, not dissimilar to that of academic grants schemes.

The Research Committee, chaired by the chief economist, has three functions (DECRS 2007:13):

(1) It assesses and advises on requests for research funding.
(2) It oversees evaluation of Bank-funded research.
(3) It advises Bank research managers on areas where research is needed.

The research agenda, a former DEC director explained, is driven sometimes by external events and thinking and sometimes by the Board or the management. 'Impetuses tend to come from various levels.' Another former DEC director added, The challenge is to anticipate topics sufficiently early to have research ready to address them when needed" (Winters 2006). DEC directors tend to emphasize the need for intellectual leadership in the broader community, while anchor staff and regional chief economists face operational issues that need support from excellent research. Even though the Bank's general policy on research is its relevance to operations, how to define relevance always varies. This is where the inherent tension lies.

World Development Reports

The *pièce de resistance* for the DEC is always the WDR, an annual publication that draws together the debate over some areas of broad interest that goes beyond the Bank. 'We have to think of the future and be able to anticipate issues that will be important for development and the Bank work.' The chief economist, regional chief economists, DEC director, and several others toss ideas around and propose potential topics. They decide which are doable and discard those that are not. The list is vetted by the president and the Board. After consulting widely, chief economists normally can incorporate their own interests into the final decision. Once the president's support is obtained and the topic decided, the chief economist selects a team of experts. 'The topic chooses you, and you do not get to choose this job,' some said, explaining how they got involved in writing the WDR. In the following 12–18 months, members of the team are seconded from their own units. To be the leader of the team is an important career marker. The leaders often bring their visions to the project, even if they may not be in complete agreement with the initial idea of the chief economist. It is a matter of debate and persuasion.

In preparing the report, the team holds consultations with the EDs, NGOs, and sometimes shareholders and stakeholders directly (Broad 2006; Wade 2002). Heated debates can always be expected. 'We knew whatever we were going to write about would be opposed by NGOs,' recalled one leader. 'We also knew our message might contradict what the president was advocating at the time,' said another. 'Because we were able to anticipate issues, we could work around them and convince the opposition with our research and evidence.' The open and consultative process helps solve the problems of disagreement.

WDRs are not official documents in the sense that they do not need approval from the Board, and each of them includes a statement:

> This volume is a product of the staff of the World Bank. The findings, interpretations, and conclusions expressed herein do not necessarily reflect the views of the Board of Executive Directors of the World Bank or the governments they represent.

WDRs have the capacity to set directions for debates and raise the profile of certain issues on development because of their extensive coverage, backed by experiences around the world. Even the DEC acknowledges that "the World Development Reports have sometimes been instrumental in changing the way that the world thinks about some aspects of development, such as poverty, health, or population" (DECRS 2007:59). Indeed this is what the chief economists and all DEC people try to achieve—ensure their research has an impact.

Reports and Studies

In addition to WDRs, the president can occasionally ask for a substantial report on a special issue. For example, at the 1991 annual meeting of the Board of Governors, Preston promised a study explaining which policies contributed to the rapid growth in East Asian economies. A team was formed in a same way as for WDRs; it was led by John Page. Quickly some of the team members assembled by him began challenging the Washington Consensus, which was still dominating the thinking and the Bank programs. Heated debates ensued. A team member recalled,

> Larry Summers was the chief economist at the time. We had to convince him first as an intellectual, as an economist, and then as the chief economist. Fortunately, John Page knew how to work

the organization. We were able to build a coalition to challenge the orthodoxy.

These descriptions of research in the Bank do not fit the image of the Bank as a medieval church where everyone followed a party line. One former director of DEC commented, 'Wide ranges of views are debated internally, and this is the ferment of ideas behind the programs and policies.' Another explained, 'The broad debate at the Bank is more collegial than universities, and therefore they are more constructive.' Getting a WDR or any major reports together is a consultative process where people with strong views debate and eventually come to an agreement. 'We live with differences,' said a former DEC director.

The Board may also request DEC to conduct a major study on a specific issue. In 2005, it wanted a comprehensive study on how the Bank could position itself on climate change. In addition to the corporate agenda, DEC sets its own research programs, on the basis of the proposals put forward by research staff. Even though the Bank was criticized for restricting researchers from following their "intellectual inspiration" (Banerjee et al 2006:20), according to a former DEC director, 'if you have an exotic interest, you can pursue in a small scale.' The research has tried to "create space for researchers to explore 'blue skies' issues before any demand for them has been expressed" (DECRS 2007:71). This can be risky, explained one director. People do not want to see the resources wasted, but unless researchers are provided with opportunities, it is difficult to see how new thinking ideas could emerge. Intellectual curiosity has to balance the corporate agenda. It is not always an easy decision.

Doing Research in Operations

The research agenda of regions and networks has to be tailored to their specific needs and the demand of client countries. The Bank makes a distinction between research, defined as analytical work "designed to produce results with wide applicability across countries or sectors," and the economic and sector work (ESW), "which take the product of research and adapt it to particular projects or country settings" (DECRS 2007:37). Operations spend time and resources on ESW.

People in operations seldom apply for research money. If they do, their applications often are not as competitive as those of research specialists. Even though the Bank emphasizes that its research "must be relevant and useful to Bank operations and to policymakers worldwide, as well as being academically sound" (DECRS 2007:61), DEC research-ers have to think about publications in books and journal articles. They are required to have, for example, two articles in a rolling 30 months published in peer-reviewed journals, and their research is assessed by citations by their peers outside the Bank. None of this is a concern for operational staff. They need specific knowledge that can help in their operations, whether building a country program, pulling the CAS together, or designing a project, rather than communicating their knowledge to researchers outside the Bank. Their research has to be specific and targeted because of demands from client countries. As a Brazilian minister for planning put it,

> When we need financing for something on which we know exactly what to do, we go to the Inter-American Development Bank. But when we need financing and we do not know exactly how to go about addressing an important issue, we seek the Bank's help. (quoted in Nankani 2005:73)

This research is often commissioned or even done by operational staff—combining knowledge (AAA or TA) with lending. It is sup-ported by the operational budget or a trust fund. A little less than 10 percent of total research budget is spent by the regions and net-works, while about 25 percent of operational budget was used for non-lending activities, predominantly AAA, TA, and other analytical work. CDs can purchase research from DEC, whose researchers have to sell 30 percent of their time to operations anyway. They can also purchase research from anchor staff or contract out to consultants. Unlike the research done at DEC, this work is policy based and ori-ented. Thus, serious studies can run to 75 pages, including surveys of literature, summaries of international experiences, collections of data, and analyses of the issues. They often do not include strong recom-mendations or proposals for loans. The purpose is to raise interest and explore possibilities. It is packaged in a way that allows the client to understand the options.

Some may not consider AAA and TA research because they tend to be specific, and their findings include few efforts at generaliza-tion. Because this kind of research is and "should be entirely tailor-made to the needs of individual countries, and thus varies greatly" (Marshall 2008:68), it is not research many researchers would like to see—the kind that "tests the theories that underlie the rationales for policy or programs intervention can thus be useful in practice"

(Ravallion 2007:4). Furthermore, research done by operations staff is not regarded as genuine because "it is not subject to the same level of scrutiny as the research coming out of DEC and may be of a lower quality, and more subject to ideological manipulation" (Banerjee et al 2006:125). This is the constant debate between researchers and practitioners who do research—theories or their applicability?

Knowledge Dissemination and Application

"Research that is not well disseminated, both inside and outside the Bank, cannot have its full impact" (DECRS 2007:31). Whether the emphasis is on internal or external dissemination, however, has been a serious question for the Bank. For DEC researchers, publication in books and journal articles is important because

> it requires clear and open disclosure of the elements on which research findings are based and opens up our work for scrutiny and challenge by peers and for public debate. It is a means both to prove and to improve the quality of our work. When research meets high academic standards, it becomes credible and hence effective. (Winters 2006)

Despite demands that research at the Bank should be empirical and "concerned with results on the ground, not just theory or methodology" (DECRS 2007:71), researchers at DEC are evaluated by their publications in peer-reviewed journals or in books. As the current director of DEC says (Ravallion 2007:7),

> The publication process is an important screening and disciplining device for researchers. Publishing in referred professional journals helps establish a researcher's credibility (although one should never assume that publishing in even the most "prestigious" journals is a perfect indicator of research quality, given the mistakes made in editorial processes). Publishing also helps DECRG attract and keep the best researchers (whose career options often lie outside the Bank, mainly in academia).

They are also assessed on citations, an indicator that is used in academia. Many academics question the correlation between citation and impact.

It is even more difficult to establish the relations between citations and impacts on operations. An independent review group commented,

> On the one hand, Bank researchers have to take care to frame their results in a way that will pass serious professional scrutiny, often in highly critical and competitive refereed journals. The editors and referees of these journals are typically tough on papers that overstate their claims. At the same time, Bank researchers have to satisfy their operations counterparts who want to see research that has clear policy implications, ideally in line with policies they are already espousing. (Banerjee et al 2006:124)

There is always a risk that, in order to disseminate knowledge, researchers might become champions of their own work. "Balancing advocacy and rigor can be difficult," said the director of DEC (Ravallion 2007:2). This is true whether the research is done by DEC or by operational staff. After a policy paper was published in 1992 on electricity reform (which will be discussed in Chapter 9), operational people in both areas and sectors organized a series of events to promote the reform formula—workshops were organized, and people from developing countries were trained with Bank assistance to learn the model; consultants were brought in to help translate the formula into activities. Research had been completed, but no decisive conclusions were reached about its applicability to operations. Yet, those who had done the research became the 'sellers' of the ideas. As advocates, it was difficult for the researchers to see its shortcomings until it was too late (Xu 2005). It is not suggested that these researchers at the Bank were eager to sell their research products to operations in their pursuit of fame or reputation, as many Bank critics assume. It was a natural enthusiastic response.

Finally, there is a potential clash between loans and knowledge dissemination. Research in operations seeks to combine knowledge with funds to deliver the assistance the country needs, whether it is a project or a program. The combination of research and operations provides staff with opportunities to craft creative solutions. The Bank may still be criticized for its 'loan culture,' but in practice, it has long passed that practice. The best assistance the Bank offers is not knowledge alone in the form of articles, manuscripts, or even analyses. It is a combination of knowledge and loans. As one VP commented,

> We want a package of value-added products for our clients through lending and knowledge transfer. Lending gives us a seat at the table

because projects get into the nitty-gritty. If we want to suggest changes, we know how the system works through project preparation and implementation.

Client countries want a package too. They are keen to accept a loan because they know that the Bank can continue to provide knowledge and support for the duration of the project. When Thailand was developing a pension scheme, it wanted (even if it did not need) a loan—with the loan, the Thai government had realized that the Bank would help develop the ideas, set up the programs, and implement them. If anything went wrong, the country could tap the Bank's skills and expertise. If it had only benefited from a diagnostic report, identifying the problem and ways to tackle it, it might or might not be able to implement it without help, and then there was no follow-up available.

Knowledge and loans come together.

Knowledge Meets Operations

If global knowledge and local applications are the Bank's comparative advantage, there is also a potential downside. That combination encourages the development of ideas of best practice, spelt out in Bank templates. These templates can encapsulate the experience of the Bank over a number of countries into a form where it can be readily applied in other places. From one perspective these distillations of wisdom can be described as part of the Bank's comparative advantage, the ability to transcend national and even regional boundaries, to apply the lessons of research to particular circumstances: the researchers' ideal. To practitioners in client countries, however, there was concern that the templates and research findings might not be sensitive to local conditions. The external review argued that the "Bank does too little in the way of cautioning people on the many reasons why policy conclusions may be subject to qualifications or depend on the specific circumstances of countries" (Banerjee et al 2006:136).

Does the Bank thereby set templates of best practice whereby global knowledge is applied across the board? DEC provides evidence of the impact of the group's findings on the reduction of poverty. The WDRs concentrate the thinking in one area. Operations look for good precedents they can utilize. To some extent all these ideas will come together in some notion of best practice. After all, the whole point of undertaking research and describing itself as a knowledge bank is to ensure that every loan proposal or analytical note does NOT start from scratch, but can build on the experience developed elsewhere. The purpose is to reduce the levels of trial and error, to find patterns of effective behavior and identify the best way of solving problems.

Bank research staff work the same way as other members of a broader epistemic community. Some ideas are in 'good currency.' There is a prevailing wisdom among their profession. When, however, operational staff seek to apply these ideas to Bank proposals, they have to present them in the established format for the preparation of proposals, the standard operating procedures that structure the way ideas are organized and presented, and determine what points provide the greatest weight and what issues have to be addressed. The temptation is to adapt successful earlier formulae. That is no more than the practices adopted elsewhere. Good practice is a combination of process and content.

This practice sometimes can result in useful advice. Sections of the Bank can develop guides to assist project staff in very specific areas. Thus, there is an *Urban Bus Toolkit*, developed by the Public–Private Infrastructure Advisory facility and complete with an interactive compact disc. It is described as a companion guide, tools and options for reforming bus systems. It is one of many. Others may be of greater importance. Templates for reform of electricity systems were influential and perverse.

Such a position can be taken to the level of caricature: the idea of Bank officers arriving in any country with the plan in their pocket that will be applied in any circumstance. Bank staff like to dispel this idea, but not always successfully. The IMF and the Bank, claims Woods,

> "tame" the most intractable problems by reducing them to core elements that the professional expertise can digest and prescribe from... The downside is that there is little room for local knowledge. Local knowledge is messy, political, intractable, and very difficult to make judgments about. (Woods 2006: 54, 55)

Few Bank staff would agree with this picture (Ritzen 2007). However, the potential tension is obvious. Staff in the regions do not see themselves as mere conduits for the transfer of settled ideas or predetermined templates into local loans, but the institutional requirements for loan assessment and approval can push them toward standard responses.

> "You Bank people always say that one size does not fit all, but when push comes to shove, that is the way you act." An NGO

representative in Phnom Penh said that to me recently, and there is much truth in his statement. The diversities of countries is an obvious lesson, yet it is one on which we often do not act. Basic models need to be adapted to meet the needs of particular countries and even parts of the same country, yet doing so is difficult for a large bureaucracy. Our headquarters-based structure with a very heavy oversight function of the executive directors makes it even more difficult. (Kavalsky 2005:29)

The Bank wants to transfer knowledge and experience; its comparative advantage is to let one country know what was done elsewhere and with what consequences. Those lessons get digested into strategies and best practice: one size fits all.

This process can go too far. Ideas are adopted as viable before they have been given the chance to be adequately tested; the mere fact that they have been adopted elsewhere seems to be enough. When existing situations are parlous, any solution can look encouraging to those suffering its consequences, even an unlikely panacea. The pull can be as powerful as the push. One practitioner was at times struck by the Bank's propensity to continue to search for—and sometimes claim it has found—the ultimate answers to development.

This pattern reflects the surprising belief that there may be a ready-made, relatively simple, permanent, and definitive response to a specific problem of development that can be applied universally and the belief that, if it worked well here, it will work well there...The blueprint method applied to the Bank's proposed remedies and recommendations for Latin America just as it did in Africa. Essentially, the approaches, remedies, and instruments were all the same, so much so that, within the Bank, the procedural aspects were also the same, whether we dealt with middle-income countries or low-income ones. (Lafourcade 2005:182–183)

The point is whether the Bank is flexible enough to adjust to different paths and speeds of implementation. In Africa, said one senior official, 'we assumed there was a private sector capable of buying assets, but there wasn't one.' After some years, a template for electricity reform had to be reevaluated. No one wants to just adopt a preconceived plan, but equally no one wants to start from scratch.

So Bank staff are faced with a dilemma. On the one hand the comparative advantage of the Bank is the global research they can bring to bear on a local problem. They know what has been done elsewhere and even what has worked. On the other hand they need to adjust any solution to meet local capacities and conditions. Officers will reject the notion that they imposed solutions just because they were the orthodoxy, although many would see the IMF as doing that. Rather they took what they saw as best practice and sought to adjust that to local conditions. Sometimes they succeed; other times they may be insufficiently sensitive to the transition from one environment to another.

Images remain hard to shake. One staff member had formerly worked for an NGO that was highly critical of the Bank; she completed a Masters degree in development. Asked how her essays for the Masters stood up to the experience inside the Bank, she said that she had got it completely wrong. She had assumed that the Bank imposed conditions. Even though the country on which she now worked was poor and needy, she said she and her colleagues did nothing unless the country wanted it and was prepared to sign off. Country ownership was real; often the poorer countries were the most defensive, determined that the Bank would not dictate to them. The dilemma remains: knowledge is transferable; are solutions?

Conclusion

The research and operational staff provide two images of the Bank's knowledge generation and dissemination. The former is concerned with the development and creation of knowledge that can assist development. The latter is driven by the clients; knowledge is a commodity to be shaped to serve their purposes. It is the application of useful knowledge that becomes important and sometimes the further refinement of that knowledge so it can be applied again.

DEC is keen to show its impact; its annual reports to the Board emphasize how its research contributes to improving the Bank's policy advice to its member countries, to broadening the understanding of the development process, to assisting in developing research capacity in the client countries, and more importantly, to supporting the Bank operations. Not everyone is persuaded. An external review of the Bank's research during 1998 and 2005 found it hard to assess whether the research had any impact. It traced the rise and fall of citations to the Bank's work, particularly to the WDRs. It looked at the extensive record of publications of the DEC staff. It was not able to state at the end that there was a clear connection.

Other sections of the Bank would not be surprised. For operations, research is a means to an end: better interaction with the client countries and better packages of services delivered as a consequence useful in operations It is a difficult challenge for the Bank. One Bank researcher argued,

> Operations may often protest that research stands in the way of doing work when findings which question current practices are presented. This may lead Operations staff to feel that research is not useful. Research which is supporting what is happening is more easily integrated into operations, but it does not mean that research is actually having an impact in this case. (quoted in Banerjee et al 2006:124)

As one former director of DEC commented, the role of research was not necessarily to make operations happy, and there had to be a free atmosphere where criticism of projects was permitted and people did not have to be too concerned about pleasing the hierarchy (Banerjee et al 2006:127).

Operations staff agreed the Bank needed a research capacity, but they were less convinced it was useful. They suggested that DEC was 'invisible' and concentrated on broad issues that were not regionally relevant or specialized. One regional economist commented 'research looks backward; operations have to look forward.' It was also uneven. Few seemed interested, for instance, in doing regional research on Africa. As a consequence some regional staff sought to do their own research, which in turn received a scathing reaction from a DEC economist:

> Research outside DEC—with a few notable exceptions—is even more practical. It is essentially a form of rhetoric. It is often not about doing research to discover new knowledge but to justify some previously determined policy. It is not unusual to be told "we should do an evaluation to prove that X program works," for instance. (quoted in Banerjee et al 2006:125)

For operational staff, what is done has to have a directly pragmatic purpose: an analytic study or a country sectoral review with the objective of further work through a grant or loan. They are not full-time researchers.

The problem is likely to remain and may not even need a solution. If, for instance, all research focused on specific regional or country issues, who would do the cross-national research? There is always likely to be tension between the different conceptions of research and debate over its applicability and value. That creative tension is inherent in the research tasks the Bank staff must undertake.

CHAPTER SEVEN

Self- and External Evaluation

The Bank must be among the most evaluated of institutions. It is evaluated *ex ante* and *ex post*, internally and externally. "I sometimes wonder," stated the then MD Shengman, "if there is anything we do in the Bank Group that is not evaluated!" (Zhang 2003:91). In addition, constant dialogue among colleagues and with borrowing officials provides informal evaluation—what works, what does not, and why. The Bank, its staff, and its operations are also under the microscope of the U.S. Congress, other governments and institutions and NGOs. These constant evaluations create opportunities for people (insiders and outsiders) to have an impact on the institution.

The Bank prides itself on being a knowledge bank and a learning organization. It seeks to identify the best practices and apply them, as appropriate. That requires self-examination. The Bank is also an institution whose activities attract extensive, often critical, external reviews. The group '50 years is enough,' which challenged the Bank a decade ago, is but one of the NGOs that sought to change the Bank. Many more make their living by watching and criticizing the Bank. There are different and, often, even contradictory expectations regarding what the Bank should or should not do and what standards it should apply.

In general, the Bank is remarkably open to both internal and external evaluations. Yet what satisfies the internal demands—tight professional evaluation, for example—may not satisfy those who tend to be emotive or have narrowly focused interests. The demand for evaluation by one group of shareholders may not be what other stakeholders want, and vice versa. The Bank staff are in the front line in facing these constant evaluations. So how does this process empower staff of the Bank and to what effect? This chapter examines the processes of both internal and external evaluation and seeks to understand the opportunities and constraints they have created for the Bank staff.

Development of Internal Evaluation

From its beginning, the Bank established a set of complex *ex ante* evaluations to ensure the feasibility and quality of its projects and programs. In the late 1960s, McNamara introduced the idea of *ex post* evaluation—assessment of a completed project or program, its design and implementation and any possible lessons. McNamara's list of "things to do" included "analyze the time required to process loans and credits, establish standards, and keep records of performance against the standards" (Kraske 1996:174). Reporting success and failure of the Bank's work could not satisfy McNamara's "untiring interest in the countries that the Bank was trying to help" (Kraske 1996:172). He wanted to know more about the nature of the problems, the extent of poverty, and the progress achieved. He also wanted to know how the Bank could improve.

Several developments triggered the formalization of self-evaluation. First, in the late 1960s, several well-known studies assessed Bank projects. In 1967 alone, there were three: Albert Hirschman evaluated 11 Bank-funded projects across economic sectors and geographical areas and concluded that "a very large portion of the decision-making process" was dominated by " 'seat-of-the-pants' judgment" (1967:8). Instead of searching "for a ranking device that would presume to aggregate the direct and indirect effects of projects" (1967:188), project evaluation should be adopted. John C. de Wilde's *Experiences with Agricultural Development in Tropical Africa* looked at the successes and failures of agricultural development programs in tropical Africa. John A. King's *Economic Development Projects and Their Appraisal: Cases and Principles from the Experience of the World Bank* illustrated problems in preparing and appraising projects. These studies called for more systematic evaluation of Bank operations.

Second, when the Bank's operations expanded quickly in size and in number, some staff asked "whether quality was being sacrificed on behalf of quantity" (Kapur et al 1997:41). Similar concerns were raised in public. Finally, "the US Congress and its audit arm, the US General Accounting Office (GAO), began to press for evaluation from the Bank, or to undertake them on its own" (Willoughby 2003:6).

Internally, there were concerns about who would conduct evaluations (those from the countries concerned or those in charge of projects) and about their independence. In 1970, McNamara instructed the Programming and Budgeting Department (PBD) to evaluate "the contribution of the Bank's operations to the development of member countries" (Willoughby 2003:3). Under the PBD, he created an Operations Evaluation Unit that consisted of five to six professionals (mostly new graduates in the YP Program).

In 1973, the unit was placed under the Joint Bank-IFC Audit Committee and changed its name to the Operations Evaluation Department (OED). In 1974, McNamara proposed the establishment of the director general (DG) at the rank of VP without operational responsibilities to ensure independence. According to McNamara, DG was a better "indication of independence from the normal operations of the Bank." His logic was that

> all large organizations, and all administrators, managers, and professionals, if they're honest with themselves, will admit that they have successes and failures... We should learn from these experiences of success and failure. It was for that reason that I set up the Operations Evaluation function in the Bank something on the order of 30 years ago. In particular, it's very, very difficult for any of us who take pride in our activities to admit failure, and it's very difficult, therefore, for us to examine the causes of it. That can be done by an independent organization, and that was the structure that we provided for Operations Evaluation in the World Bank. (2003:ix)

An independent group of professionals examining the activities of their peers was seen as the key to ensuring the quality and effectiveness of evaluation. Independence of evaluation was further confirmed in 1974 when the management and the EDs reached an agreement:

> OED's independence should be further institutionalized by placing it under the sole charge of a director-general, Operations Evaluation, with rank of vice president, selected by the executive directors from a short-list [up to three names] provided by the president, removable only by the executive directors, and ineligible for reappointment to the Bank Group staff except in unusual circumstances... OED would report, through the director-general. (Willoughby 2003:9)

OED was expected to reach its own conclusion about the Bank's projects. It was supposed "to call attention to the implications of projects for the Bank's overall policies, practices, and procedures" (Ayres 1983:46). With its project performance auditing and project completion reports, OED started engaging in "social and political analyses highly rare in Bank reports" (Ayres 1983:46). After its heyday in the 1970s, OED experienced a difficult time in the 1980s and then gradually recovered in the 1990s. Despite its continuity, OED staff always faced several predicaments—standards for evaluation, its independence, limited resources, and complicated relationships with the Board, management, and operation staff.

First, the evaluation was done according to triple-E principles: "Effectiveness (extent to which objectives fulfilled), efficiency (cost/benefit analysis), and economy (reasonableness of unit costs)." Three aspects of the operations would be assessed: "The physical project, institution-building aspects, and use of the Bank's administrative budget" (Willoughby 2003:6). Often it is difficult to apply all three principles. For example, as the first DG of OED, Mervyn L. Weiner, recalled, the evaluation of a project supporting a beef export industry showed that the project was successful in supporting the large ranch owners and therefore cattle production for export, but failed to address the Bank's mandate of poverty alleviation and "should thus no longer be eligible for financing by the Bank" (2003:24). At the core is whether OED should assess the results of work already done or the policies behind the project.

Second, accountability is always an issue. OED staff do not have direct clients. Should it act in the interests of the Bank as an institution? If so, what are the interests of the Bank? This is a particularly difficult issue for OED when the Bank is facing criticism, from either large shareholding countries or the public in general.

Independence

When OED was created, McNamara emphasized that its independence was absolutely necessary if evaluation would have any impact on the Bank's operations. This principle continues. The selection and remuneration of the DG are under the oversight of the Committee on Development Effectiveness (CODE) with advice from the Bank's HR VP. The DG can hold office for renewable terms of five years and be removed only by the EDs. To ensure the independence of OED, its DG can never be eligible for subsequent appointment to the staff of the

Bank Group except in unusual circumstances. In other words, DGs of evaluation can never (re)enter the ordinary service of the Bank. In its over three-decade history, almost all its DGs served two continuing terms (ten years), no matter whether OED reports were positive or negative.

OED is entirely separate from the operation staff of the Bank. Its DG has the power to appoint the staff. Most are reassigned from elsewhere in the Bank, although recruitment from outside is possible. OED relies heavily on consultants to do evaluations, many of whom are retired Bank officials. It prefers Bank staff for two main reasons: it is difficult for the outsiders to understand the intricate working relationships within this large institution and its client countries. OED staff can also appreciate the complexities of the work done at the Bank. Some regard OED as a 'preretirement home', while others argue that experience there allows them to appreciate the entirety of the Bank's work. The critics argue that the independence of OED is compromised when it remains part of the Bank and its staff can return to it. They demanded an independent institution, outside the Bank, be created. For its supporters, keeping OED as part of the Bank and integrating it with the management is a necessary condition for meaningful evaluation. "Whatever may be thought about the (re)entry policy, the sacrifice of knowledge and experience would be too great if only outsiders were hired by OED," explained one former ED (Stek 2003:492). The interaction of operational staff and evaluators is the key for successful evaluations and for lesson learning.

OED, now called Independent Evaluation Group (IEG), has its own budget, staff, and functions, independent from management. Its budget approval "was the weakest aspect of OED's independence" (Kopp 2003:57). Officially, the Board decides OED's budget; yet, the Board rarely deviates from management-submitted proposals. Thus, "the work program and its content and directions were subject to strong influence by the Bank management through the backdoor of budgeting" (Kopp 2003:57). The budget often restricts OED from hiring higher-level staff. Yet those in IEG think they can conduct the evaluations the way they should be done.

Complexity of Its Products

OED initiates its own work program, which is then endorsed by the Board. Initially, two pilot studies were tried: a study of the Bank's 20-year development work in Columbia and a summary evaluation of lending to seven important electric power borrowers in Latin America, Asia, and Africa. These pilots set the parameters of the OED's work: evaluation would consist of two fairly ambitious but "very different studies—a deep one of everything the Bank had done in one country, and a wide one covering loans to a broad spread of borrowers in one sector" (Willoughby 2003:4). OED's evaluations cover projects (implementation completion and project performance); countries (CAS completion reviews); sectors (such as financial or prime education); themes (gender, poverty, environment, etc.); and global issues (IDA review) as well as process (such as AIDS coordination, knowledge management) and corporate evaluations.

When a project or a country program is completed, the operational staff are supposed to conduct a mandatory self-evaluation, which is then subject to OED's evaluation. 'Self evaluation is often honest.' OED validates the rating from the corporate perspective. What is the rate of return? What is institutional development? Is it sustainable? These are quick turnaround reviews, 12–15 pages long and take no more than three months. Such auditing work used to take 70–75 percent of the OED's resources in the 1970s and 1980s. In 1996, project evaluation accounted for 50 percent of the OED work program and was closer to 20 percent by 2003. More resources are now used for in-depth studies.

Then 25–30 percent of these mandatory reviews are subject to in-depth reviews—project performance assessment reports. "In selecting operations for assessment, preference is given to those that are innovative, large, or complex; those that are relevant to upcoming studies or country evaluations; those for which Executive Directors or Bank management have requested assessments; and those that are likely to generate important lessons" (OED 2005).

The third category of reviews examines country programs or sector/thematic studies. They normally cover big swathes of projects.

Table 7.1 Evaluation Coverage: World Bank

	ICR reviews	Project PPAR	CASCR reviews	CAEs	Sector reviews
No./year	280	70	~20	~7	~8
(% of total)	(100%)	(25%)	(100%)	(100%)	
Site visit		yes		Yes	Yes
Elapsed time	90 days	6–12 months	3–5 months	1 year	1–2 years

Note: ICR—implementation completion report, PPAR—project performance assessment review, CASCR—country assistance strategy completion report, CAE—country assistance evaluation.

Six to ten such studies are initiated by OED each year. Each will normally take a year or a year and half to complete. If it is a study of a country program, it is normally comprehensive, covering ten years and many different sectors and projects. It can be politically sensitive not only with the country team but also with the borrowing country under review. For sector or thematic evaluations, OED can initiate the idea and then float it past sectors and regions concerned. It is important to receive support from the latter because demand-driven evaluation makes it easier for OED staff to collect the data. As one officer put it, 'Otherwise, regions or sectors would say they lost files or could not find data, etc.'

OED can also initiate evaluations on corporate matters as it sees fit. Its actual evaluation can take place if it gets a green light from the CODE. In May 2007, for example, in the middle of the Wolfowitz imbroglio, the DG of IEG suggested to the Board it might be the time to evaluate several key issues of the World Bank Group's internal governance:

1. The process for the selection of the president and senior management.
2. The role and functioning of the Board.
3. The internal system of institutional safeguards.

Nothing happened.

Limited Resources

Staffing of OED/IEG has always been an issue. If OED wanted to have any impact, it needed high-calibre staff. Yet, it was difficult to recruit experienced staff who knew both the Bank's operational policies and country management and who were willing to come. For those who did want to work at OED/IEG, the question is, can they go back into operations after several years of evaluating the work done by staff there? If they do want to return, how can the DG expect them to be frank and fearless in assessing the work of their past or future colleagues?

OED started with "a small staff of two Bank economists, three graduating young professionals, and several research assistants" (Willoughby 2003:5). It has now expanded to about 90 staff with 25 or so in senior positions. It accounts for about 1.5 percent of the Bank's administrative budget. It depends heavily on consultants and retired Bank staff to do the actual studies. In its early years, YPs were often assigned to the OED as part of the rotation. They got out at the first opportunity. In general, OED is not considered a good career move. As OED's first DG stated,

> Since a major intended benefit of evaluation work was feedback to operational staff, recruiting experienced operational staff for limited periods and then having them move back into operations seemed to be the most appropriate staffing policy for OED. But this proved very difficult to implement...Managers were understandably reluctant to release their best people, and only too happy to transfer their poorest performers! To dissuade staff who expressed interest in OED work for a period, some managers even threatened re-entry difficulties after their evaluation stint. There was nobody to manage staff reassignments in the best interests of the Bank. (Weiner 2003:23)

Some consider OED as a preretirement home for crusty old men. "You went at the end of the day to review projects after they were completed," said another former OED staff (Stout 2003:149–150). One operations staffer explained his interest: his sector was not doing well in the region, and the portfolio had declined steadily. He had worked in the same region for about 25 years and had one and half years left before retirement. 'Working at the OED may not be a bad idea, and it would allow me to see the whole process of an operation.' Many are transferred to OED against their will (Donaldson 2003:45). OED needed high-calibre people to interact with operational staff if it wanted to have an impact on the quality of operations. It ends up with some good staff but also "some pretty weak ones" (Donadson 2003:45).

The 1987 reorganization was a golden opportunity for OED. Because all except a handful of staff 'lost their jobs' overnight and had to apply to be rehired, a process that took over a year, the then DG Yves Rovani was able to fill "OED with top-level performers and dropped lots of 'strong individuals'" (Donaldson 2003:50). Once the dust settled, many talented people left again for operations. A few who stayed have been able to undertake some evaluations that at least have had an impact on the policy direction of the Bank. The 1987 reorganization also started a rotation system that allowed people to move into OED and back to operations. The view that OED staff were less than welcome, however, prevailed. Those who worked at OED were often constrained by the knowledge that candid treatment of results might put them in a bad light. There has always been an issue whether OED is a mouse under the table or a frank and fearless lion.

Conflicts with Operations

A former DG of OED described it as "the new kid on the block," but "lives in a tough neighborhood—at the intersection of two highly contested fields" (Picciotto 2003:125)—development and evaluation. From its beginning, operations staff complained that OED's staff and consultants had little experience with real operations or direct knowledge of their history and context. They challenged OED observations, accepting some criticisms but disregarding others. Even after OED brought in operations staff, they are often ignored. The mentality is 'if you are good, you are either with operations or research or both.' but not in evaluation. OED is somewhere out there. Operational staff take on projects or programs without the hindsight that OED staff have. The typical reaction to OED's reports is "to dispute the factual details and to question the usefulness of the finding" (Kopp 2003:55). Sometimes, when handed the evaluation reports, the operational staff simply said, "Well, that's very nice, but we don't do this type of operations any more," or "it's old stuff" (Rovani 2003:35). The friction between evaluation and operation often undercut the feedback benefits of OED's work.

Operations staff not only have the experience but also control the information of what and how they are doing. OED needs access to information from both operations and borrowing countries. Getting cooperation has not always been easy. In its early years, OED people would visit the operation unit responsible for a particular project and expect to find binders with the relevant records there intact. Sometimes operations staff had a bad system of record keeping or were reluctant to submit all reports. In 1980, as responsibility for preparing project completion reports was shifted away from Bank operational staff to the borrowers, "the whole system as conceived by McNamara—which was for comprehensive evaluation, with self-evaluation by operation staff as an essential component—was about to crumble" (Rovani 2003:34). The 1987 reorganization affected the evaluation even more when "some records were broken up, others just disappeared" (Weiner 2003:26).

When they undertake evaluations, OED staff not only examine project/program files and interview operational staff, in most cases they also need to visit the borrowing country for onsite discussion with project staff and beneficiaries. They may or may not have the access. For example, in 2004–2005, the country team of China asked OED to evaluate the resettlement program of several energy projects. At the same time OED was conducting a project performance assessment on three power projects in China. China had no objections to the latter and gave it full support. The resettlement, however, was a completely different story. The objective of the evaluation was to find out whether China had adopted best practice and what lessons could be learned. They wanted to ask the Chinese to 'tell us the story on resettlement, social development, and safeguards.' The OED team was first asked to supply the questionnaires to the Chinese government, and then was told to come back at a more convenient time. Several rounds of communication led to no action. In this case, the country team had decided to use OED as leverage to draw attention of the Chinese government to certain practices that it was reluctant to confront directly. It turned out what was difficult for the country team was difficult to OED team as well, but the message was sent out.

Occasionally, staff can take advantage of OED evaluations to 'get them off the hook' of bad projects. They would suggest OED evaluate projects with which division chiefs had been tarred. "Because once OED comes out with a fairly—even a hard-hitting—report, it allows the Bank to say, okay, we see it, and to turn the page and put it behind them" (Donaldson 2003:53).

Conflicts with the Board

In its early days when OED presented the Board its first working program, one 'important' ED commented,

> We already know the Bank is a pretty good organization and that most of the things the Bank does are sound and will probably turn out well. So that's not what we want to hear. What we want to learn about are *the problems, the failures, and how these shortfalls should be addressed.* (italics added, Weiner 2003:21)

Such a noble endorsement by the EDs can be heard in a general discussion on OED. "The board is highly appreciative of OED's evaluations" (Mackay 2002:84), and, over the years, has in general supported the OED which "was and is always a trusted adviser to the Board" (Zhang 2003:92). This positive view may not hold when specific evaluation reports are concerned. 'Evaluation is independent; its reports, however, sometimes are not well received by some EDs,' especially when evaluations concerned their own countries, said a senior OED officer.

However, American ED Jan Piercy once commented,

> I wished that some newspaper reporters and congressional staff were in this room, because to understand the genuineness of the Bank's

search for improvement is to come away with a different under-standing of the Bank. Very often, institutions on the development arena are criticized without due regard for the dire conditions they address. We're criticised because poverty has not been more reduced, because education hasn't reached all, and yet we need to look at the other side of the equation, and that is what our open self-assessment significantly contributes to doing. (Piercy 2003:100)

Uneasy Relationship with the Management

OED has to walk a fine line—evaluating projects and programs, but not making judgments on policies. OED can initiate studies on sector or thematic programs over a period of time to see their effectiveness and their impact on 'development' in general. The finding sometimes con-firms what operational staff have already realized. A director at OED said, 'In evaluation, the smartest are beginning to shift, but good people in operations are already shifting.' At other times, the findings can be "inconvenient" for the management, as Shengman put it (2003:92). One example would be the annual reviews of evaluation results done at the end of the 1980s, which identified steady declines in satisfactory ratings of projects. Its 1991 review showed that the proportion of Bank-financed operations judged unsatisfactory at completion increased from 15 per-cent of the cohort evaluated in 1981 to 30.5 percent of the 1989 cohort and 37.5 percent of the 1991 cohort. This was a big embarrassment.

On September 21, 1993, the Board took an unprecedented step of creating an independent panel to address the issue of poor performance. The result is the well-known Wapenhans Report. This opened the door for NGOs to be involved in the Bank's activities. OED was proud of its honest evaluations. The Bank, however, "was given little credit for self-criticism, [and] the press lionized the negative findings of the report" (Kapur, et al 1997:33). Consequently, "by the time of the Wapenhans Task Force report in the early 1990s, we [the management] looked very much to the OED results as a critical ingredient," and "OED really played a very important role and continues to do so in signaling what's right, what's wrong" (Salop 2003:97).

The management team knows better than to intervene directly in any evaluations. OED still sometimes feels the pressure.

No, I don't think we were ever forced to kill a study. I think we'd avoid them strategically rather than waiting to get blocked. But there was always opposition to any study we want to do. Evaluation is quintessentially a political process. Every time we had to ask, 'Okay, is it worth it?' but I don't think we ever backed off entirely. (Donaldson 2003:53)

One dramatic example of impact is the OED's study on *Power for Development*. It covers 154 projects, involving IDA, IFC, MIGA, and the IBRD. Ten years after changing the Bank's lending policies to the power sector, there were signs that while the Bank had moved out of the sector, the private sector had not moved in as anticipated. There was talk that the Bank's policies were out of date and, to some, created disasters. OED floated the idea of conducting an in-depth study of the Bank's operations in the electricity sector and received support from the Board.

In such in-depth studies, OED provides recommendations, and the management is supposed to respond. On this evaluation of power sector reform, OED recommended a fundamental shift of the Bank's lending (OED 2003). When the report went to the Board, two network VPs, three SDs, operations and OED people were all present. Both the Board and management responded positively, despite some grumbling among operations staffing in the sector. However, OED does not always have the support from management and some responses can be long and sensitive.

To strengthen the view that the Bank was a self-evaluating institution and to ensure high quality of its work, in 1997, Wolfensohn created the Quality Assurance Group (QAG), as a 'watchdog' to bring greater discipline to the project process while also providing positive input in operations. QAG gives real-time evaluation of the quality of Bank-financed loans, ESW, and other activities. QAG also has corporate responsibility for managing the Annual Review on Portfolio Performance, which assesses the status of the entire Bank portfolio.

Rising External Discontent and Challenges

The Bank has always attracted public attention partly because it needed to convince the public it was a reputable bank, partly because what it does always has supporters and opponents and partly because what it does in some developing countries cam make a difference. Initially, a biweekly presidential press conference was used to win public support. "In addition to finding our operational feet, we were also faced, in those days of beginnings, with the task of establishing the Bank's public image" recalled the assistant to presidents Meyer, McCloy, and Black. "We issued press releases whenever we could find anything we thought the newspapers might report...to create a market for the Bank's obligations by convincing investment institutions" (Chronology 9). Presenting a good public image has become increasingly important since the 1980s when media started providing instant reports from around the world.

In the 1980s, civil society campaigns against multilateral financial institutions escalated. Anti-dam campaigns targeted several Bank projects in Africa, Latin America, and Asia. They raised concerns about river basins, tropical forestry, and biodiversities, which quickly spilled over to other related issues: involuntary resettlement of communities, protection of indigenous people's lands, accountability and transparency at the Bank. NGOs, especially those from developed countries, vociferously chastised the Bank and brought the cases to the Board, and their own governments and onto the streets. Under increasing pressures, the Bank conducted its first comprehensive review of big dams after being in the business for 40 years. In early 1990s, the Bank management renewed its pledge to prioritize issues of environment, resettlement, and tribal and indigenous people in project lending. A substantially revised policy, Operational Directive 4.01, was completed in October 1991. The Bank significantly cut its involvement in these projects. Funding for hydro projects reduced from $11 billion between 1978 and 1982 to an estimated $4 billion between 1993 and 1997. To the staff, 'there are numerous ways to help the poor, and we did not have to confront NGOs in these projects.' Retreat was seen as acknowledgment of being 'guilty.' Yet, 'just pullout was not an answer—critical NGOs got louder and more militant.'

In 1992, two Bank-sponsored studies, the so-called Morse Commission, which investigated India's Sardar Sarovar projects, and the Wapenhans reports, which reviewed the Bank's loan portfolio, attracted a lot of attention. These self-evaluations that identified the steady decline in satisfactory ratings for projects and the exponential growth of activist NGOs worked in tandem to put more pressure on the Bank staff. The mission of many NGOs was to demand international organizations, especially multilateral financial institutions, be 'accountable.' Their voices reached a crescendo when they identified the Bank's alleged lack of compliance with its environmental and social standards. Yet, ironically, much of the information used by them came from the Bank's own published self-evaluations. Even though in the early 1990s the Bank management adopted new measures to ensure environmental and social protections "partly from love and partly from fear" (Wade 1997:709), anti-Bank campaigns had escalated by the time Wolfensohn became president.

It became clear that self-evaluation was no longer enough. In 1993, the Board created an Inspection Panel (IP) to serve as an independent mechanism to ensure accountability. Although an integral part of the Bank, IP was to enjoy complete independence from management and staff. It was created, as Wolfensohn stated, to be "a vehicle for private citizens, and especially poor people, to access directly the World Bank's highest governing body—the Board of Executive Directors—and to seek redress for what they may perceive to be harmful operational consequences of the World Bank" (World Bank 2003a:vii). This did not calm many NGOs; indeed, more were organized. Armed, ironically, with the ammunition provided by the Bank itself (its OED's annual reviews, the Wapenhans Report, and the simple fact of the establishment of the IP), they demanded the Bank become more open, accountable, and responsive. The '50 Years Is Enough' campaign brought this 'anti-Bank' (more accurately, anti-IMF) movement to its peak. The Bank was asked not only to be accountable to its shareholders and borrowers, but also to those watchers whose very existence depended on their criticism of it. How could the Bank be accountable to a group of NGOs whose own accountability was in question? What did this change mean to the staff and their work? When Wolfensohn became the Bank president, he decided to open the Bank to NGOs. Its staff were to work closely with NGOs, as a way of responding to criticisms from civil societies.

The Bank had started engaging NGOs in its operations in the early 1980s. Indeed, "many powerful NGOs in industrial countries pursued agendas that helped them with their fund-raising activities" (Burki 2005:143). The Bank was an easy target. At the time no NGOs from developing countries were involved. While some resisted the Bank's proposal to bring southern NGOs into the Bank-NGO Committee, others openly criticized the Bank for excluding developing country citizens (Cahn 1993). Even after the mid-1990s, when Wolfensohn expanded the Bank's consultation with southern NGOs and involved them in Bank's activities, northern NGOs led most of the fights against international financial institutions (Mallaby 2004). Southern NGOs did not enjoy the same status or same trust. Their image was undermined by corrupt politicians or businesses setting up NGOs to siphon funds or evade taxes. Those which received funding from multilateral or bilateral institutions were seen as instruments of developed countries. Furthermore, their quality was questioned because they had difficulties attracting professional staff.

In the second half of the 1990s, several cases were brought to the IP by NGOs even though the operational procedure of IP clearly states that

- requesters must claim that they live in the area affected by a project or program financed by the IBRD or IDA or that they represent people who do, and
- requesters must allege that they are or are likely to be harmed by IBRD- or IDA-financed activities, and they must describe the harmful effects (World Bank 2003a:7).

One example is the Qinghai Project (voluntary settlement on newly irrigated land, also known as Gansu-Hexi Corridor project), a component of the proposed China Western Poverty Reduction Project. Its objective was to reduce absolute poverty in remote and inaccessible villages of three provinces—the Inner Mongolia Autonomous Region, the Gansu, and the Qinghai provinces—and to assist about 1.7 million people. In all three locations, the project expected to increase income and productivity in both farm and off-farm activities. It included a component designed to move 57,775 farmers from heavily eroded hillsides in the eastern part of Qinghai through voluntary resettlement 300 miles further west on the barren plains in Haixi, an area inhabited by about 4,000 people. The Bank was contributing $40 million to this part of the project that would benefit the 57,750 who were to move, the 110,000 who were staying, and the 4,000 who live in and around the new area. The Bank staff had spent time and resources assessing the environmental, voluntary settlement, and other social impacts. On April 30, 1999, hundreds of people gathered in the park across from Bank headquarters, holding signs, 'Save Tibet' and 'World Bank Kills Culture.' No one at the Bank had anticipated this reaction. Less than two months later, IP received a request for inspection of the Qinghai component from the International Campaign for Tibet, "a US-based non-governmental organization, acting in representational capacity for people who are living in the project area" (IP 1999). None of its members lived in China or in the region that would be affected. None of those 57,775 farmers who would have benefited were part of the protest.

In response, the Bank staff again scrutinized the environmental and social impacts of the projects. Nothing short of abandoning the project seemed to satisfy NGOs. As Mallaby observed,

In the confusion of June 1999, it was hard to sort out the reasonable criticisms from the unreasonable ones. The Clinton administration announced it would vote against the project when it came up for board approval; it had no desire to face down the Tibet lobby in Congress. Most journalists accepted the NGOs' view of the project; there is tendency to assume that small, underdog groups must be the good guys, where big outfits like the World Bank are presumed to be the malign. (2004:274)

The sad part of the saga was that the IP interrogated the Bank staff involved in preparing the project "like a court-martial—with the slight difference that in most court-martials you have a right to an attorney" (Mallaby 2004:279). The morale of the Bank staff in East Asia region was destroyed—within a short period of time, the RVP, his deputy, and many others left. By the time the Chinese government, "fed up with the controversy and high costs of remedial measures, withdrew its request for the Bank to finance the project, and proceeded with its own resources" (Marshall 2008:128), many in the Bank still wondered whether the people and environment in Qinghai would have been better protected if the project was supervised by Bank staff. One comment was , 'Learn to bend before you are broken; don't be a martyr for a day but lose the battle.' Saddened by the development, EAP VP Jean-Michel Severino ordered a review of full risks involved in the Bank's work in the region. At risk was not only the Bank's relationship with China, but its own reputation in conducting development projects.

NGOs' efforts to influence Bank's processes have generated some positive changes. For example, the Bank has always developed country assistance strategies, even though they became known as CAS only in the 1990s. "The CAS—once the most secret Bank document—is now subject to extensive consultations in a growing number of countries and in several cases is widely disseminated, published in the media, and posted on websites," the Bank told the ministers and the media at the 1999 spring annual meeting (IP 2000). The change was adopted mainly because of the complaints from NGOs about transparency in the Bank, but despite the opposition of some governments who saw the CAS as their document.

In the second half of the 1990s, the Bank revised several of its social safeguard policies, conducted strategic reviews of its more controversial lending practices, added extra fiduciary responsibilities to project work, and engaged more NGOs in consultations. However, one of the "unhappy consequences of the Bank management's willingness to give in to the pressures of the northern NGOs" is that

it has made the managers who are responsible for operations risk averse; most managers do not relish the prospect of facing the

Inspection Panel. That outcome is singularly unfortunate because economic development is a business full of risks. Mistakes have been made and will continue to be made. By scaring the staff, the Bank has hurt its ability to do innovative work. (Burki 2005:144)

Staff are used to being evaluated internally and externally, by their superiors and their colleagues. However, when their work became a political football kicked around by NGOs, Congress, and other governments, some talented staff left. Even though NGOs have now become part of *modus operandi*, the general mood is, 'if it's highly controversial, who needs it—not the Bank, not the country.' CDs have to identify where and how collaboration can be done with local NGOs. In some countries, NGOs are accepted as part of the Bank-supported projects by governments. In others, like Mexico and China, NGOs, especially those from developed countries, are not welcomed. In many cases, CDs are asked to mediate between the government and NGOs.

The increasing involvement of NGOs and especially of community-based organizations (CBOs) in the Bank's projects has created new dynamics with borrowing countries. The Bank encouraged CBOs to organize resettler participation and intervene at grassroots levels. CBOs undertake citizen surveys on the quality of government services; the Bank then sends these citizen report cards to the government as a way to push for reform. For Bank staff, the challenge is to select good credible NGOs. In the past five to seven years, OED has conducted several evaluations on NGOs' participation. One message is clear: NGOs do not equate civil society, nor are they necessarily community based. Large international organizations can easily become large bureaucracies with their own agendas. Small ones can be narrowly focused interest groups. Staff work with those that can benefit the poor.

New Challenges

At the end of the 1990s, another agency was created to watch over the shoulder of Bank staff—the department of institutional integrity (INT). Corruption had long been assumed to be so quintessentially 'political' that the Bank was prohibited from dealing with it. In the 1990s "many of the Bank's employees were troubled and embarrassed" by the problems of fraud and corruption, and some brought issues into the discussion with the "reference of 'rent seeking,' 'leakage,' or some similar euphemism" (Thornburgh et al 2000: 9). Wolfensohn put the issue of corruption on the agenda at the annual conference of 1997 when he announced, "Let's not mince words: we need to deal with the cancer of corruption." On May 12, 1998, the management outlined the original mandate of the Oversight Committee on Fraud and Corruption. It was to investigate Bank staff who involved in fraud or corruption. The investigation would be conducted by either the Internal Audit Department, Office of Professional Ethics, or any outside investigator appointed by the Bank. In October 1998, the president expanded its mandate to encompass responsibility for the supervision of all investigations into allegations of fraud and corruption (including those involving Bank staff and Bank-financed contracts). Shengman chaired the Oversight Committee. By 2000, it had 47 staff and a budget of $6.9 million. Two Bank employees were found guilty in 1999 for embezzlement and accepting bribes in giving out contracts. It made its first debarment of a Canadian consulting firm in the same year.

In 2001, the Bank merged three smaller units and created the INT. One part of its mandate was to investigate potential staff misconduct, which included serious corruption cases, such as accepting kickbacks from Bank contractors. Other misconduct covered a wide variety of ethical and behavioral issues ranging from failure to meet court-ordered alimony or child support payments, to allegations of sexual harassment, and violation of Bank policies on dissemination of confidential information (Thornburgh 2003:10). An independent team recommended separating the responsibilities and giving the less serious ones to HR, but nothing had been done by the time Wolfensohn left the Bank.

Should INT play a proactive, reactive or preventative role in investigating corruption cases? Should it focus on the Bank staff or the client governments or the consulting firms? How much resources and time should it invest in serious corruption issues and how much on misbehavior of the staff? Adding to the complications was the issue that many Bank staff felt INT was used as instrument by Wolfowitz to achieve his overt political agenda.

Wolfowitz announced to both the staff and the public that he was taking a 'tough stand' on corruption. One of his first steps was to name a new director for INT. In doing so, he violated the norm that "the Director of the Department should be appointed for a five-year term by the President from a list of no less than three persons recommended to him by an international panel of five experts from outside the Bank who are experienced in the investigation and prosecution of fraud and corruption cases" (Thornburgh 2000:44). Before his arrival, the Bank had enlisted the help of an executive-search firm, which, out of a large pool of candidates, identified nine on a short list. Wolfowitz rejected all of them and appointed his own counselor, Suzanne Folsom, to head the department. Folsom "had strong ties to the Republican Party (her husband, George Folsom, a foreign-policy specialist, worked for the Administrations of Ronald Reagan and George H.W. Bush)" (Cassidy 2007). Her subsequent decision to retain her title as counselor to the president, despite her responsibility to represent an independent and authoritative voice on questions of corruption and institutional integrity, was seen as a conflict of interest. Later the Volcker Report confirmed this: "The role of the Director as independent investigator might be compromised" by carrying another title as Counselor of the President (Volcker et al 2007:14).

The concerns about INT came on two fronts. Most staff agree that corruption is a problem, yet few see 'zero-tolerance' policy as a way to deal with the client countries. 'Corruption is a symptom and an integral part of underdevelopment.' The Bank's work is associated with corrupt governments. This is just part of what the Bank does. Cleaning up corruption is a slow gradual process. The Bank staff had to develop a strategy to help its client countries build capacities to deal with corruption. When Wolfowitz suspended projects in several countries without much input of the Bank staff, questions were raised by current and former Bank officials and the shareholding governments:

> Why were projects being suspended in India and not in Indonesia, which by many measures is more corrupt? Why Uzbekistan and not Tajikistan? Why Congo-Brazzaville and not the Democratic Republic of Congo? (Cassidy 2007)

Meanwhile, since INT was in charge of both serious corruption cases as well as 'misconduct,' it created an atmosphere at the Bank that everyone was under its watch—'be careful if you want to get a pencil from the office; INT is investigating,' an official said scornfully. In some cases, the INT was "bypassing internal rules on investigating the email records of a number of employees" (Ball and Alden 2006). When the Bank Staff Association raised concerns, the management refused to do anything about it. To calm Bank staff, Wolfowitz said that INT should be treated as an 'ally' helping to root out corruption rather than a "watchdog" that held the staff under suspicion (Ball 2006). But this was exactly how INT behaved against Bank staff. Then when the Bank staff brought complaints to the INT about the pay rises for Wolfowitz's girlfriend, the open-ended contracts for Wolfowitz's two political appointees, and the consultant contracts for a third, INT refused to respond or take on the investigations.

"Investigators—even well-trained investigators acting with the highest professional standards—are not typically candidates for popularity prizes in any organization," acknowledged the Volcker Report. The unpopularity of INT within the Bank was particularly problematic, most importantly because of the belief among the Bank staff that "a strong anticorruption effort would somehow be anti-development and 'penalise the poor twice' by curtailing lending in corruption-prone countries or sectors" (Volcker et al 2007:8). One CD told the INT frankly, "there is no basis for the government in his country to recognise any authority for INT's investigators to conduct investigations 'in country'" (Thornburgh 2003:8). Thus, in the past decade, especially under Wolfowitz, the efforts to watch its staff on corruption issues through the INT have subjected staff to another level of evaluation and one often seen as negative.

Conclusion

The Bank lives within a web of internal evaluation and external review. Few are as critical or, at times, as damning as its own staff. The variety of reviews has at times led to changes of direction, to reconsideration of policies and to a comparatively open assessment of performance. What is more, the critiques are often open. The Bank itself gave ammunition to its critics when it concluded that many of its projects have not succeeded or fallen short of their objectives. They in turn, often from a narrow and ideological perspective, condemn the Bank staff for what they do. There is never likely to be a complete unity of intent because the objectives and starting assumptions are so different. As in all large organizations, the senior management prefer that the debates about the processes and problems of management remain internal, but do not discourage analysis of projects and programs. Their most informed critics are often their own staff, formally charged with the responsibility for review.

CHAPTER EIGHT

Governance: Political, not Politics

In 1997, Wolfensohn identified 'the cancer of corruption;' he declared that corruption and poor governance undermined social and economic development. This recognition of governance as important for development was partly a response to the external criticism that the Bank had ignored corrupt political processes in its client countries.

In practice senior officials had long admitted that "it's the politics, stupid" (Kavalsky 2005:28), but they always had to work around it for the Articles of Agreement declares,

> The Bank and its officers shall not interfere in the political affairs of any member; nor shall they be influenced in their decisions by the political character of the member or members concerned. Only economic considerations shall be relevant to their decisions, and these considerations shall be weighed impartially in order to achieve the purposes stated in Article I. (Article IV, Section 10)

The Bank had always faced challenges linking its commitment to project-related funds and its concern over institutional development. Requiring borrowing countries to change their policies and institutions as a condition of lending had not been formally adopted as Bank policy before 1980.

Many Bank officials saw this shift to policy, rather than project, lending as a temporary reaction to the urgent need to stabilize the debt crisis. It was difficult enough to *agree* on how to change the broader macroeconomic system without getting involved in politics. Those who defended the shift argued that, while other donors funded projects, the comparative advantage of the Bank was "certainly in handling policy issues."

> The staff of the World Bank has the capability in terms of sector specialisms and professional disciplines for policy analytical work and it has a long history of undertaking such work. Moreover, its autonomy from national interest groups and its proven record of commitment to support development in a non-political way make the Bank uniquely able to develop an operational involvement in policy issues. (Please 1984:12)

Policy-oriented lending allowed the Bank to protect developing countries from the duress of the donor countries. The Bank, not beholden to any individual donor, needed to provide policy advice and institutional reforms in its package of loans (Please 1984).

The intrusive policy-oriented structural adjustment lending in the 1980s created widespread resentment of the Bank but achieved little change in the poorest countries. As conditions deteriorated, the Bank had to engage in capacity and institution building, which in modern parlance is part of 'governance.' Wolfensohn gave it formal recognition as a target for Bank assistance. Wolfowitz, too, as incoming president, demanded an anticorruption drive. He announced in a speech in Jakarta that a campaign against corruption was his priority, leading to a controversial Bank paper designed to strengthen its good governance and anticorruption (GAC) projects. Presidents thus gave both attention and legitimacy to the initiative.

Our concern here is not to describe the story of governance in the Bank or the impact of governance loans on clients; that can be found elsewhere (e.g., World Bank 2008a, 2008b; Thomas 2007). We want to show how the story illustrates the dilemmas that we have explored: the need for staff to turn the visions of presidents into practicalities, the problems faced by sector anchors in developing applicable cross regional lessons, the importance of staff on the front line in determining what can be done, and the difficulty in evaluating programs with long time spans and unclear indicators of success.

This chapter will illustrate the dilemmas of governance. At the highest level there are debates over what the Bank could, or should, do: edicts laid down by the legal counsel, aspirational statements from presidents, and broad visions reflected in policy documents. At the other pole are the programs, developed at national level, negotiated with officials who may well be beneficiaries: programs that must be designed for local conditions, often small in dollar terms, but still complex to devise and hard to assess. Benefits are invariably dispersed, long term, difficult to link precisely to inputs. There is no infrastructure to point to, and no rate of return that can be readily calculated.

The Articles of Agreement

Governance had received attention in the early 1990s, both as a reaction to the continuing ineffectiveness of structural adjustment loans and the need to assist countries emerging from the collapse of the Soviet empire. Yet, governance had to be approached with care.

In a series of memoranda, the Bank's legal counsel, Ibrahim Shihata, insisted on a narrow interpretation of the Articles. He stated that conditionality could not be used to introduce political transformation. He conceded that good governance depended on the existence of a set of rules and their effective application. Since effective investment required good order, Shihata argued that the Bank could become involved where it believed the rule of law was a prerequisite for success; therefore, areas of public administration, such as civil service reform, accountability for public funds, and budget discipline, were legitimate targets (Thomas 2007: 733; see also Shihata 1991, 2000). If corruption was defined as a technical problem interpreted in economic terms and needing procedural solutions, the Bank's assistance could then be used to deal with the problem under the Articles. That is how Wolfensohn explicitly argued,

> I decided in 1996 that I would redefine the 'C' word not as a political issue but as something social and economic. That got me under the wire of the Articles of Agreement. (quoted in Thomas 2007:742)

Governance in the Bank

The Bank's definition of governance grew more complex as its aspirations expanded. In 1994: "Governance is the manner in which power is exercised in the management of a country's economic and social resources for development." There were four aspects: public sector management (PSM, especially efficiency); accountability; legal framework for development; and transparency and information (World Bank 1994).

By 2006 the concept had become more detailed and nuanced. It was defined by the WBI as

> the traditions and institutions by which authority in a country is exercised for the common good. This includes (i) the process by which those in authority are selected, monitored and replaced, (ii) the capacity of the government to effectively manage its resources and implement sound policies, and (iii) the respect of citizens and the state for the institutions that govern economic and social interactions among them.

So the Bank's activities were extended to ideas of the common good, the attitude of citizens, and an assessment of governmental capacity. Redefinition added scope.

The Framework

Bank staff working on governance are part of the PREM network. PREM is the home of the Bank's macro- and country economists, who dominate to the extent that debate is often carried on in their language and concepts. Economics is seen by its advocates as the means to integrate perspectives and provide strategic overviews for each country program. There are few political scientists or people with other management skills in the network.

PREM is divided into a number of five sector boards: economic policy, gender and development, poverty reduction, public sector governance, and (very small) trade. The Public Sector Governance Board is chaired by a director who heads the Public Sector Group (PSG); it includes his deputy representing the Anchor Group, the SMs from the six regions, and one or two people from each of the seven thematic responsibilities: Legal Institutions of the Market Economy, Public Expenditure Analysis and Management, Tax Policy and Administration, Decentralization, Administrative and Civil Service Reform, Anticorruption, and E-government. An IEG evaluation on public sector reform (PSR) noted that in 2008 there were 99 people in PREM in the regions under the PSG umbrella: 60 in public expenditure, 28 on the civil service, 5 on tax, 13 on anticorruption, and 15 on political analysis. A further 111 worked in Operations and Policy Country Services (OPCS), providing support across the regions in financial management and procurement (World Bank 2008a:31). The commitment to governance, despite the rhetoric, remains small.

The Anchor Group manages knowledge and provides support across the regions because every country office cannot develop its own tax or legal expertise. It provides briefs or information that are then adjusted for local needs. It can offer just-in-time advice, training, peer review of analytical studies, or workshops. It also deals with external bodies: the UN Convention against Corruption, the OECD convention on Combating Bribery of Foreign Public Officials, and the State Stolen Asset Recovery Initiative. The WBI staff develop cross-country indicators of governance and corruption and explore the effectiveness of legislatures.

Each region has a SM for public sector governance, with responsibility for delivering projects that CDs commission, ensuring their quality, allocating staff, and managing the careers of the staff under their tutelage. They have direct lines of accountability to the PREM SD in their region, but work with the Anchor director and the resident country units.

In a few places, notably Bangladesh, India, and Indonesia, a senior governance adviser, equivalent in rank to the country economist, oversees the governance programs and ensures that governance receive adequate attention when projects are developed. The senior advisers argue that governance ought to be integral to all the Bank's loans. They see the need to 'mainstream' the issues. In the country policy and institutional assessments (CPIA), devised to allocate IDA funds, 5 of the 16 questions relate to governance, and then they are weighted twice. It is, therefore, they argue, everyone's business, even if the issues often receive low priority in other operational areas.

The Strategic Directions

Over the decades the Bank has produced extensive reports on governance; we cover here just a few to illustrate the dilemmas. In 1994 a team from the Operations Policy division, under the general guidance of Jim Adams, produced a summary of its performance: *Governance: the World Bank experience.* Total lending for governance in 1993 was $US 609 million in the context of "a smaller state equipped with a professional bureaucracy that can provide an enabling environment; for private sector-led growth, to discharge effectively core functions such as economic management and to pursue poverty reduction" (World Bank 1994:xvi).

The most common subject for assistance was PSM—"the capacity of governments to make and implement public policy, the effectiveness of public programs, and the strength of public institutions." PSM included financial management and civil service reform. A total of 40 CASs were reviewed. In 29 of them, PSM was the only governance topic raised. Only 8 went further; 3 made no mention of governance at all (World Bank 1994:38). The dilemmas were recognized. Because issues of governance were highly sensitive, Bank staff were reluctant to commit ideas to paper because they feared to tread too near the boundaries of the Articles of Agreement. Besides, they were unfamiliar with the territory and lacked the skills (1994:39).

The impact varied by region. In SA there was little interest in programs of governance. In EAP most countries did not want advice; where they did, in Papua New Guinea or the Philippines, for instance, dialogue had been intensive, but results elusive. As the report noted,

> As mandated, the Bank's work has been exclusively on the economic and social dimension of governance. The Bank, nevertheless, may find itself close to the political dimensions in the policy dialogue with governments. (World Bank 1994:57)

The 1997 WDR, entitled *The State in a Changing World*, argued that an effective, rather than a minimal, state was vital for economic development. It wanted to improve the states' capabilities by reinvigorating public institutions and addressing the incentives and pressures both inside and outside government. The report laid out an agenda for public sector reform that provided core themes for analytical approaches and lending instruments. It began the process by which, according to its own assessment, the Bank "is now recognized as the leading centre of knowledge on governance and public sector reforms and a champion of anti-corruption issues world-wide" (WDR 2007:4).

In this context Wolfensohn's 'cancer of corruption' speech provided the impetus to expedite an agenda that had been bubbling along inside the Bank for some time. The 1997 fiscal crisis merely reinforced the message that governance was a problem.

In 2000 the PSG in PREM, drawing on experience across the Bank, published *Reforming Public Institutions*. It noted the Bank has sometimes taken a rather narrow and "technocratic" view of public sector reform, interacting exclusively with "government interlocutors." The paper concluded that "it has sometimes relied on models of 'best practice' that have not been feasible in the particular country." It accepted that, consistent with the country ownership mantra, a country's leaders had to be in the driver's seat (World Bank 2000:xv). Voice and partnership were needed. Appreciating local conditions was essential.

> We need to start with a thorough understanding of what exists on the ground and emphasize "good fit" rather than the one-size-fits-all notion of best practice. The Bank's unique advantage is its ability to combine expert cross-country knowledge with in-depth understanding of specific, situational client countries. (World Bank 2000:xv)

In the following years a number of regional updates both explored regional programs and sought to learn the broader lessons.

In 2004 the WDR, *Making Service Work for Poor People,* emphasized the need for targeted and effective government services. It was, one cynic said, the old concept of public administration revisited. By 2006 it was reported that $4.5 billion had been lent in areas related to governance, the rule of law, and PSM.

In 2006 in Jakarta the new president, Paul Wolfowitz (2006), announced,

> I will be asking my staff in high-risk countries to develop a strategy to mobilize all World Bank instruments, loans, grants, technical assistance and private sector investment, to strengthen and fight corruption. We will increase our investments in such key areas as judicial reform, civil service reform, the media, and freedom of information and decentralization of public and service delivery.

The speech set the tone for his term.

Governance became a battleground between Wolfowitz and his Executive Board. His suspension of loans in India and a number of African countries because of corruption had been seen as punitive. It raised questions. What were the standards against which decisions would be made? Was an investigation by the Office of Integrity by itself enough to suspend a loan? A draft paper of "Strengthening the Bank Group's Engagement on Governance and Anticorruption" was requested by the Board. It was carefully drafted by the PSG staff, but then heavily redrafted in the president's office and sent to the Development Committee of the Bank (made up of ministers of finance, not EDs) at its meeting in Singapore in September 2006 without further consultation.

Feedback before its presentation had already warned against the Bank acting as a global arbiter or referee; it should "engage," "consult," "stick to what it was good at" (World Bank 2006a:5). Consultation, noted the Bank, was held in 47 countries with 3,200 people.

The Development Committee gave the president's paper a frosty reception; there was, by one account, 'blood on the floor.' Its chair argued that "disengagement from client countries based on governance considerations would set back efforts toward achieving the MDGs." He stressed the need to consult the Board if "any financial disengagement or scaling down because of governance concerns is proposed by Management" (World Bank 2006b:21). The Japanese minister warned it was "essential not to make arbitrary assessments, thus ensuring equal treatment." The British argued, "None of us should walk away from assisting poor people, even where the situations are difficult." The minister from Côte d'Ivoire, on behalf of 26 African states, said, "The Bank should not suspend its assistance based on the mere presumption of corruption in countries." The Indian minister, "Development cannot wait for improved governance and a corruption-free world. Both must go 'hand in hand'." China's minister of finance emphasized "sticking to development as Bank's core mission…Disengaging countries with aid on the ground of weak governance would set back the efforts towards achieving the MDGs" (World Bank 2006b:28, 42, 49, 67, 97). Everyone stressed the need for country ownership. The Development Committee sent the proposal back for consultations and redrafting. It was rare for the Development Committee to reject a paper, but there was widespread concern about the informal power structure that was dictating policy.

The new draft softened the original that had bluntly laid down a series of steps that would be taken at country, project and global level. The new version was indirect, providing a strategy, not just a set of demands. It repeated the initial diagnosis but added a set of guiding principles, emphasizing the mandate to reduce poverty, with governance as a means to that end. It accepted that there is no one-size-fits-all solution and the need to include multiple stakeholders. The purpose, it proclaimed, is "to strengthen, rather than bypass, country systems." It sought "entry points." Instead of eight dot points that listed the initiatives the Bank would take at country level, there were a number of paragraphs that emphasized partnership, country involvement, and contingency.

Even in the most poorly governed countries, the WBG will seek to stay engaged, in some cases with shorter interim strategies while agreement is pursued with the government on medium-term priorities. (World Bank 2007:5)

The approach was cooperative, even when the clients did not want to cooperate.

> In exceptional circumstances where the central government cannot adequately administer the proceeds of Bank-financed operations, the WBG will seek innovative ways of engaging to provide services directly to the poor using instruments such as community-driven development and third-party delivery systems which do not rely on central government administration for disbursing resources. The Bank also will seek to use policy dialogue, analytic work and technical assistance to try to build support for a stronger engagement on governance. (World Bank 2007:6)

All else failing, staff would provide an "interim strategy note."

Softly, softly and keep the channels of communication open. That governance was hard was recognized. The paper was sufficiently general that almost any strategy of direct involvement or careful engagement would satisfy its objectives. Loans were not seen as the target; any analytic involvement was desirable if that was the best that could be achieved. There was also an appreciation that the Bank should "seek out and support leaders and institutions that are committed to improving governance." The redraft was taken directly to the Board and approved for release on March 30, 2007.

Here is the classic dilemma. At the senior level, the Board and president had broad ideas, but knew progress depended on local actions. The challenge for staff was to turn these aspirations into projects on the ground.

Delivering Governance

The Anchor: A Pivot

The Anchor unit acts as advisor to the presidents and VPs; its staff were heavily involved in drafting Wolfowitz's paper on anticorruption, before it was rewritten in his office It was also a pivot, to be used or ignored by the SDs and SMs. The PSG staff develop general lessons to supplement local analysis. If a country is emerging from war, what sequence helps institutional reform? They warn against raising expectations too high or failing to recognize the limits of the possible. The desire is to provide some products, in terms of political economy, that assist their frontline staff.

And yet Anchor staff recognize that top-down pushes seldom work; success is based on sustained interaction to gain local support. As one Anchor person put it, just before enthusiastically heading off for a field position, 'The Bank needs an officer somewhere who understands the politics; this is where the political economy takes place.' The Anchor staff's challenge is to make those studies of political economy more effective, to provide products that assist in determining when reform projects might best work.

When a QAG report assessed the lessons to be drawn from the analysis of 25 at-risk public sector projects, its recommendations were sensible, but general. They reiterated the wisdom that had been repeated for years. Inter alia, local staff should do the following:

- Encourage local participation
- Tailor plans to local characteristics
- Undertake political economy studies
- Conduct simple stakeholder analyses
- Avoid using standard Bank diagnostic tools as automatic design templates
- Assess whether the Bank is deploying the right skills
- Avoid underestimating country ownership risk and implementation capacity
- Encourage TTLs to report candidly (World Bank 2008a:27–28).

The advice is well directed and emphasizes, yet again, how much the calculation of possibilities lies at the local level. Sectoral lessons may be persuasive but can clash with country understandings. No one at the country level would disagree with, or be surprised by, these exhortations.

Governance on the Frontline

The governance agenda touches on areas of political sensitivity at the heart of a country's structure of power. As M.A. Thomas (2007) suggests, when a country's political processes are ingrained or, in her examples, neo-patrimonial, it is unlikely that proposals for reform will be enthusiastically implemented (even if the funds are welcomed amid promises of improvement). Changes might undercut power. So staff face a number of challenges.

Comparative Advantage: There is no clear route that takes a country from poorly governed to well governed, from corrupt to constitutional. Assuming a gradual transition there will inevitably be times when, during that process, a country may be 'less' corrupt. Should the Bank support the process, while admitting that levels of corruption remain, thus being seen as condoning the status quo, or is it required to condemn all corruption at all times? If it works only with governments who are entirely clean, its activities would be minimal in places where they are most needed. If the Bank (quite reasonably in some cases) refuses to believe those who protest their willingness to support change, then nothing would happen. It may be possible to generate a template that gives guidance in other areas; it is hard to do persuasively in governance.

As a senior adviser explained, many people did not think the Bank had—or should have—a comparative advantage in questions of governance. The Bank could not become explicitly involved in politics, so the staff had to present all issues as technical: better case management of judicial workloads, schemes for tax collection, civil service pay systems, customs reform.

Skills and expertise: The Bank is technically involved only because corruption and governance are seen as economic issues, that is, they undermine possibilities of economic advancement. Consequently, solutions may be seen in economic terms too. The economists' calculus of levers and incentives, and the search for identifiable lessons of transferable good practice, may not be best suited to local cultures. It is true almost every report states that in issues of governance 'one size does not fit all.' There are still complaints that, at least until recently, too few staff have the background to interpret local politics. (Structural functionalism, said one of the few political scientist employed in the 1970s, was useless as training; 'perhaps a smidgin of Marxism might have helped'). As one skeptic discussed,

> It is essential that donors stop appointing untrained people (usu-
> ally economists) into public management reform, social impact
> assessment and community involvement jobs. The reverse would
> never be tolerated (say, asking social impact experts to do eco-
> nomic analysis). (quoted in Jenkins and Plowden 2006:138)

'Economists' said a governance adviser, 'can't model institutional culture.'

The dominance of economists may be changing, but only gradually. Of the Bank's senior public sector experts based in Indonesia, Bangladesh, and India, one was formerly on the Harvard faculty; others have doctorates from Columbia and Oxford. One governance job was advertised as 'the most challenging job in the Bank.' Their numbers remain few. When Wolfowitz declared war on corruption, there were only 12 anticorruption experts employed as such in the Bank

Staff are aware of the realities. 'To argue it is apolitical is a farce,' said an adviser. Depending on the country, governance staff may write advisory notes for both sides in an election, meet regularly with ministers, and build connections with NGOs. The process is often tortuous, as there is a need to persuade countries that governance issues need to be taken seriously. 'There was huge skepticism when we started in Indonesia, but we were gradually able to build a constituency.'

The challenge for governance advisers is to find a way to engage. Illustrations of experiences elsewhere may be a start, but there is continuing suspicion about any concept of a blueprint. In places like Afghanistan or Bangladesh, with deep-seated political crises, discussions of technical ways to improve tax collection or revise the pay of the civil servants may not attract a high priority. Indeed there is a problem 'getting a handle' on where to start in a country like Bangladesh where levels of corruption are high, where the country is politically riven or even under military rule. The Bank staff there can not just leave. Nor can they have an attitude of zero tolerance towards corruption, or no collaboration would occur.

Some of the countries are not keen to borrow in this area. India and China have long traditions of governance and believe they have nothing to learn. Middle-income countries are satisfied with AAA; they are happy to pay for the advice, but see no need for loans. Where they do, it is all about knowledge transfer.

Staff have some levers. Procurement was often noted as the best way in. To deliver a Bank-financed project, countries have to follow the Bank's rules for procurement, designed to ensure transparency of contracting and prevention of corruption. The Bank chooses to 'ring-fence' its own projects, to prevent improper activity where its own funds were being used. Governments can then transfer the procurement rules to other projects. Tax administration was easy to sell because it can be seen as technical. Much harder were areas such as cabinet decision making: how to make ministers more systematic. It may only be possible to provide a series of policy notes, to hold workshops to show how other countries manage the process.

Alternative strategies: There are a number of strategies. Top-down approaches, following well-developed guidelines, are advocated but will seldom work. In Ethiopia there was dialogue for three years before even a concept note was requested, and another 18 months before any operations began. The CD there wanted a coherent vision. Sometimes CDs wanted a bottom-up program but the government would not allow such activity and limited projects to civil service reform. In poorer countries the CD 'cooked it up' with 'ventriloquist's requests.' If broader approaches were needed (e.g., to develop public sector indicators across 22 HIPC countries), the Anchor unit or other key players would have to champion the initiative. The key was the interest of the CDs. Where they saw benefit, it was possible to achieve something. Where they lost interest, nothing would occur.

It was all slow in practice. Strategies had to be low key; to avoid humiliating the clients when nothing worked. Projects had to be possible. When one prime minister wanted the Bank to develop a vision for the public sector, the local staff did not pursue it; it would have been a waste of effort because there was no capacity to implement any outcome. Willingness without capacity was not enough. Some CDs want a strategy, but do not have the funds, and the SD refused to cross-subsidize the project. In another case a CD encouraged a number of technical analyses and judicial reform. A new CD pulled the plug. Civil service or judicial reform is long term. It takes 20 years to change the culture, said a governance expert, and the Bank's three-year cycles militate against such horizons. Sudden changes of direction, and living within the three-to-five-year cycles of CD appointments and CASs, could be frustrating.

The strategy was, wherever there was an inkling of interest, to provide a policy note or analytic study to identify what might be possible, then make contacts, and figure out how far they could go. It might be nowhere. Discussions were continued in Romania for eight years without anything but TA delivered. In some South American countries, the staff were inching forward with governments uninterested in the agenda. One adviser believed it was necessary to make the clients feel comfortable; 'we should never challenge their commitment.' Nor should they appear to dictate by saying, 'I think we should do...,' added another. In India, where the Bank had no influence at the national level, the CD developed a strategy of talking to the state governments. Even then, every cent spent in the country had to be approved by the National Department of Economic Affairs. The Bank, said one governance adviser, should 'realize influencing is itself an outcome.'

It had no capacity for 'command and control, only moral suasion.' It needed to help, not punish.

Trust: Staff in the field have to build trust. Knowing the expertise is there, ministers can use the staff as an on-call advisory capacity. There was always a fine line to judge where advice was appropriate. Locally appointed governance staff have a feel for the possibilities that, they believed, no appointee from Washington, D.C., could ever replicate.

Trust in governance staff was fragile. It proved difficult to maintain when the scandal over Wolfowitz erupted. How could the Bank staff argue that client countries needed to develop a civil service based on merit and not nepotism when it appeared the Bank itself could make appointments on the basis of personal relationships. The PREM Anchor orchestrated a public letter signed by most of the governance staff, pleading that the scandal be fixed. They could not implement any governance strategy while the Bank was so internally obsessed and needed to restore confidence in their message.

One expert argues that there are two schools of thought on governance and anticorruption activities. One wanted to get the basics right, often through technical solutions and by working with governments. The other was the 'engage the public' school that believed in the value of civil society, participation, and accountability. Both would argue that it was the presence of the Bank, not the size of the loans, that had value.

Loans were not a high priority. In the countries that most needed help, there were often no loans for years, but there was ESW, supported by IDA in countries like Afghanistan. There the Bank might organize conferences to discuss options. Many countries just wanted details of best practice. Bank officers liked loans because it gave them a seat at the table where they could better appreciate how the process really worked. On the other hand, loans had a three-year cycle; governance issues required ten years at least to become embedded.

Few governance loans were large. If the quantity of lending was to be a criterion for success, governance experts did it tough. A loan for judicial review or tax administration would take as long to prepare, develop, and receive approval as a structural adjustment loan, even if it was for far less in total. As one experienced officer said, 'We kill ourselves for 18 months for a loan worth $60m; economists come twice and lend $1.2 billion.' To some the lack of emphasis on loans was fortunate. In governance, said an expert, we are too fixated on products, not outcomes. The core skills were seen as opening doors, encouragement, making the countries feel they are players. Sometimes opportunities arrive. After the Aceh tsunami, the Bank office in Indonesia, acting as the coordinating agency for a wide range of donors, could blend the issues of governance into the disaster relief to ensure that funds were delivered effectively.

There is no single governance approach. Most officers are heavily involved in one country or region and left broader issues to others. Governance programs vary from region to region, in part because of the interests of the client countries, in part because of the priorities of the sector directors or CDs. In LAC there were a large number of projects, often worth around the $20–$30 million level; the SMs there wanted to be involved. In SA there was enough TA to keep people busy and they were also easier to sell.

One SM summarized the Wolfowitz three-level agenda somewhat caustically:

- At project level we are careful to see the money is not stolen.
- At sector level we think about governance.
- At country level we maintain an active dialogue.

Governance may be regarded as crucial; it still has difficulty in being accepted within parts of the Bank as core business. It depends on the people in the front line, on the balance of interest of CDs and sector staff and on the local capacity to develop projects that meet client needs.

Some Examples: Governance in SA and EAP

The projects undertaken in SA and EAP can illustrate what the Bank does under the rubric of governance. These projects were listed in a PSG regional update of activity in the follow-up to the 2000 Report, *Reforming Public Institutions and Strengthening Governance,* and included projects approved or proposed in 2000–2002. They cover five areas: public finance management (public expenditure reviews, budget management, procurement, financial management, accounting and auditing); administrative reform; service delivery and decentralization; legal and judicial reform; and broader governance, including civil society participation and anticorruption.

First, there is the balance between what the Bank describes as upstream engagement (ESW and Diagnostics) and lending. The former include conferences, policy notes on rightsizing and retrenchment, training, and political analyses of governance reforms in the region. In EAP there were anticorruption surveys in Cambodia, Indonesia, and Thailand; anticorruption reports to Vietnam and the Philippines; regional political analyses on governance reform; an international conference on combating corruption; parliamentarians' workshops; and a Handbook for Fighting Corruption. In SA the principal interest was in financial management studies and service delivery; none in judicial reform, only policy notes on deregulation and a workshop on anticorruption. Regions were different in their demands. Only a few loans emerge from these studies. There were more governance loans in EAP than in SA. Most of them fall under the public finance rubric, even if the bulk of the diagnostic activity was elsewhere.

Second, in SA the largest number of studies and grants are negotiated with state government: Karnataka, Uttar Pradesh, and Orissa. The Bank had more leverage where its knowledge base provided a greater advantage. Indeed there were no governance loans at the national level in India.

Third, loans in many of the countries adopt the narrow technical route; accounting standards, procurement, fraud prevention provide the bulk of the subjects. If the governance staff were to be judged by loans alone, their performance might be regarded as minimal. It would belie the levels of activity and engagement displayed by the advisory and diagnostic work they do on the ground.

Assessing Governance Impacts

Governance is an area where the Bank cannot win. If it sets conditions for loans, it can be accused of interfering in the affairs of client states, of insisting on modes of political behavior that do not suit local conditions (e.g., Cahn 1993). If it does not, many of its loans might be dissipated through incompetent administration and even corruption. The Bank staff know it. Modes of governance affect the success of all Bank projects.

So how are governance projects assessed? There have been a number of attempts to identify concrete evidence of success. There are no buildings or indisputable statistics which can show a causal link to the Bank's activities; the results must be in part impressionistic. Some comments are damning.

The Bank's internal analysis of 124 civil service reform activities between 1980 and 1997 found that only 33 per cent of completed

activities had achieved satisfactory outcomes (World Bank 1999).
"Have Bank interventions helped make governments work better?" asked a Bank staff member in 1999. She answered her own
question: "Despite some progress the answer is 'probably not'."
(quoted in Jenkins and Plowden 2006:31)

Other findings are mixed, rather than enthusiastic. An OED review
of capacity building in Africa, published in 2005 (World Bank 2005),
covered the previous decade. It provides a "could do better" report
card. In Ethiopia "ten years of experience with Bank-supported Public
Expenditure Reviews (PERs) had contributed little to capacity in the
Ministry of Finance" (2005:15). In Benin and Ghana, "the design of
public financial management projects overlooked the resistance of
officials in line ministries with responsibility for implementation"
(2005:16). There was no lack of appreciation of the problems:

> Public sectors are often weak, not just because of their lack of
> capacity, but also because their weakness benefits powerful inter-
> ests that seek to avoid taxation...External assistance can help both
> the supply and demand sides of the process by providing inputs to
> enhance the functioning of the public sector and by strengthening
> structures of demand and accountability. But it cannot influence
> the cultural norms and the political economy underpinning the
> demand for public sector performance. Therefore capacity build-
> ing will succeed only where they take adequate account of the
> prevailing local politics and institutions and are country owned
> rather than donor driven. (World Bank 2005:8)

An IEG evaluation in 2008 suggested that financial management and
tax reform did better than civil service assistance and anticorruption,
perhaps because they were less "politically and culturally sensitive"
(2008b:43, 72). IEG's exhortation to avoid unrealistic expectations and
ideas of 'one size fits all', is coupled with the comment that, even so,

> it seems important to start with a basic adaptable pattern and from
> that learn the best ways to adapt it. PFM, transparency of budget,
> and tax administration have such patterns, which the Bank...[has]
> helped develop. For civil service and administration there is no
> such pattern. (IEG 2008b:65)

That might explain variations in impact.

A QAG survey of 25 "at risk" governance projects, worth over $800 million, concluded that two-thirds of them would not meet their objectives. With the optimism that often pervades Bank analyses, it also "believed that action can be undertaken...that will improve the success rate from 32 percent to about 90 percent" (World Bank 2008a:i).

None of these findings are surprising. As the IEG report notes, those countries that need help the most, have the weakest capacity for change (2008b:70). The programs of governance may not be successful, but they are so central to poverty reduction the Bank cannot walk away from the area; if its activities appear to be as quixotic, energetic and dedicated in a lost cause, staff know that the need for better governance underpins all their other projects too.

Conclusion

Governance highlights the managerial dilemmas that face the Bank. First is the potential gap between the higher echelons at the Bank and the operations staff. The president and the Board may pronounce policy and approve projects. The work of turning those ambitions into progress depends on the front line staff. Second, the Anchor tries to identify useful patterns of experience. However the country offices decide what will be adopted and do not always maintain support for as long as governance staff would like. Third, improving governance is hard and those directly involved are as conscious as anyone of the need to understand local conditions, to work closely with governments. It explains why governance experts like to be on the ground. That is where the action is. Fourth, many projects may get a rating of unsatisfactory because there are few concrete indicators to prove causality, to tie the Bank's contribution to clear advances. The greater the ambition, the more likely that will be.

The Bank's experience with governance shows that, even if their public sector staff are nominally not involved in politics, they must understand the circumstances and engage with the local and the powerful. Every report emphasizes that improvements in governance depends on adaptation and adjustment to local conditions and political realities. In the end, as staff realize, all governance reform is local.

CHAPTER NINE

Electric Power

In no other sector has the Bank had a greater impact than in electric power. "Its successes, by and large, are not the result of groping and pioneering followed by conceptual breakthroughs, but are due rather to the relative ease of transferring technology of power generation from more developed to less developed countries if foreign exchange is made available for importing equipment" (Mason and Asher 1973:715). The same mentality, however, can also explain the failure of the Bank's operations in the sector in the 1980s and 1990s. The attention to the Bank's power projects can be partly explained by the fact that they are large, whether hydro or thermal, generation or transmission, traditional or renewable, and the developing countries need extensive financial and technical support. The Bank is also a single easy target while the private and public players are more dispersed.

The Bank's role in the power sector in developing countries can be understood by examining the actors, ideas, actions and impacts within it. Ideas are always contested even in this sector where physical features are common wherever electricity is generated. Several contending factions existed: the sector argued with country experts, electrical engineers with electricity economists, the headquarters with the field, and the Bank teams with client countries. The shifts of influence may explain some of the successes or failures of the Bank's activities in this sector better than technical factors or economics.

Power as the Core Business

The core business of the Bank, 'bricks and mortar,' was identified as soon as the Bank went into business. "In almost all developing countries, a major part of the necessary investment must be made for transportation and communication facilities, port developments, power projects, water and sewage systems and other public utilities which form the basis for the development of all other sectors of the economy," declared the Bank's third Annual Report (1948:17). The Bank actively argued that an adequate supply of electricity was a basic necessity not only for raising living standards but also for increasing productivity, labor efficiency, and general scientific, technical, and social advances. A lack of electric power conspicuously handicapped growth and thereby general development. The countries that needed infrastructure were also the ones who lacked capital. Guided by philosophy and necessity, the Bank devoted a large share of its lending to building power projects.

From 1948 when the Bank made its first power loan to Chile to 1968, over 30 percent of the Bank's total lending went to power projects ($4361 million). After McNamara became president, agriculture became the Bank's priority; its commitment to power development declined in proportion to total lending but was still over seven times that of the previous two decades in actual amounts ($31 billion between 1970 and 1989). Up to 1983, electric power remained the largest single sector for which Bank funds were used (Collier 1984:19).

The Bank by then had established reputation, confidence and leverage over borrowers in the power sector. Its advantages were particularly obvious when developing countries were hit by oil crises, world economic down-turns, and chronic shortages of public funds for large projects in the 1970s. The Bank had increased its lending to the power sector from $2814.7 million in 1960–1970 to $6981.6 million in 1971–1982 (see Table 9.1). In just three years (1979–1981), total Bank lending in the energy sector was $6549 million; 77.4 percent of it ($5070m) went to power projects (World Bank 1983:82). As some countries in Europe, Asia, and Oceania had 'graduated' from the Bank's borrowing, the share of lending to the power sector in both East and South Asia increased significantly in the 1970s–1980s.

Table 9.1 Disbursements for Power Projects by Region

US$ million	Past Borrowers		LAC		EAP		SA		Total
	amount	% of total	amount	% of total	amount	% of total	amount	% of total	amount
1960–1970	515	18.3%	1308.2	46.5%	281	10%	210.3	7.6%	2814.7
1971–1982			2438.5	35%	1315.5	18.8%	1120.7	16.0%	6981.6

Source: Hugh Collier, *Developing Electric Power: Thirty Years of World Bank Experience*, Baltimore: The John Hopkins University Press, 1984, 164–167.

The Bank's lending was split almost equally between generation and transmission, and distribution network facilities. At first the Bank "took a somewhat passive attitude toward the question of which projects to finance; it acted more or less like a commercial lender in that it was content to consider the projects proposed by borrowers" (Collier 1984:14). It soon developed its own preferences. It supported large projects that showed the advantage of economies of scale. "Consequently, new generating capacity might take the form of a hydropower plant on the most economic site and a large thermal plant whose location would be determined by the kind of fuel used" (Collier 1984:13). There were two crucial features: (a) commitment to the construction of high voltage transmission lines that eventually allowed rural electrification, and (b) a large dam culture.

Power loans loomed so large in the first two decades because there were chronic power shortages and severely limited domestic resources to finance the projects in both high- and low-income countries. Up to 1967, the Bank had devoted about 23–25 percent of its total lending to the power sector in countries such as Australia, Austria, Demark, Finland, Italy, Japan, New Zealand, and Norway. By 1971, lending to that group of countries had dropped to 1.7 percent of the total commitment, while lending to Latin American countries remained strong (66 percent). In the 1970s, power lending to Latin American countries remained at over 33 percent of total loans; in SA it was about 16.5 percent and in East Asia about 19.2 percent.

The 'large dam' culture developed more by default than conscious decision. The Bank's third president, Eugene Black, once said, "A dam sometimes can save a whole country" (Zhang 2006:136). In his 13-year tenure (1949–1962), over a quarter of the Bank's loans (over $2 billion) went to large dams. By the time he left, the Bank had become the most influential development agency in the world. The 'dam' culture was built into the organisation. The Bank not only lent money and provided technology but also built a reputation for doing large power projects. Momentum built both demand and supply. Leaders of developing countries came to believe that "a large dam was a better indicator of modernization than thousands of schools or water pumps" (Zhang 2006:136). Furthermore, as nationalisation of electricity utilities took place in both developed and developing countries, it became easy for the Bank to obtain guarantees from the governments, as required by the Articles of Agreement. Finally, power sector investment has always been capital intensive and many developing countries came to depend on external assistance.

Consequently, in its 'rise to power' period of 1968–1980, the Bank reversed its practice of "the 'reluctant Banker' period of 1944–1968, when the Bank lent small and mainly to middle-income countries" (Goldman 2005:19). This passive and conservative mode of lending to power projects was replaced by more aggressive approaches. Bank staff realized that "the sector offers an especially appropriate channel for the efficient transfer of a significant part of the capital developing countries require" (World Bank 1971:3). If lending itself was to be an objective, power projects provided an easy way of hitting targets. They were large, capital intensive and with high risks that deterred private sectors. They were relatively easy to plan, implement, and oversee.

The trend reversed in the 1990s. The Bank's lending to power projects declined steadily until it hit rock bottom with a mere 5 percent of its total commitments in 1999. Both internal and external environments had changed. The Bank had been targeted for its lending to large dams by NGOs; blamed for the high failure rates of power projects in developing countries by its shareholders; criticised for competing with private investors; and faced ever rising costs and complications in preparing projects. The Bank's lending to power projects revived only after 2003 when the Board approved the management's Infrastructure Action Plan; yet the process has been slow.

Power Lending

Power lending always meant more than providing finance to developing countries to build power projects. Technical assistance and institution building have been integral to the Bank's power lending since its inception. Proposed projects had not only been of "a high priority nature" but also "economically and technically sound" (Annual Report 1950:9). Initially, with limited in-house skills, the Bank depended on the borrowing countries to provide technical data and consultants to provide technical assistance; its principal emphasis was on prospects for repayment. The Bank's engineering team would go on mission and review the technical data submitted by the country team; as a report said: "I checked over the proposed programs of expansion and am satisfied that they are reasonable and in line with good engineering practice" (Mason and Asher 1973:159). As the Bank expanded its lending into the sector, it recruited engineers and energy economists. Not only were the inspection and review of technical aspects now undertaken by in-house engineers and technical experts, the Bank staff also developed an elaborate project cycle—project identification, preparation, appraisal, negotiation, implementation and supervision and evaluation—to standardise the process.

Physical construction of power projects, according to the Bank, had "to be accompanied by substantial institutional changes in the organisation of the sector, the handling of its financial problems, and the planning and implementation of investment" (Collier 1984:13). The financial performance of power projects drew most attention; it was approached "largely from an engineering point of view and evaluated projects primarily in financial terms" (Mason and Asher 1973:715–716). Power tariffs were a key to the financial strength of power utilities and hence the ability of the borrowing country to repay loans. Often negotiations with the borrowing countries were not about whether the Bank would lend, but rather about how to set or review power tariffs. These have never been purely economic questions; they are also political because electricity is not only a public good but also a precondition for social and economic development.

Facing the problem of distinguishing between reasonable or unreasonable tariff increases, the Bank formed an internal working party in 1961 (Collier 1984:28). It adopted the rate of return approach and the provision was often written into the final contract signed between the Bank and the borrowing country. The rationale was that the utilities should earn an adequate return on their invested capital to be able to pay the current interest rate for new capital and expand to meet rising demands. Consumers should pay the full costs incurred by producers. The system worked in the 1950s and 1960s, partly because most power lending went to countries which soon graduated from the Bank or to Latin American countries which had better economic conditions than most developing countries. By the 1980s, the system started collapsing as the rate of return dropped in many borrowing countries: in Columbia, for example, an average annual rate of return of 7 percent in the 1960s dropped to 0.2 percent in the 1970s and then negative for several years (Collier 1984:173, 175). In the 1980s, "average real power tariffs in developing countries declined from 5.2 cents to 3.8 cents/kwh, the quality of service deteriorated, technical and non-technical losses and fuel consumption continued to be high, and poor maintenance of plants persisted" (World Bank 1993d:12).

Since not every borrower had "the necessary organization, management, and experienced manpower" to implement power projects, the Bank took the responsibility to "strengthen its borrowers' ability to carry out projects" by providing technical assistance that covered "a broad range of services such as engineering, management and organization, financial or accounting procedures, the preparation and operation of training programs for the borrower's staff, or the study of future investment needs or of the structure of tariffs" (Collier 1984:7, 3, 20). To mobilize domestic resources, for example, the Bank assisted El Salvador in the creation and distribution of a local bond issue (Mason and Asher 1973:161). It "was also directly involved in establishing the Swaziland Electricity Board and the Electricity Authority of Manila" (Collier 1984:71).

Integrating institution building into power projects allowed the Bank to 'influence' the policies of the borrowing countries through its "long familiarity with the sector, its ability to extend large loans that are open to worldwide procurement, its flexible approach in lending to different types of investments, and its analytical work in the area of sector studies" (Guhan 1995:25). By the end of the 1960s, the Bank had assembled a large team of engineers, energy financial specialists and energy economists. In addition to financing large power projects most developing countries could not afford, the Bank's central project staff produced a series of studies, varying from major research projects to short notes. The first staff occasional paper promoted by then Bank president George Woods analyzed economic choice between hydro and thermal power plants. With a diagnostic analysis of rates of return over a life-period of hydro and thermal power plans, the paper concluded that rapid expansion of the market would favor hydro over thermal development in the near future (Van der Tak 1966). The study not only confirmed the Bank's approach but also provided an economic analysis to justify it. It started "seeking out projects and making suggestions to borrowers about suitable projects" (Collier 1984:14). Consequently, in the 1970s, the Bank expanded its dam projects, undertaking over 400 around the world.

Since many developing countries did not have the human capital or resources to engage in research, particularly on the pricing issue, Bank staff undertook the research. Turvey and Anderson's *Electricity Economics* and Munasinghe and Warford's *Electricity Pricing* analyzed the theoretical and practical problems of public utility pricing. Their solutions were then integrated in negotiations on specific power projects with little input from borrowing countries. This practice was also strengthened by the formal rules—for the Bank to approve lending, the borrowing country must agree not only to retain a sound financial position, but also follow prescribed rules on procurement, the use of consulting engineers, or other aspects. At the time, this seemed the best way to assist the borrowing countries build up their institutions in order to make the power projects work. Of course, later, this combination of loans and conditions was severely criticized by NGOs and some governments in developing countries.

Following the oil crises in the 1970s, several donor countries pooled resources to create the Energy Sector Management Assistance Program (ESMAP) as a joint technical assistance program between the World Bank and the UNDP. It operates, however, out of the Bank and on trust funds put in by the 13 donor countries to support energy development. ESMAP provides knowledge and expertise, a site for staff development, and a pool of experienced people for the client countries. Its concentrated research and expertise have allowed the Bank to play an important role in the global shift in analyzing the power sector. For better or worse, its close working relationship with the Bank staff, whether in the anchor or regional offices, has made possible the spread of new models.

Power Pendulum

In the early 1990s, the Bank remained a large financer of the power sector devoting about 15 percent ($3–3.5 billion a year) of its lending there. Faced with poor performances, the staff started reviewing its policies. In 1993, the Industry and Energy Department produced a policy paper, written by a single author but with input from experienced energy experts. As a policy paper, it did not need approval from the Board, which endorsed it anyway. "The World Bank's Role in the Electric Power Sector" (1993d) quickly became the Bank's formal lending policy. The paper discussed some fundamental changes that had been under way in Britain. Reforms would contain three main components: ownership reform could go through commercialization, corporatization and eventually privatization; structural reform would entail unbundling (separating generation, transmission, distribution and retailing) in terms of accounts, operations and management; and regulatory reform would require the creation of an independent regulatory agency to make the market system work in the sector. Even though the policy paper never said these reform measures should be used as a condition for lending in the power sector, it did suggest these were the right ways to make power sector development sustainable.

By issuing the policy, the Bank took reform into uncharted waters. Reform in the power sector along these lines had occurred earlier in

Chile and the United Kingdom. Yet, even before the success of these reforms could be assessed, some economists inside and outside the Bank decided that they were the panacea for the problems the Bank was facing. Furthermore, despite the seemingly sequential reform measures, many ignored the sequence and considered the 'policy paper' prescribed 'commitment lending,' which meant that assistance would be given only when a country's institutional and structural reform policies were satisfactory.

There were a number of reasons for rushing into the reforms. First, in the 1980s, the Bank's dam projects were under severe criticism, particularly because of the costs of these projects in terms of indirect environmental and social effects. Some people took "the extreme view that all large dams [were] bad and that new construction should be stopped or greatly modified" (Dixon et al 1989:3). The large dam projects in the 1950s and 1960s had helped the Bank establish its reputation as the most influential development agency in the world. By 1989, the Bank had lent over $28 billion to 93 countries for over 600 large dams for electricity as well as irrigation and flood control. The Bank staff in the 1960s pioneered the modelling of river basins and new methods of economic analysis of multi-purpose projects in developing countries that were eventually accepted as the standard for the justification of large dams. From the 1970s, its staff brought the social and environmental effects of large dams into their analysis.

In addition, the Bank adopted guidelines on dam safety in 1977; on involuntary resettlement in 1980, 1986, and 1990; on safeguards of indigenous people in 1982; on natural habitat in 1986 and 1995; on environmental aspects of dams and reservoirs in 1989; and on environmental assessment in 1991. Little of this achievement had been recognised. The Bank had directly or indirectly assisted only 3 percent of the dams in developing countries between 1970 and 1985, and its rate of involvement fell to about 2 percent by the end of the 1990s. With its loans for dams merely 0.6 percent of the world's financing for new dams in developing countries, the Bank was targeted for building large dams. 'When big dam projects blew up, the Bank retreated into its cave,' described one Bank staff. Instead of explaining itself, the management decided to cease involvement in hydro projects. In the face of pressure and sometimes even disruptive behaviour from NGOs, some Bank staff also decided it was not worth the fight. There were so many other projects the Bank could assist, especially at a time when macroeconomic issues took priority anyway.

Second, at the end of the 1980s, the success rate of Bank-financed projects came into question in general. Power lending projects were particularly in trouble. Rates of return had fallen; quality of services had deteriorated. It was not only these symptoms that bothered Bank staff; it was the frustration they felt: "Almost everything else has been tried," stated one of the working papers out of the Industry and Energy Department's energy series. "The World Bank, for example, in over four decades of lending, has supported a broad range of measures to improve and modify existing institutional structures" (Churchill and Saunders 1989:2). Instead of improving, the performance of power utilities had actually deteriorated. The Bank had to do *something*.

Third, the Bank faced increasing challenges from private investors freed up by financial deregulation. With the power market saturated in developed countries, private investors were looking to other places. They, however, had no intention of taking risks, whether due to currency demand or political and corporate incompetence. They called, through their governments, on the Board for Bank's support, especially its cofinancing and guarantees. This led to the creation of MIGA in 1988 and contributed to the shift of policies from public to private financing of power projects.

Finally, neoliberal economic thinking was spreading. The Bank was not spared. In the 1980s, the acute problems of structural adjustment and debt drew researchers to the issue of getting prices right. In the power sector, although research "was initially dominated by engineers, economists came to play a role, and important analytical work on...pricing took place at the Bank" (Stern and Ferreira 1997:554). At this time applied research was reduced—after the 1987 reorganization, all-inclusive large country departments were created and the research people were pooled into the newly created policy, planning, and research complex.

After the fiasco of the 1987 reorganization, the director of the Industry and Energy Department, Anthony Churchill, brought some specialists from the regional technical departments back to the centre to strengthen "the links between research and policy formulation and operational activities" (Annual Report 1988:71). They worked on reform strategies in the power sector without getting involved in application. They launched an energy paper series, with research on power pricing, investment, and other issues relevant to the Bank's power lending. Some 50 papers were produced; all, to some extent, showed frustration over the poor performance of utilities. Even though state-ownership and vertically integrated structures were not identified as the root of the problem, the poor performance of the utilities in developing countries were analysed from the macroeconomic, rather than access, angle. The diagnosis provided by these studies included "(a) inappropriate government interventions; (b) poor institutional frameworks and inadequate incentives for efficient management; (c) insufficient manpower and other resources; (d) weak analytical tools; (e) inadequate policy instruments; and (f) market distortions and low incomes" (Munasinghe and Saunders 1989:23). The structural adjustment program was consequently seen as a part of the solution to problems in the power sector.

Meanwhile, the wind shifted outside the Bank. After over a decade of preparation, in 1990 the Thatcher government adopted comprehensive ownership and structural reform in its electricity sector, yet in limited geographic areas—England and Wales only. Breaking up the monopoly went hand in hand with the privatization of generation and supply. The Electricity Act of 1989 divided the Central Electricity Generation Board, with its 74 power stations and the national grid, into four companies—60 percent of the conventional generation capacity was placed in National Power and the remainder was placed in PowerGen. The 12 nuclear power stations were placed in Nuclear Electric and the high voltage transmission grids, with some pumped-storage generation capacity, were transferred to the National Grid Company. When the 12 distribution companies were privatised at the end of 1990, competition was also introduced in supply. The Office of Electricity Regulation was created as an independent agency from the government and the utilities to regulate the market competition (Newbery and Green 1996; Newberry 1999).

Even though it took another decade for Britain to complete the restructuring, the model was immediately championed by many in developed countries and at the Bank where officers were looking for solutions to 'unsolvable' problems. Professional journals were flooded with the articles supporting such simultaneous and comprehensive reforms. The *story* about electricity—that electricity is no different from other commodities that could and should be bought and sold in the market and the electricity industry, if left alone, would produce the greatest efficiency—had not been invented by the Bank staff, but by joint efforts of politicians looking for ways to reverse the state-involvement in the economy and economists independently developing a means of achieving the political objectives: 'perfect' market models for changing the state-owned and vertically integrated, monopolized electricity industry. The story was soon adopted by the economists inside the Bank.

Frustrated by the failure of Bank policies, sector specialists looked into the reform experience in Chile and UK. One Bank power expert recalled, '1991 was calamitous for me.'

> We were facing a crisis. Support for public utilities had produced nothing. We were stuck and decided to go for a new direction and desired to make an impact. We looked at reform in UK and Chile; this was the wave then. We focused on theories—shudder at the thought—and produced a policy paper on corporatization or privatization, unbundling and independent regulation. We knew there was no track record of the reform but we accepted it without qualification.

Once the Board endorsed the 1993 policy paper, the signal was sent to the Bank staff, its clients, consulting firms and civil societies that the Bank was shifting its lending policies. The package of unbundling, arm's length regulation, competition and privatization to replace the failed state-owned monopoly was treated as a panacea for all the problems in the electricity sector. Workshops were organized, often jointly by the Bank; regional development banks, such as ABD, EBRD; and bilateral donors, in Cancun, Tokyo, Jaipur, Beijing, and Washington, D.C. (World Bank 1993a, 1993b, 1993c). Those in Cancun and Jaipur were seen as 'landmark' regional efforts to push through reform. Scholars and consulting firms were brought in to confirm and reinforce the story (Frischtak 1995).

This, however, should not be taken as a sign of consensus. Within the Bank, engineers and energy experts raised concerns; staff in the field particularly questioned the applicability of the template: 'a lot of debate on actual implementation of the template' continued, said one Bank sector expert, including the wisdom of the template's adoption in Orissa, India. Their voice was drowned in the wave of calls for radical and fundamental change. The combination of knowledge and loans in this case worked effectively in pushing through the radical reform. The Bank staff took the template to the borrowing countries with both 'carrots' and 'sticks'—if the government agreed to reform its public utilities following the template, the Bank promised to bring financial and technical assistance as well as private investment. Otherwise, no help would come from the Bank for power projects (Dubash and Rajan 2002; Xu 2004, 2005).

By then, the Bank "no longer believed that infrastructure was the route to human betterment" (Mallaby 2005:337), and lending was no longer considered important: 'Wolfensohn came to the Bank and within months triumphantly announced that the Bank would reduce its power lending from 15 to 25 percent of the total commitment to 5 percent,' many Bank staff stated. 'No one went against him, and lending declined quickly everywhere except in China.' The Bank's business went to education, health care and social programs, and, more importantly, to what the Bank had focused on since the 1980s, structural adjustment loans. In the 1990s, policy loans increased rapidly, from 25 percent to more than 60 percent. Traditional project loans accounted for less than 40 percent. Lending to infrastructures had also declined when some Bank people decided that it was not worth the effort to jump the hurdles in preparing power projects or to combat the hostilities from international and local NGOs. Project preparation had become increasingly complicated as a series of measures on social and environmental protection, resettlement, procurement, et cetera, was added by the management and thereby prolonged the process of getting one project adopted.

Most people in the Bank, including the EDs, knew the reform was experimental and the performance in Chile and UK had not been properly assessed. In an interview in 1997, the U.S. ED, Jan Piercy, made it clear, "We are still very much in the learning stages" (1997). Efforts were made to 'sell' the model for change anyway: workshops were organized; officials in developing countries were sent at the Bank's expense to the earlier reform countries (Britain, New Zealand, and Chile) to learn the lessons; and consulting firms were brought in.

The template, at least the ideas behind it, was adopted quickly even in countries that were least suited for this kind of reform because of the 'push' from the Bank staff in the field and the 'pull' of local officials. The most discussed case was in Orissa, India. It was a disaster for the people, the state budget and business. Orissa was chosen as the guinea pig for reform because the state government was desperate for funds to complete a hydro project financed by the Bank; its newly elected Chief Minister 'was clear about the problems but had no solutions,' recalled a Bank specialist in charge of the project. He decided to accept the Bank's conditions and advice to reform the power sector in return for the funds. The Indian central government pushed the reform so that the state electricity board (SEB) could improve its financial situation and the state could reduce its dependence on the central government's subsidies. Consulting firms from developed countries took advantage of the reform agenda to get themselves business funded by the bilateral and multilateral donors (Dubash 2002; Xu 2005). For the

Bank, once the chief minister gave a green light, it 'was useful to use Orissa as a model'. The Bank staff mobilized donors' money, especially from DFID, provided TA and coordinated actions from donors, consulting firms, and private investors. Looking back, the Bank staff involved in the Orissa power reform admitted that 'it was a disaster,' it was 'unfortunate,' and 'Orissa should have never been the reform case because it was so poor.'

By the beginning of the 2000s, the Bank's lending to infrastructure had dropped so low that something had to be done. The Bank's lending to power projects had declined from 14 percent of the total in 1992 to less than 5 percent in 2001 (see table 9.2).

One assumption in the 1990s was that when the Bank pulled out of power lending, private investors would fill the gap. Private participation in infrastructure did increase, but only for a few years and never to capital-poor developing countries. It declined after the Asian financial crisis in 1997–1998.

Table 9.2 Lending to Power Sector, 1992–2001 (US $ million)

	1992	1993	1994	1995	1996	1997	1998	1999	2000	2001
IBRD/IDA	21706	23696	20836	22522	21312	19147	28594	28996	15276	17250
Power	3042	2613	1613	2242	3247	1889	2067	440	994	824
Power/IBRD/IDA	14%	11%	7.7%	10%	15.2%	9.9%	7.2	1.5%	6.5%	4.8%

Source: World Bank, *World Bank Annual Report*, various years.

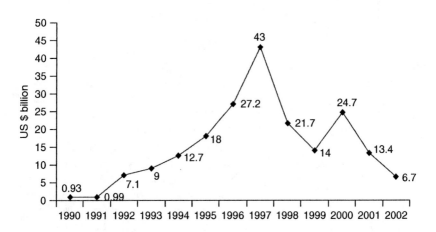

Figure 9.1 Private Investment in Electricity in Developing Countries, 1990–2002

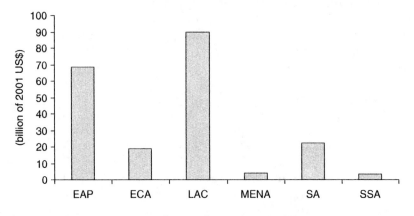

Figure 9.2   Private Investment in Electricity by Region, 1990–2001

Source: Ioannis N. Kessides, Reforming Infrastructure: Privatization, Regulation, and Competition, Washington, D.C.: The World Bank, 169.

Between 1990 and 2001, more than two-thirds of the total private investment went to two regions: 33 percent to EAP and 43 percent to LAC. Sub-Saharan Africa (SSA) where an average access rate to electricity was in single digits (except South Africa), attracted only 2 percent of the total. Most private sector flows went to only 12 countries in these two regions. This left a minute portion for the rest of the world. Yet demands for access to electricity were rising everywhere.

Bad experiences of reforms alarmed those in the energy sector at the Bank when private investors pulled out and left the government cold in India, Brazil, and several other countries (Bacon and Besant-Jones 2002; Besant-Jones et al 2004; Besant-Jones 2006). Not only investors suffered; local people did too. In places where access to electricity was low to begin with, the poor hardly benefited at all. Instead, in places like Orissa, the state government had to take on more debt; those with access to electricity saw their electricity bills soar; and the utilities suffered serious problems of power theft. There was a vicious cycle— unaffordability led to problems of power stealing; non-commercial losses forced utilities and regulators to raise tariffs even further. Access to electricity in some places even declined. The only countries where the reform may have benefited some sections of the society were South American ones which already had high access rates. By the early 2000s, it had become clear the reform template was not working.

Reviving Business

Major changes in Bank policies need a combination of internal leadership, demands from its main shareholders and stake-holders, and, more importantly, realization by Bank staff that they are required. Even with this combination, changes are difficult because of its widespread coverage and the diversity of the people involved. The management decided in early 2002 to place infrastructure back on its agenda because of demands from some client countries and its realization that the Bank was losing its relevance in world development.

Some EDs, especially from large developing countries, argued that developing countries needed more capital to help them meet rising energy demands. Meanwhile, the U.S. Congress decided to push management in the opposite direction. The Meltzer Commission, formed by the Congress, recommended in 2000 that IFC, the Bank's private sector arm, and MIGA, its political insurance unit, be abolished; the Bank stop providing finance to countries with annual income per capita of more than US$2500 and those that had access to private capital markets; the Bank shift towards providing poor countries with grants rather than loans; and the Bank pull out of Asia and Latin America, leaving the ground to the Asian Development Bank and the Inter-American Development Bank. The Meltzer report, particularly its demand that the Bank abandon lending to middle-income countries and concentrate on grants to the poor, sent chills through Bank officials. It was clear that some people in Congress wanted the Bank to have "a UN-type dependence on its rich donors" (Mallaby 2005:341) and to give up its independence.

According to Shengman,

> One day when I went to see Wolfensohn, he was sitting there staring outside the window. I sensed that something must have happened. He told me that morning at a Senate hearing on appropriation, some senators demanded the Bank cut its lending and business in middle-income developing countries, such as China; otherwise, the Congress would cut the funding to the Bank (Zhang 2006:155).

Lending from the Bank had already declined significantly after a short increase after the 1997 Asian financial crisis. In 2000, it had dropped to $15.3 billion, about half of what it lent in 1998. In 2001, the situation did not improve. The proportion of total lending to infrastructure shrank, from 60 percent in 1991 to merely 28 percent in 2001. The decline in lending threatened the financial stability and political independence of the Bank vis-à-vis both the shareholding and borrowing countries. In late 2001, instead of reducing lending and pulling out of the middle-income countries, management decided to expand the Bank's activities in both poor and middle-income countries. This decision was made not because the management decided to defy Congress or the Bush administration. Rather it was a natural response of the Bank as an organization—for its survival and its relevance.

Lending to infrastructure was at the centre of this revival. To justify infrastructure lending, the management tied it to the United Nations Millennium Development Goals (MDG)—no development could be possible without providing people with access to water, electricity, and roads. The decision that the Bank would get back into the business of financing infrastructure, with public-private participation if possible, was first revealed in December 2002 by the Bank's MD. Asked why the Bank had abandoned the financing to infrastructure in the first place, Shengman explained that

> there were many reasons, such as external pressures from private investors who wanted to get into the infrastructure. There were internal problems as well: we did not then have the comprehensive capacity to do a good job on environmental protection and resettlement when infrastructure projects were launched. Moreover, we retreated from the infrastructure also because of our complicated and long process of getting a project on its way, from its identification, preparation, appraisal, etc. The fundamental issue, however, was that we had not fully understood the close connection between economic development and infrastructure. (Zhang 2006:139–140)

This was the first time management acknowledged it was a mistake for the Bank to pull back from infrastructure projects.

Bank staff in infrastructure made a significant contribution to this change. Staff in the field demanded changes; researchers revaluated the Bank's templates and its experience in implementing the reform; and the OED decided to conduct a stocktaking of the ten-year experience in infrastructure. These initiatives apparently were uncoordinated. They demonstrate that the Bank is a flat organization where anyone can make a difference.

First, people, like John Briscoe, working on water resources in the 1990s, identified a significant gap between the demands from the client countries and the concerns of developed country constituencies, namely the NGOs. The former had appreciated the embankments, roads, and access to electricity the Bank had helped build while NGOs emphasized the social and environmental impacts these infrastructures brought (Mallaby 336–373). The clients launched a campaign to get the message across to management and EDs, using civil society, politicians, governments, and the press to counterbalance the pressures from the NGOs.

Second, OED initiated its own study in 2002 on the so-called private participation in the electricity sector. The evaluation found that, as the Bank left the power sector in 1993, private investors did not move in, at least not to the extent expected. By shifting its portfolio away from power generation to sectoral adjustment, the Bank staff had provided analytical and advisory products on climate change, energy access, and poverty reduction. Nothing could be achieved when there was no capital for developing countries to expand their generation capacity and thereby access to electricity. By the end of the 1990s, many developing countries were suffering from power supply crises. The evaluation called on the Bank and IFC to move back into the power business; the rationale behind the call was that countries could not develop without providing their people with access to electricity. Management agreed (OED 2003).

Third, in 2004 two major studies indicated a shift of thinking about lending to the power sector. One was the Operational Guidance Note for the Bank staff, developed by the energy anchor, *Public and Private Sector Roles in the Supply of Electricity Services*. The main message was "'cookbook' solutions for power sector reform clearly have to be avoided" (Besant-Jones et al 2004:4); Bank staff in the field should tailor solutions to the starting conditions in a country. A second study by the lead economist in the research division, Ioannis N. Kessides, was backed by the Bank's chief economist, François J. Bourguignon, and offered an opportunity for some senior Bank officials to express their views. The study drew the similar conclusion to the OED's report: (a) there is no single template for reform, even in a sector which "around the world is physically and operationally similar and where the technical complexity exists everywhere" (Hunt 2002:12, 13); (b) privatisation was oversold and it was no panacea, nor was unbundling; and (c) reforms of the electricity sector require proper sequencing (Kessides 2004; Besant-Jones et al 2004). These reviews were particularly critical of the insistence that borrowing countries had to adopt the reform template:

Today's industrial countries relied on the old, vertically integrated model to develop good infrastructure and have only recently pursued unbundling. So why should developing and transition economies take a new approach? This question is especially relevant given that the new model poses significant risks if not accompanied by appropriate structural and regulatory safeguards. (Kessides 2004:4)

In presenting the study to the press, the Bank chief economist first re-emphasized that "there is no universal reform model" (June 14, 2004) and then explained that private sector participation in infrastructure, including the power sector, might have prompted increased investment and expended service coverage. Private investors, however, were not interested in developing country utilities, especially in poor countries. If private investment did occur in places where the regulatory system was either lacking or ineffective, it might have negative impact on poor people in terms of access to electricity.

The OED's report on *Power for Development* raised some sensitive issues for the management—mainly the direction of power lending and conditions and sequences for reform. Its suggestions were eventually integrated in the Infrastructure Action Plan. The Bank "will continue to lend to well performing *public* utilities, including to subsidise connections and consumer charges for poor households...there will be greater flexibility in determining the period of time over which staff increases are imposed" (World Bank 2003b:7). The Bank, as many its own officials proudly stated, 'is very open minded about its mistakes and internal criticism is much greater than that from outside.'

After the management decided to revive activities in infrastructure, it needed to convince the Bank staff. "The World Bank is like a large elephant," commented Shengman, "no one strategy or a policy could be adopted and implemented overnight" (2006:140). There has always been internal debate. Shengman argued that the Bank must expand its business for self-preservation:

I have never seen any bank with shrinking business while maintaining high morale and high profits. In the World Bank, for every $1 billion lending, it can employ 200 people. If we allow lending to go down further, how could we support our staff? Every one could see this simple logic, but most behaved like ostriches and did not want to face the reality. (Zhang 2006:163)

The vice president in charge of infrastructure was asked to develop an operational plan, to add $1 billion each year to infrastructure in the following five years. The media immediately asked whether the Bank would go back to its 'old' businesses at the expense of quality and social and environmental protection. Many staff also questioned whether it was a wise decision because of the sensitivity of the infrastructure projects. Even some senior staff were concerned whether quantity and quality could be achieved simultaneously.

Shareholders were cautious. The British government wanted to make sure that an expansion of the Bank's lending to infrastructure would not lead to competitive lending among multilateral and bilateral donors; the French questioned the timing of the expansion; the Germans wondered whether lending to middle-income countries would affect assistance to poor African countries; and the Scandinavians demanded that increases in lending would not affect project quality. After intense 'shuttle diplomacy' by the Bank management team, all shareholders, including the Americans, fell into line (Zhang 2006:151-60). The Board endorsed the management's "Infrastructure Action Plan" in September 2003:

> The Infrastructure Action Plan was developed in response to client demand to revitalise the Bank Group's infrastructure business. The Action Plan signals Management's and the Board's commitment to infrastructure and the recognition that intensified engagement in infrastructure...is essential to begin to address the vast unmet needs for infrastructure service delivery. (World Bank 2003b:1)

Instead of emphasizing the macroeconomic conditions, as the Bank did in its 1993 policy paper, the Action Plan refocused infrastructure lending on access—access to modern energy was the necessary condition for poverty alleviation, development, and climate change. Improving access requires the Bank return to power lending to both poor countries, especially the Sub Saharan African countries, and the middle-income countries, such as Brazil, China, or India. The Bank had something to offer to these countries: global knowledge on how to attract private investment to the power sector; how to build an independent regulatory regime as a pre-condition for private investment; how to improve energy efficiency. Learning the lessons which forced the Bank out of the business in 1990s, the management emphasized that quality, environment and resettlement would all be taken seriously. To ensure cooperation from the middle-income countries, the management also streamlined project approval.

Implementation took a painfully long time. There had to be an attitude change. Even though the Bank as an institution was open-minded about the mistake it had made, its staff on the ground had to change their ideas and redevelop faith in infrastructure projects. This turned out to be difficult, especially when the research done by the anchor only provided analyses, not specific solutions, which would have to be adjusted according to local conditions. Adding to the difficulty was the limited number of specialists remaining at the Bank. Many had left the Bank when its lending to infrastructure was axed. Those who stayed took on other responsibilities, such as evaluation or project financing in general.

Many TTLs have little time to read professional journals to develop new ideas. They fell into routines and kept their eyes on the template of the 1990s. Even after research showed that new thinking was needed and after management changed direction, some still insisted owner-ship, structural and regulatory reform were necessary. 'If they cannot afford to pay for it, they do not need electricity,' one Bank specialist in SA declared. 'Therefore, private ownership is the only solution to the problem of high noncommercial line losses.' Others were reluctant to go back to infrastructure projects.

The consulting firms that TTLs proposed to manage projects tended to think the reform of the 1990s remained what the Bank wanted too. While the Bank management insisted that infrastructure development was the key to achieving MDGs and access to electricity was the focus, consulting firms emphasised the profitability of the utilities. Finally, governments in many poor countries resented the idea that they were told that they could not do what had been adopted in some developed or higher middle-income countries and therefore insisted on the 'most' advanced models for electricity reform. They sometimes simply told the Bank's country team 'we want that' (meaning the reform imple-mented in the United Kingdom, Chile, or somewhere else).

The complicated local conditions and a wide range of nonspecific suggestions provided by the anchors might explain the slow process of changing ideas and practices in the field. One Anchor specialist expressed his frustration:

> We have shown liberalization was not workable in most devel-oping countries and we have understood the Bank staff need guid-ance. We have developed many studies on the subject, especially the 2006 study on "Reforming Power Markets in Developing Countries: What Have We Learned?," in which we drew lessons from the ten years of experience with power market reform in developing countries, provided empirical evidence from 30-plus

countries and listed a sourcebook of about 240 published documents about reforming power markets in these countries. Then some staff in the field are still singing the chorus of the "World Bank model" of market liberalization.

Prospects

With expansion of the infrastructure lending the corporate priority, power lending was at the centre of the initiative. Since then, the total energy portfolio has increased steadily:

For those in the energy sector frustrated with the rigid requirement for reform, the decision of senior management was timely. The direction could be changed because of a combination of leadership and a shift of emphasis—instead of the 1990s emphasis on efficiency and profits for utilities, now the agenda was to improve access to electricity for the poor. 'Once access became the driver, all else followed,' stated an energy specialist. A few power specialists still at the Bank have welcomed the change but also realize the difficulties of policy implementation:

Five years ago, we could not even talk about hydro projects and we thought the Bank did not need power engineers any more.

Table 9.3 Energy Portfolio by Financing Source, FY03–FY08 (US$ million)

Product Line	FY03	FY04	FY05	FY06	FY07	FY08
World Bank	1,194	938	1,956	3,164	2,017	4,518
IBRD	468	259	677	1568	504	2,673
IDA	579	551	715	1457	1070	1420
Carbon Finance[a]	10	35	79	88	144	196
GEF[b]	62	63	105	51	128	145
Guarantees	75	30	377		160	
Others			1		10	83

Note: Carbon Finance [a]:the World Bank Carbon Finance Unit (CFU) uses finance contributed by governments and companies in OECD countries to purchase project-based greenhouse gas emission reductions in developing countries and countries with economies in transition.

GEF[b]: Global Environment Facility provides grants and concessional loans to help developing countries meet the costs of measures designed to achieve global environmental benefits. The World Bank is one of the three implementation agencies of the GEF.

Source: World Bank: http://web.worldbank.org/WBSITE/EXTERNAL/TOPICS/EXTENERGY2/0,,contentMDK:21651596~menuPK:4140787~pagePK:210058~piPK:210062~theSitePK:4114200,00.html.

When you tell people that their expertise was no longer needed, they either switched to doing something else or simply have left the Bank. Now we can talk about hydro projects, but we just do not have the people who are able to do the projects any more. If we hire consultants, they still think the market liberalisation is what the Bank wants.

It has taken a couple of years for the Bank staff in the field to put power projects together. How these reforms will continue remains to be seen.

The list of electricity projects approved by the Board in 2008 confirms several messages we try to make in this chapter: (a) the assistance from the Bank to the power sector is back; (b) the focus is on access and energy efficiency; (c) there are varieties of instruments the Bank staff can use to provide the necessary assistance the country needs; and (d) projects vary significantly in terms of the amount of funds the Bank provides, even though all projects have to go through the same steps before they can go to the Board.

Table 9.4　Loans and Credits on Energy, 2008

Date Approved	Title of the Project	Purpose	Funding Agency	Amount
Jan 17, 2008	Mexico: GEF Integrated Energy Service	Access	GEF	$15 million
			IBRD	$15 million
Feb 07, 2008	Philippines: Bicol Power Restoration Project	Transmission towers	IBRD	$12.94 million
Mar 18, 2008	India: Fourth Power System Development Project	Transmission	IBRD	$600 million
Apr 17, 2008	Madagascar: Additional Financing to the Integrated Growth Poles Project	Basic service	IDA	$40 million
May 1, 2008	Tajikistan: Energy Emergency Recovery Assistance Project	Winter emergency	IDA	$6.5 million
May 13, 2008	Burundi: Multisectoral Water and Electricity Infrastructure Project	Access	IDA	$50 million
May 15, 2008	West Bank and Gaza: Electric Utility Management Project	Access	Trust Fund	$12 million
May 15, 2008	Guinea: Electricity Distribution Rehabilitation Project	Distribution	GEF	$4.5 million
May 20, 2008	Dominican Republic: Electricity Distribution Rehabilitation Project	Distribution	IBRD	$42 million
May 20, 2008	Zambia: Increased Access to Electricity Services Project	Access	IDA	$33 million
May 29, 2008	Indonesia: Geothermal Power Generation Development Project	Renewable	GEF	$4 million
Jun 17, 2008	Bangladesh: Power Sector Development Policy Credit	Access	IDA	$120 million
Jun 17, 2008	Pakistan: Electricity Distribution and Transmission Improvement Project	Services	IDA	$83.1 million
			IBRD	$173.6 million
Jun 24, 2008	Cameron: Energy Sector Development Project	Rural access	IDA	$65 million
Jun 24, 2008	Cameron: Environmental and Social Capacity Building for the Energy Sector	Capacity building	IDA	$20 million
Jun 26, 208	Eritrea: Power Distribution and Rural Electrification Project	Access	IDA	$17.5 million
Jun 26, 2008	Benin: Energy Services Delivery Project	Services	IDA	$7 million
Jun 26, 2008	Argentina: Energy Efficiency Project	Efficiency	GEF	$15.155 million
Jun 26, 2008	Jordan: Promotion of a Wind Power Market Project	Renewable	GEF	$6 million
Jul 08, 2008	Solomon Islands: Sustainable Energy Project	Services	IDA	$4 million
Sep 04, 2008	Mali: Household Energy and Universal Rural Access	Access	IDA	$35 million
Sep 25, 2008	China: Jiangxi Navigation and Hydropower Complex Project	Renewable	IBRD	$100 million
Oct 21, 2008	India: Fourth Power System Development Project	Transmission	IBRD	$400 million
Oct 30, 2008	Bangladesh: Peaking Power Project	Access	IDA	$350 million

Source:　World Bank, "Loans & Credits on Energy," at http://web.worldbank.org.

CHAPTER TEN

A Life at the World Bank

On October 26, 2006, a crowd of former and current Bank staff packed the area outside the Preston Auditorium in the Bank's main complex to attend the farewell for Christiaan Poortman, universally known as Chrik. 'The pain, the anger, and the anguish were just unbelievable,' recalled one former Bank staffer. 'Meanwhile, there was this pride for this man who was the best of the institutional insiders, who would not want to see the institution go down the drain or his boss screw up his client countries or his colleagues.' For those in the lower ranks, the dismay was apparent: 'Chrik is of the absolute highest integrity; he was not a rebel or defiant or trying to undermine the president. If this can happen to someone so smart with such a strong career and such an institutional guy,' colleagues asked, 'what could happen to me?' 'Then and there,' a former official observed, 'I just saw the institution reject Paul Wolfowitz.'

Poortman had been the VP for MENA when Wolfowitz became the Bank president. In the following 13 months, there had been a number of disagreements over Palestine, Iraq, and issues of anticorruption in general. The straw that broke the camel's back was Lebanon—whether the Bank should have high-level representation at a donor conference in Rome, convened by Secretary of State Condoleezza Rice, to discuss the rebuilding of Lebanon while bombing continued with U.S. acquiescence. 'To me this is hypocrisy to the extent of hypocrisy,' said Poortman and advised against it. Wolfowitz disagreed and went. Soon after, Poortman was offered the position of CD for Central Asia as a demotion, an insult, and a way to force him out. Poortman decided to resign from the institution he had respected and worked for over three decades. To assist a smooth transition, he was prepared to stay on for a couple of more months. Against all the norms, practices, and with a blatant lack of respect, the president immediately announced a replacement, to be effective at once, and Poortman was asked to clear his desk in a matter of days.

Poortman was in many ways an exemplar of a generation in the Bank, a generation that became interested in and did development work before joining the Bank in the 1970s, was passionately committed to development, and served several presidents and many rounds of EDs. He and his colleagues spent their careers in the poorest and sometimes conflict-stricken regions, working on macroeconomic policies as well as various projects. His career is thus not only the story of one person, but of a whole group of talented, dedicated Bank officials. It provides insights into the way the Bank operates, the development work it undertakes, and, more importantly, the people working in it.

Working for Development

Poortman joined the Bank in 1976 after working for four years as an economist at the Ministry of Finance and Planning, Swaziland, helping to establish the ministry following the country's independence in 1969. He was one of the elite recruits in the YP program, yet an exception, trained as a macro/development economist but without a doctorate and not from a U.S. ivy league or leading UK university (University of Groningen, Netherlands). At 30, he was older than most of his cohort, and what he brought was experience in the field and a commitment to development.

During his first year YP rotation, Poortman was sent to work on an irrigation project in Indonesia where he had spent his first ten years of life and where his father, a second generation Indonesian-born Dutchman, had practiced as a doctor. He went from village to village, talking to farmers, developing farm and community budgets, calculating crop yields, and trying to discover how best support could be given. This activity might be basic, but was necessary for the local villagers and the Bank projects.

After completing his YP rotation, Poortman spent six years as an economist working on the Philippines and giving advice on fiscal reform, balance of payments, trade policies, and debt management. The Bank worked with the government in developing the first structural adjustment loan. The work was led by the director of the Country Programs Department in EAP, Kim Jaycox. A YP himself in 1964, Jaycox had already built a reputation in the Bank as a no-nonsense, hard-driving, and extremely dynamic manager. He impressed Poortman and vice versa. 'Chrik was a very good economist and an outstanding performer there,' recalled Jaycox. Poortman had a similar positive view of Jaycox: 'He was a very dynamic leader with a lot of charisma.' From then on, Jaycox became Poortman's mentor. In the Bank, career development is often left to the individual. Mentors and patrons who encourage and promote are invaluable for both the careers of younger staff and the Bank's operations.

Just when Poortman was finishing his assignment in the Philippines, 'the house came down.' Aquino was assassinated; the foreign creditors pulled out of the country, and all of a sudden, the Philippines plunged into a big hole of debt that it could not repay. The Bank was very exposed. The Philippines taught Poortman, as a macroeconomist, his first lesson: 'Economic management is not just a matter of tinkering here and there. There are fundamental principles that have to be obeyed; as a banker, one has to be careful and be aware of the broad economic, social, and political context into which one is lending.'

The links with Jaycox led Poortman's career back to his initial passion—Africa. As incoming VP in Africa, Jaycox asked Poortman back. 'I did not need much encouragement,' recalled Poortman. 'In those days if someone like Jaycox told you that he needed you, that was very important.' For Jaycox, known as 'Mr. Africa' in the Bank, Africa needed people like Poortman, who were not only good economists and high performers, but also outgoing and sympathetic to the client countries. More importantly, he 'had a lot of humility and respect,' which were greatly needed in Africa. Jaycox was then persuading the Bank's leaders that Africa was the acid test for anybody who wanted to make a career in development.

In 1983, Poortman became a senior country economist in the Sahel department, covering Mali, Burkina Faso, and Niger. There he had similar responsibilities as in the Philippines, which had a more developed economy than those in Africa. He focused more on issues of food security and debt management rather than macroeconomic policies because of the sheer poverty and lack of human capital or economic sophistication in the region. 'People were not just poor; they were absolutely and totally poor,' recalled Poortman. Some places 'were utterly destitute.'

In 1987 Poortman shifted direction from being a macroeconomist to doing project work as a division chief for Industry and Energy Operations in West and Central Africa. There he received recognition from the Bank's senior management, not just for developing new projects, but for his willingness to work in difficult environments. He also learned how to become a good manager: 'If your manager is asking you to do something that is necessary, but may not be in the spotlight, you will do it if you have a certain amount of trust that he or she is a person who will look out for you and your career in the future.' To trust and be trusted are essential for the smooth operation of a large and diverse institution.

In those years, Poortman worked, as almost all the Bank staff did, out of the HQ and traveled on missions, often for weeks on end. Seeing Zimbabwe as a potential development success story and a country that might change people's perceptions about Africa, the Bank management decided to establish a large office in Harare in 1990. This was ten years after independence. Difficult as it is to believe today, Zimbabwe was then a showcase in Africa. Poortman was appointed as the second resident representative in Zimbabwe in 1990, partly because of his seniority and partly because of his reputation of working in difficult countries in West Africa. He moved to Harare with his family. Although President Mugabe was suspicious, even hostile, to any international organization, Poortman worked closely with the finance minister, who wanted to open up the country's economy and adopt structural reform measures. 'Being a resident in Harare was very important then because the government was making big decisions requiring technical input and advice on a real-time basis.'

Poortman was given a lot of trust, discretion, and support by his CD, Sven Sandstrom, later an MD, and his VP, Jaycox. As the resident representative, Poortman was also left exposed as the local face of the Bank. Over a decade later, critics of the Bank, and especially those opposed to the structural adjustment program, targeted him personally, as though he alone made the decisions (Bond 2005, 2006). They argued that Poortman imposed policies on an unwilling government while ignoring the social implications of the economic reform program. While Poortman did not deny that at times the Bank made mistakes, he and his colleagues sometimes express their frustration that the outsiders so overestimate their capacity and underestimate the willingness, even keenness, of many African leaders to 'adopt what other countries are doing.'

Building Bridges

In 1994, following the Bank's practices of regular rotation, Poortman joined ECA as a division chief in country operations, working mainly on Bulgaria, Romania, Macedonia, and Turkey. There, he formulated country strategies, engaged in macroeconomic dialogue with Turkey on structural adjustment programs, and worked on economic and social transition issues with former Soviet satellites Bulgaria and Romania. His work did not escape the notice of the RVP, Johannes Linn, who selected Poortman as CD for Bosnia and Herzegovina. 'Chrik just seemed to be the natural person for the job,' commented Linn. 'He had this *rare* combination of being a good economist and an effective manager, levelheaded and efficient, and he had also had hands-on operational experience in difficult situations.'

In post-conflict countries, CDs have to work with different factions and bring client countries and donors together. The country program set up by Poortman's predecessor was a complex operation under a joint management of the Bank and the EC. Being able to work with the EC and other donors was as important as working with the clients. Like other CDs, Poortman was responsible for formulating the CAS, determining the composition of the lending program, assessing and deciding what financial assistance, TA or AAA, the country needed, and then allocating the budget accordingly for projects and programs. Unlike other CDs, his main focus was to "manage the Bank's crucial involvement in post-conflict reconstruction of the Balkan states" (Gill and Pugatch 2005:197). This job was as much about politics as economics: 'From a technical point of view, dealing with such issues as fiscal policy, privatization, or banking reform was straightforward, but getting together different factions, which had not long ago been killing each other and would have had little hesitation in doing so again, turned out to be extremely difficult', he said. Integrating all parties and sharing power was the precondition for establishing a common economic space—the linchpin for strengthening the new single state created by the Dayton Accord. "My training in economics revealed its limitation when the solutions most often available were not second best, but fifth or sixth best" (Poortman 2005:200).

The Dayton Accord created a joint multiethnic and democratic government charged with conducting foreign, diplomatic, and fiscal policy, but it also established a second tier of government comprising the Bosniak/Croat Federation of Bosnia and Herzegovina (known as the Federation) and the Bosnian Serb-led Republika Srpska (RS) (World Bank 1996; Bosa 2002). 'It was a very tense situation in which you had a three-ring circus where everyone tried to bull and get out of the ring,' explained Poortman. 'In that kind of environment, it was a complete nightmare to help put together an economic policy and economic reform.' The hatred among the parties ran deep, and many had no hesitation in embarrassing the Bank people either. "Our role at the Bank was the difficult one of ensuring joint responsibility for the debt, while at the same time being careful not to take sides in the underlying political dispute" (Poortman 2005:204). The donors did not make the job any easier.

Donors had pledged $5.1 billion for repairing damaged infrastructure and utilities, clearing mines, providing employment, and demobilizing combatants. Poortman cochaired the donor conferences with an experienced official from the EC. The Bank later sent a veteran officer to Brussels with responsibility to mobilize resources for the country and coordinate the reconstruction efforts of the Bank, the EC, and other donors. The challenge was to ensure that the donors would pledge sufficient amounts of assistance for the right projects for reconstruction, the pledges would materialize, and, more importantly, the assistance would be provided evenhandedly. Some donors insisted on re-imposing sanctions against the Bosnian Serb Republic (Republika Srpska) for its failure to meet obligations stated in the Dayton Accord. To convince the donors that 'the peace dividend' must be widely shared and that 'the Serb minority was not shut out of development' was difficult. Poortman worked, more as a diplomat than a normal Bank staff, closely with his team, the donor community and all the factions. He had to operate in the HQ, the field, and Brussels. When the insistence by some donors that political preconditions be met refueled hostilities, it became very dangerous for the Bank people working in the field. "Part of my time was being worried about my staff being in the wrong place at the wrong time and caught up in protest," recalled Poortman.

> When I traveled to eastern RS and encountered angry residents trying to stop or stone my car and that of other foreigners, I could not but think that political conditionality was a very blunt policy tool. (2005:202)

Poortman internalized the lessons he had learned from Sandstrom—delegating and trusting his staff. 'Chrik was an inclusive manager,' recalled a staffer, 'a new style of people manager giving a great deal of trust to the people who worked in the field.' 'While you are in the field, it is very important to make sure you have a safe base in the HQ and know there is a reasonable or good degree of trust between you and your manager. Chrik was able to inspire that trust.' Poortman, who worked out of the HQ, delegated responsibilities to the field officers. He expected honest advice from his team in the field, and neither wanted surprises.

The situation in the Balkans did improve. More countries were then added to Poortman's portfolio—Kosovo, Albania, and Macedonia. When the Bank was asked by the UN and the EU to help Kosovo rebuild itself, the first question Poortman and his colleagues asked was, 'What have we learned so far?' Learning the lessons from self-evaluation, often through informal processes, is one of the attributes of the Bank as a knowledge bank. Poortman and his team handled development issues in Kosovo "with much greater appreciation of the political constraints involved" and made sure that the new country would not return to the old state-controlled economy by supporting small and medium enterprises. After the fall of Milosevic, "I could only smile when the Bank had me assume the additional role of Country Director for Serbia and Montenegro" (Poortman 2005:208).

The Bank offers opportunities for its staff to exercise innovation and initiative. To build trust and cooperation, Poortman and his team undertook a major symbolic project in which the Bank would normally not get involved—reconstructing the historic Mostar Bridge, which 'was literally a bridge between the ethnic groups Bosnia Muslims and Bosnia Croats' and which had been destroyed by the Croats in 1993. Pooling funds from UNESCO and various bilateral organizations and foundations was not nearly as difficult as getting the agreement from Bosniaks, Bosnia Croats, and Bosnia Serbs to undertake the project. 'If we were going to take $5 million out of IDA allocation to the country, we needed to have the approval of all factions,' recalled Poortman. 'This was also an opportunity to get Croatia involved, and we convinced the Croats to put money into the project at one of the many meetings I cochaired in Brussels.' When the bridge was opened on July 23, 2004, after Poortman had already become the VP for MENA, the Bank's MD told the audience it was true that the Bank normally would not "do" reconstruction of old bridges and towns, but

> putting the bridge and its surroundings back together again provides an extraordinary opportunity for reconciliation among the people of Bosnia-Herzegovina. This kind of reconciliation is a prerequisite for revitalizing the economy and rebuilding the social fabric of a land that was a synonym for suffering and conflict less than a decade ago. (Zhang 2004)

For Poortman, the bridge was inspiring and emblematic: "It is a powerful symbol not only of the country's history and recovery, but also of the catalytic role that we in the World Bank can play in promoting development" (Poortman 2005:212). He still keeps a piece of stone from the old bridge in a glass box in his office.

Providing Leadership

As the CD for the Balkans, Poortman consolidated his reputation in the Bank for his ability to obtain cooperation from donors, his effectiveness in working closely with Balkan factions, and his support for staff in difficult post-conflict situations. He had also received exposure to the Bank's president and Board. In 2003 he returned to Africa to become the director for operations. Just four months later, he was appointed as the VP for MENA. His experience of working in post-conflict regions was an important factor for his selection. The situation in the Middle East became very difficult for the Bank after 2001. Wolfensohn wanted a new VP, a capable and strategic leader and manager—able to get things done, sensitive to both donors and clients of all sorts, able to work with both—but not someone who would compete with the president for the agenda.

Indeed, as "the transatlantic rift caused by Iraq dwarfed the worst fighting between Europe and the United States over the Balkans" (Mallaby 2004:362), the Bank needed somebody who could navigate the minefields among its shareholders while respecting the interests of its Middle East clients. Poortman had been observed while working in Bosnia and Herzegovina, and his work there made him an obvious choice. It helped, marginally, that he was not from any of the nations embroiled in the region.

Poortman's appointment as VP surprised him and many others, particularly those who never considered him a 'political player' or politically astute in the sense that he would not speak up unless it was to his advantage. He was a straightforward, competent manager and a good technocrat. It was even a surprise to his former boss. Outside his immediate circle, Poortman's promotion received extensive approval. One senior officer commented, 'His appointment was seen as part of a process in which more weight was given to technical excellence and contributions to development than other considerations.'

Poortman replaced a VP who was well liked by staff in the region and who did not want to leave. 'When I got there, clearly the mood was not of great jubilation,' he admitted. With his long experience at the Bank, Poortman had worked with many of his new colleagues before. Without much knowledge of the region, he understood that he needed to be extremely careful, modest, and humble. He told his staff, 'I am not going to come in here and pretend I know everything; I need everybody's help; we have a job to do, and we will pull together and do it.' He listened and sought advice and suggestions from those who had been in the region for some time on the important regional and country issues. In addition to many formal meetings and consultations, 'Chrik, being Chrik, also had a lot of informal interactions with people, every hallway and every cafeteria line was an opportunity for communication.' He traveled frequently, listening to and consulting with government officials and staff in the field, getting a real feeling for the region. After 14 months into the job, he had visited all his countries, except Syria where there were some difficulties. He made an effort to know 'what was going on in the trenches' and 'understanding and listening to the frustration and problems facing the staff, not just about the office work, but about their families and their long absence from home.'

New VPs sometimes create turnovers in personnel for opportunities to build their own teams. MENA had just gone through several rounds of reorganization under his predecessor. Poortman kept the regional operations director, an equivalent to a deputy VP, and the regional chief economist. He also retained an adviser who was from the region and had worked in MENA for some years. In a short period of time, mutual trust between him and the team was built: 'He had this trust in you that you are willing to do a lot,' one staff member commented. He had unreserved confidence in his deputy, Hasan Tuluy, who acted in his place in Washington, D.C., for the 40 percent of the time when he was away in the region.

Poortman understood that CDs were the first line in dealing with client countries; they needed discretion and autonomy as well as trust. He also understood that trust did not come overnight or by virtue of the position. He was good at seeking others' opinions; he was also willing to make difficult decisions when it was required. 'That is the kind of leadership you are looking for,' one CD said. 'You want to be heard, and you want a decision to be taken too. It may or may not be the decision that I or somebody else would have taken, but that is okay because no one is right all the time. Chrik was very good at this.'

Poortman also worked closely with the EDs representing the countries in the region and those of major donors, the British, German, and American EDs, inside and outside the boardroom. He established regular interaction with the EDs from the region, who 'first looked at me with big eyes, wondering whether they were given an amateur to handle the region.' They soon struck a mutual respect and trust. 'I felt responsible vis-à-vis the Bank and also vis-à-vis the international community that was putting a lot of money into the place and fully expecting the Bank to be in the driver's seat, to be able to show that there was progress and improvement in the situation.' Briefing, reporting, and seeking advice and support from EDs was necessary for the success of the Bank program. Even though the relationships sometimes were difficult, communication allowed the EDs to appreciate the work the Bank was undertaking in the region. In MENA, according to his colleagues, 'because he communicated with the EDs frequently, a lot of preventive work was done before the crises hit.' Later these EDs effectively became colleagues, people Poortman could go to for information, wisdom, and guidance; they became close allies during his difficult time with Wolfowitz.

The MENA region covers some 20 countries. It has the 'poorest of the poor' (Yemen, Djibouti); middle-income countries (Morocco, Algeria, Egypt, Jordan, Iran); countries in conflict (Iraq, Palestine, Lebanon); and high-income countries (Gulf countries, including Saudi Arabia). Poortman had his hands full from the beginning. One important issue was the safety of his staff. Working in the field had always been dangerous, but the Bank staff had in the past never been a target. They were respected by and large by all factions because they were there to help. This included the West Bank and Gaza. The situation in Iraq, however, was different. In August 2003, soon after Poortman became VP, a truck bombed the UN headquarters in Baghdad and killed 22 UN staff, including its special representative. A Bank official was killed too. A month later, another suicide bombing targeted the UN office in Iraq. The Bank had pulled its staff out because according to the Articles of Agreement it was prohibited from working in conflict regions. There was no reconstruction or development to talk about if fighting continued. Nonetheless, the issue whether the Bank should put people on the ground in Baghdad became a focal point of disagreement between Poortman and Wolfowitz when the latter became president in July 2005.

Other difficult issues in the region involved the West Bank and Gaza, Lebanon, and Iran. Should the Bank support an integrated land and water management project and a city water and sanitation project in Iran? How should the Bank react after Hamas won the election? What role should the Bank play in Lebanon? All these were the thorny issues for Poortman as VP for MENA. Bank teams in the field did extensive analytical work, including studies that developed a language of 'sustainable security' and 'absolute security' for the Israelis, whose support was needed for the Bank's work in the West Bank and Gaza, and that produced a statistical master plan for Lebanon when no other work could be done. In all these situations, the Bank's work was more about political calculations, even if presented as technical and economic problems, than the traditional development project or program work. This required leadership from the VP.

Being Dutch

Most of Poortman's colleagues described Poortman simply: 'You know, he is Dutch,' as if that explained everything about him. What they meant was that he was straightforward, never shy telling his boss about his views, very persistent in his quiet way, but not confrontational. Poortman, according to his staff, was courageous in telling his bosses, Johannes Linn, for example, what was wrong and what should be done: 'When he felt that the things were not going right, he would come and tell me not in a confrontational way, but in a clear and concerned way,' said Linn. 'He would say what he thought and thought what he said,' explained other bosses. He did not see why he should kowtow to superiors just because of the position they held. He expected the same from people who worked for him. Most people appreciated his frank views because Poortman was an institutional man—he would not do anything to undermine the institution. When he expressed disapproval of certain actions or policies of the Bank in private, he did it because he believed that was right for client countries, his colleagues, or the Bank as an institution. One former Dutch ED simply said, 'I wish all Dutch would be like Chrik.'

Poortman was passionate about development and deeply cared about the countries he served. That passion and commitment was both a strength and a weakness. He was an insider, steeped in the Bank's history and its beliefs. That could make him cautious and careful, as he saw the development tasks through the lens of the Bank and its way of working, whether in structural adjustment lending or concepts of country ownership. There is often a Bank orthodoxy, a position from which he would start. On arriving in Bosnia, 'I expected to be successful if I could apply the Bank's general approach to transition in its broad outlines, with some adjustment to suit the post-conflict reality' He learnt otherwise. Political difficulties limited the possibility of designing any economic policy on the basis of preexisting formula. "Policies that we think are right at one point in time or space may be inappropriate in other situations," Poortman stated. "Our approach can veer into dogma if we do not account for the role of luck" (2005:210).

This passion, however lofty, could bring him into conflict with his superiors. Poortman was Res Rep in Harare when the Bank president, Preston, visited. In his view, Preston ruffled local sensibilities by using apartheid South Africa as an example for best practice; he did not show sufficient respect to the government officials, nor for the Bank staff who prepared meticulously for his visit. Poortman felt he had to mollify some of his governmental contacts and his staff. He also told Preston, however tactfully, about his concerns. Preston then consistently blocked his reintegration into an appropriate position in the Bank in Washington, D.C. To have a president as an enemy is not career enhancing.

Straightforward and frank advice is regarded as constructive only when those in power are able to see themselves as part of, not above, the institution. Wolfensohn was known for his short temper, self-centeredness, and egotism. He was also known for his charm, talent, and managerial skills (Mallaby 2004; Ferguson 2004; Zhang 2006). Poortman was skeptical when Wolfensohn came to the Bank and was particularly critical about his first trip to Africa and his treatment of Jaycox.

His views were known to Wolfensohn too.

> I received a phone call from Jim Wolfensohn, asking me to become the VP of MENA. I was very surprised because I never really thought that was anywhere near possible. When I went to his office for a discussion, he asked me whether I could work with him as he had heard that I was not always in favor and sometimes even critical of what he had been doing.

In fact, Poortman had come to appreciate Wolfensohn. For almost two years, they worked together in the Middle East when the Bank was under pressure from the Bush administration to 'enter into Iraq on the back of American tanks.' They both thought that would drive the Bank backward in its relationship with the Arab countries for years. Wolfensohn was nervous because he was walking a very thin line—he wanted to improve the relationship with the Bush administration, and "he also had to respect the feelings of his other Board members" (Mallaby 2004:264). The Coalition of the Willing wanted him to provide funding and assistance to Iraq, while the Germans and French were explicit that 'those that do the damage carry the main burden for reconstruction.' The Bank created the Iraqi Trust Fund to help

Iraqis restart delivery of basic services and rebuild infrastructure. After the bombing of the UN building and the pull-out of Bank staff, the work was done by Iraqis and monitored by Bank staff in neighboring countries. In the fall IMF/World Bank Annual Meeting of 2003, Wolfensohn was extremely preoccupied with the Iraqi situation; he was under pressure from the British and American governments to put the Bank staff back on the ground, in turn putting Poortman under severe stress. This was symptomatic of political minefields Poortman had to navigate among donors, clients, the president, and the management. 'At the end I was genuinely sorry not to be able to work with him any more when he left,' recalled Poortman. 'It was a lot of difficult work, but we worked together very well.' Wolfensohn cared about the people working for the Bank; Poortman appreciated that.

In sharp contrast, Wolfowitz never visited the region and never gave specific instructions during Poortman's tenure. Despite his promise that he would start by "listening" (Anonymous 2005:20), Wolfowitz was never prepared to listen, to have open discussions on difficult issues, or to take the responsibility by providing specific directions. This made the VPs' job almost impossible. Poortman and his team sent briefings to the president on the issue of the Bank presence in Baghdad, with recommendations. Wolfowitz never responded. When he was confronted, Wolfowitz simply refused to talk about it or to take decisions. But he expected his VP to do so. 'I refused to make the decision for him, and I was determined that no one would die under my watch,' said Poortman adamantly. *After* he left the Bank, Wolfowitz explained in an interview, "It is easy to think of supervising contracts long distance, but when the real purpose is dialogue with policymakers it is hard to do that long distance" (Cassidy 2007). It was too late: Poortman had already been forced out for not being willing to make the decision on Wolfowitz's behalf.

Poortman, like all his colleagues, was prepared to work with his new president and understood that VPs served at the president's pleasure. He was, however, not prepared to sacrifice the interests of his clients or his staff and determined to speak his mind: 'I made a decision soon after Wolfowitz came on board that, if I wasn't going to speak up, how could I expect younger managers to do so who had much more at stake in terms of their career, their children at school, or their pension? So I decided it came with the territory that I must speak up for my client countries and for the Bank.' He duly spoke up; so he had to leave.

Despite these challenges, and while making difficult decisions, Poortman occasionally showed his staff his 'true' personality, very different from the picture of seriousness he presented when people first met him. Concerned about the birds who were nesting on the building opposite the Bank complex, he could suddenly jump up from his chair in the middle of a meeting, grab his binoculars to watch a bird across the top of the roof, 'Oh boy, did you see that hawk!' Then he would sit back and say calmly, 'Now, let's transfer $500 million to...' After traveling with his VP "through the Balkans by car along highways, byways and rutted tracks" for ten days (Linn and Poortman 2002), the two of them sat in the middle of Corfu, waiting for their plane. There 'we started watching a game of cricket, a sport, it turned out, we both loved'— slightly unusual for two continental Europeans. His comic performance of karaoke surprised his superiors as well as his peers. His colleagues could give him grief about his golf and the Dutch football team, which was always the runner-up. A colleague commented that 'Chrik was not a person for shoulder slapping and that sort of stuff,' but he always took personal interest in his people. He would reach out to people whether it was a celebration of a wedding or a birth of a baby, a sickness or retirement. He would always be there, and he genuinely cared about people. That earned him the trust of his colleagues at the Bank.

Chrik Poortman was a World Banker through and through. His is but one story among many.

CHAPTER ELEVEN

Conclusion: The Bank Is Less Than the Sum of Its Parts

The experienced Bank officer who turned the familiar adage on its head had worked across three regions over 20 years. He was not an economist and had participated in and watched many aspects of the Bank's activities, a broader range than many of its critics. He has a point. After all, what is the Bank? When critics and observers talk of the Bank, to whom do they refer? Who represents it? We can suggest several interpretations.

- EDs, who represent the member states and direct the Bank to do the wishes of their political masters.
- Presidents, who set the scene and can dominate the institution. What the presidents say is the policy of the Bank *is* the policy of the Bank. They can frustrate and energize, as Wolfensohn did, or anger and paralyze, as Wolfowitz managed to do.
- Regional vice presidential barons, who oversee activities in their regions and determine what is done there with a degree of independence.
- CDs, especially when they are based in the field, determining what will be funded and working with, and accountable to, their client countries.
- Sector specialists, who bring expertise in education, climate change, electricity, roads, health, governance, and sundry other disciplines, far beyond the perceived notion of the Bank as a cadre of economists or an international commercial bank.
- Researchers in DEC, pushing at the forefront of knowledge in development, recognized as leaders in their field.

- The staff in country offices far from Washington, D.C., providing insights and contacts, encouraging local participation, to achieve better health and commitment to education.

The list could go on and on. They are all part of the Bank, all delivering the programs, all committed to the mission of 'development,' which may be interpreted in various ways and with different emphases.

What does the Bank represent? The Washington consensus? Neoliberal economics? These are very western-centric views of the Bank. Go elsewhere and ask what the Bank is known for, what the images of the Bank might be, what uses it can serve.

- In China it promises innovation and technology transfers
- In Indonesia it brings lessons on governance
- In India it assists the state governments
- In Bangladesh it can advise on flood mitigation
- In Vietnam it offers advice on anticorruption measures
- In Bosnia it helped reconstruct the Mostar Bridge
- In Tunisia it supports girls' education
- In South America it lights parks to reduce crime

And on and on. To these countries, the Bank is represented by the local staff, by the projects and programs they bring, by the support they give. Washington, D.C. is a long way away.

We can also ask how different people see the Bank. In Washington, D.C., where many of the Bank watchers and NGOs gather, the Bank is represented by its daunting edifice and soaring vestibule. To most clients, the Bank is the small office with 50–100 employees, most of them local, where negotiations take place. To the poor villagers, the Bank is what it brings—roads, clinics, levee banks, schools, textbooks, wells, and even cows. Clients may have differing views on the Bank and the way it works. Some are suspicious, other welcoming. That impression may in part be based on experience and part of image and reputation. Perhaps the best indicator of the Bank's performance is what clients and donors do. Donors still contribute substantial grants to IDA and Bank trust funds. Clients still want assistance in all forms. In difficult times the Bank still has its 'authoritative voice.' The Bank staff must be doing *something* right if these hardheaded governments still want to participate.

The Bank has many faces, and observers see but one or two of them. Their views will depend on where they look, what their interests are, whether they want to accept help or challenge its foundations. Like a blind man finding an elephant, they will seek to interpret the whole from the part they encounter.

We have sought to emphasize a number of themes. The Bank is contested; there are different interpretations of what it represents, and the staff fight over them. Its staff deliver a daunting array of programs all over the world. They are often innovative, challenging, even ingenious in the solutions they seek to bring. Diversity, discretion, local autonomy, country ownership, these are some of the Bank's watchwords.

Too often the Bank is demonized and misunderstood. The Bank official who acknowledged she would have to rewrite all her graduate essays on development, because from outside she just got it all wrong, may be typical. A senior domestic civil servant who had written critically about World Development reports and their use of statistics was stunned to be told about a program like the one seeking to deliver access to justice in Indonesia: 'I never knew they did that,' he commented. And he was more interested in the institution than most. The snigger that often greeted our comment that we were writing on the Bank was derived from a general impression that it was no more than a neocolonial tool or a vehicle for American hegemony. The details of what the Bank did were unknown. It is hard to change those images and preconceptions, even with evidence. If the desire is there, any project, however innovative and locally empowering, can be painted as an example of the Washington consensus.

The Bank as a bottom-up institution is often hard to appreciate because it presents a totally different image from the Bank of legend. We do not deny the validity of other impressions. Of course it is a presidential institution where presidents have the ability to inspire or demoralize, where they can preside ineffectually or bring visions for change. Of course it is a large, bureaucratic, sometimes badly managed institution. Of course there are examples of poor treatment of individuals and insensitive management of careers. Of course it has fashions in its approaches and modes of thinking; all institutions do. The Bank is far from ideal. Sometimes its staff are too optimistic in their evaluations of success. At times they have been wrong in their diagnoses. On occasion they have changed their collective mind about the best solutions (to do them credit, often after self-evaluation).

Nevertheless, internal debates flourish. It is therefore so much more than the caricature allows and so much more interesting as a result. It is a place of energy and ideas, of commitment and dedication, an institution to which bright people dedicate a career. Even those who wanted to tell us (occasionally persuasively) about the problems of the Bank, to complain of its poor management, and to wonder that anything got done in that bureaucratic morass soon began to talk with excitement about the fascination of the challenges and the quality of their colleagues.

This picture of the Bank as the place where ideas are contested and autonomy dispersed is different from the images provided by the theories with which we began. Indeed they have problems accounting for the diversity that our empirical evidence supplies. PA analysis concentrates on principals, the Board, and the Bank as agents. Because the Board formally has the authority to 'endorse' all decisions, PA analysts assume it to be a principal who seeks to control actions and prevent slippage away from its intentions. We have shown how wrong that picture is. PA analysis examines the small part of the iceberg above water and ignores the nine-tenths out of sight. It often interprets autonomy and discretion as attempts to pervert the wishes of the principal and argues that procedures then need to be designed to bring the recalcitrant staff into line. But the Board does not have views on most issues and shows no sign that it wants to; it is content to react because the EDs know their limitations, regardless of what the Articles of Agreement say. It is representative, not managerial in style. Staff do not necessarily seek to thwart the Board out of self-interest when they develop projects; usually there are no opinions to ignore. The staff take the initiative, plan the projects, propose the ideas, and present the final draft for approval because that is the only way the Bank could work as a semi-independent agency. Such an institution is beyond the limited world in which states delegate and control and IOs seek to develop arenas for independent action. The theory cannot explain the practice.

Nor can the approach of interpreting the Bank solely as a bureaucracy with a mission to defend and self-interest to drive. The Bank staff may have developed new activities and extended its terms of reference. The institution of the 2000s would never have been imagined in the founders' philosophies. Those extensions were never foreordained; they were contested and reinterpreted, creating winners and losers, the powerful and the frustrated. The Bank has never been a single bureaucracy with a united vision. Ideas are taken seriously and fought over, sometimes bitterly. There may be agreement on the need to maintain and protect the Bank, but how it might be done is a matter of dispute.

In these battles there is never a single exclusive ideological monopoly, whether defined as Catholic, Leninist, or economist. Economics remains the dominant discipline, but neither the only one, nor a single school of thought. Its truths are challenged, even by other economists. Other professions compete for their place in the sun, and the need for additional disciplines is acknowledged (even if only just in some corners). Some ideas and solutions, perceived as current best practice, may temporarily be in good currency, but their periods of dominance will end, and new solutions are provided to tackle the intransigent issues of development. Again the significance is the degree of internal debate over best solutions. If Bank staff do not always fight in public, to protect the standing and reputation of their institution, they do so readily in private.

So we needed a more embracing approach—a set of ideas that accept the Bank as an institution with ideas to argue, careers to pursue, and challenges to meet. We need to see the world from the perspective of the staff, their hopes, opportunities, and ambitions, their networks and careers, as they move from position to position. The structure of the institution shapes their world, but they in turn shape the institution and its image. They work within an institution that is ever changing and where the soul of the Bank is open to persuasion.

That is the reason we see the Bank as an institution with many faces; hence the neatness of a picture that portrays the Bank as less than the sum of its parts.

REFERENCES

Abbott, K.W. and Snidal D. 1998. "Why States Act through Formal International Organizations." *Journal of Conflict Resolution*, 42 (1): 3–32.

Allison, G.T. 1971. *Essence of Decision*. Boston: Little Brown.

Anonymous 2005. "If the New World Bank President Calls..." *The International Economy*, 19:2, 20–31.

Ascher, W. 1983. "New Development Approaches and the Adaptability of International Agencies." *International Organization*, 37 (3): 415–439.

Ayres, R.L. 1983. *Banking on the Poor*. Cambridge, MA: MIT.

Bacon, R.W. and Besant-Jones, J. 2002. "Global Electric Power Reform," World Bank, Energy & Mining Sector Board discussion paper series, no. 2, June.

Ball, A. 2006. "World Bank Staff Told to Treat 'integrity' unit as ally." *Financial Times*, January 23.

Ball, A. and Alden W. 2006. "Questions Raised about Wolfowitz Style." *Financial Times*, January 23.

Banerjee, A., Deatib, A., Lustig, N., and Rogoff, K. 2006. "An Evaluation of World Bank Research, 1998–2005," The World Bank.

Bapna, M. and Reisch, N. 2005. "Making the World Bank More Democratic Is Just as Important as Appointing a New Chief." *Financial Times*, January 13.

Barnett, M. and Finnemore, M. 1999. "The Politics, Power and Pathologies of International Organizations." *International Organizations*, 54 (94): 699–732.

Barnett, M. and Finnemore, M. 2004. *Rules for the World*. Ithaca: Cornell University Press.

Bartlett, C.A. and Ghoshal, S. 1990. "Matrix Management: Not a Structure, a Framework of Mind." *Harvard Business Review*. 68 (4): 138–145.

Bennis, W. and Nanus, B. 1985. *Leaders*. New York: Harper & Row.

Besant-Jones, J., Harris, C., Stuggins, G., and Townsend, A. 2004. "Operational Guidance for World Bank Staff: Public and Private Sector Roles in the Supply of Electricity Services." The World Bank Energy and Mining Sector Board, February.

Besant-Jones, J.E. 2006. "Reforming Power Markets in Developing Countries: What Have We Learned?" World Bank Energy and Mining Sector Board discussion paper series, no. 19 September.

Bevir, M., Rhodes, R.A.W., and Weller, P. 2002. "Traditions of Governance: History and Diversity." Special Issue of *Public Administration*, 81 (1).

Birdsall, N. 2002. "Why It Matters Who Runs the IMF and the World Bank." Centre for Global Development, working paper #22.

Blough, R. 1968. "The World Bank Group." *International Organization*, 22 (1): 152–181.

Bond, P. 2005. "Should the World Bank and IMF be 'Fixed' or 'Nixed'?" *Capitalism Nature Socialism*, 15:2, 85–105.

———. 2006. "Zimbabwe's Hide and Seek with the IMF: Imperialism, Nationalism and the South African Proxy." *Review of African Political Economy*, 32:106, 609–619.

Bosa, S. 2002. *Bosnia after Dayton: Nationalist Partition and International Intervention*. London: Hurst.

Bowley, G. and Sciolino, E. 2005. "Wolfowitz Reassures Europeans on His Goal." *International Herald Tribune*, March 31.

Broad, R. 2006. "Research, Knowledge, and the Art of 'Paradigm Maintenance': The World Bank's Development Economics Vice-presidency (DEC)." *Review of International Political Economy*, 13 (3): 387–419.

Burki, S.J. 2005. "World Bank Operations: Some Impressions and Lessons," in *At the Frontlines of Development*, ed. Gill and Pugatch. Washington, D.C.: The World Bank, 126–149.

Cahn, J. 1993. "Challenging the New Imperial Authority." *Harvard Human Rights Journal*, 6, 159–194.

Cassidy, J. 2007. "The Next Crusade." *The New Yorker*, April 9.

Caulfield, C. 1996. *Masters of Illusion*. New York: Henry Holt.

Chronology 2007 . World Bank Historical Chronology at http://siteresources.worldbank.org/ EXTARCHIVES/Resources/WB_Historical_Chronology_1944_2005.pdf.

Churchill, A. and Saunders, R.J. 1989. "Financing of the Energy Sector in Developing Countries." The World Bank, April.

Claude, I.L. 1971. *Swords into Plowshares*. New York: Random House.

Collier, H. 1984. *Developing Electric Power*. Baltimore: The Johns Hopkins University Press.

Cox, R.W. 1969. "The Executive Head." *International Organization*, 23(2): 205–230.

Cox, R.W. and Jacobson, H. 1973. eds. *The Anatomy of Influence*. New Haven: Yale University Press.

Darrow, M. 2003. *Between Light and Shadow*. Oxford: Hart Publishing.

de Groote, J. 1981. "Address Following a Farewell Dinner, the F Street Club," June 29, in *A Collection of Farewell Speeches on the Occasion of the Retirement of Robert S. McNamara*, Washington, D.C.: The World Bank.

DECRS. 2007. "Report on the World Bank Group Research Programs: Fiscal years 2004 and 2005, and future directions," January 18.

Dixon, J.A., Talbot, L.M., and Le Moigne, G.J. 1989. "Dams and the Environment," World Bank technical paper # 10.

Donaldson, G. 2003. "From Working Methods to Business Plan, 1984–94," in *World Bank Operations Evaluation Department*, ed. Grasso, Wasty and Weaving, Washington, D.C.: The World Bank, 45–52.

Drake, E.G. 1981. "Statement before the Board of Executive Directors, the World Bank," June 30, in *A Collection of Farewell Speeches on the Occasion of the Retirement of Robert S. McNamara*, Washington, D.C.: The World Bank.

Dubash, N.K. 2002. ed. *Power Politics*. Washington, D.C.: World Resources Institute.

Easterly, W. 2002. *The Elusive Quest for Growth*. Cambridge, MA: MIT Press.

Einhorn, J. 2001. "The World Bank's Mission Creep." *Foreign Affairs*, 80 (4): 22–35.

Emadi-Coffin, B. 2002. *Rethinking International Organization*. London: Routledge.

External Review. 2004. "Report of the External Review of the World Bank's Evaluation Function and DGO's Mandate," February. The World Bank.

Ferguson, N. 2004. "The Real Mr. Wolfensohn." *The Washington Post*, October 3.

Frischtak, C.R. 1995. ed. *Regulatory Policies and reform*. Washington, D.C.: The World Bank, no. 15372.

Galambos, L. and Milobsky, D. 1995. "Organising and Reorganising the World Bank, 1946–1972." *Business History Review*, 69 (2): 156–190.

George, S. and Sabelli, F. 1994. *Faith and Credit*. Boulder, CO: Westview Press.

Gilbert, L.G. and Vines, D. 2000. eds. *The World Bank*. New York: Cambridge University Press.

Gill, I.S. and Pugatch, T. 2005. eds. *At the Frontlines of Development*. Washington, D.C.: The World Bank.

Goldman, M. 2005. "Tracing the Roots/Routes of the World Bank Group." *International Journal of Sociology and Social Policy*, 25 (1/2): 10–29.

Grasso, P., Wasty, S., and Weaving, R.V. 2003. eds. *World Bank Operations Evaluation Department*. Washington, D.C.: The World Bank.

Guha, K. 2007. "How Wolfowitz Fell Out of His Own High Standards." *Financial Times*, April 12.

Guhan, S. 1995. *The World Bank's Lending in South Asia*. Washington, D.C.: The Brookings Institution.

Hass, P.M. 1992. ed. "Knowledge, Power, and International Policy Coordination." *International Organization*, 46(1).

Hawkins, D. and Jacoby, W. 2006. "How Agents Matter," in *Delegation and Agency in International organizations*, ed. Hawkins, Lake, Nielson and Tierney. New York: Cambridge University Press, 199–228.

Hawkins, D.G., Lake, D.A., Nielson, D.L., and Tierney, M.J. 2006. eds. *Delegation and Agency in International Organzsations*. New York: Cambridge University Press.

Heclo, H. and Wildavsky, A. 1974. *The Public Government of Public Money*. London: Macmillan.

Helleiner, G.K. 1986. ed. *Africa and the International Monetary Fund*. Washington, D.C.: The International Monetary Fund.

Hirschman, A.O. 1967. *Development Projects Observed*. Washington, D.C.: The Brookings Institution.

HR. 2004. "Towards an Operational Skills Framework: A Concept paper," February.

———. 2007a. "Strategic Staffing Update Paper," June.

———. 2007b. "Young Professional Program: Academic Background & Credentials."

Hunt, S. 2002. *Making Competition Work in Electricity*. New York: John Wiley and Sons Inc.

IEG. 2008. *Public Sector Reform: What Works and Why?* Washington D.C., The World Bank

Inspection Penal. 1999. "Request for Inspection: China Western Poverty Reduction Project," June 18, 1999. The World Bank.

Inspection Penal. 2000. "Inspection Report: The Qinghai Project," April 28. The World Bank.

Jenkins, K. and Plowden, W. 2006. *Governance and Nation-building*. Cheltenham, UK: Edward Elgar.

Kahler, M. 2001. *Leadership Selection in the Major Multilaterals*. Washington, D.C.: Institute for International Economics.

Kapur, D.; Lewis, J.P., and Webb, R. 1997. *The World Bank*. Washington, D.C.: The Brookings Institution.

Kavalsky, B. 2005. "Pictures and Lessons of Development Practice," in *At the Frontlines of Development*, ed. Gill and Pugatch. Washington, D.C.: The World Bank, 19–45.

Kessides, I.N. 2004. *Reforming Infrastructure*. Washington, D.C.: The World Bank.

Kopp, H. E. 2003. "Promoting Professional and Personal Trust in OED," in *World Bank Operations Evaluation Department*, ed. Grasso, Wasty and Weaving. Washington, D.C.: The World Bank, 55–60.

Kraske, J. 1996. *Bankers with a Mission*. Washington, D.C.: The World Bank.

Lafourcade, O. 2005. "Lessons of the 1990s," in *At the Frontlines of Development*, ed. Gill and Pugatch. Washington, D.C.: The World Bank, 163–195.

Langrod, G. 1963. *The International Civil Service*. New York: Oceana Publications.

Libby, D.T. 1975. "International Development Association." *International Organization*, 29 (4): 1065–1072.

Lim, E. 2005. "Learning and Working with the Giants," in *At the Frontlines of Development*, ed. Gill and Pugatch. Washington, D.C.: The World Bank, 89–119.

Lindblom, C.E. 1968. *The Policy-making Process*. Englewood Cliffs, NJ: Prentice-Hall.

Lindblom, C.E. 1977. *Politics and Market*. New York: Basic Books.

Linn, J. and Poortman, C. 2002. "Staying the Course in the Balkans," at http://lnweb18. worldbank.org/ECA/eca.nsf/General/0CB7E3D97038C3E485256C3F005AF3A9?Open Document.

Mackay, K. 2002. "The World Bank's ECB Experience." *New Directions for Evaluation*, 93: 81–99.

Mallaby, S. 2004. *The World's Banker*. Sydney: University of New South Wales Press.

Mallaby, S. 2005. "Saving the World Bank." *Foreign Affairs*, 84 (3): 75–84.

March, J.G. and Olsen J.P. 1989. *Rediscovering Institutions*. New York: The Free Press.

Marshall, K. 2008. *The World Bank*. London: Routledge.

Martin, L.L. 2002. "Agency and Delegation in IMF Conditionality," paper for the Utah Conference on Delegation to International Organizations at http://www.internationalorganizations.org.

——. 2006. "Distribution, Information, and Delegation to International Organisations," in *Delegation and Agency in International organisations*, ed. Hawkins, Lake, Nielson, and Tierney, New York: Cambridge University Press, 140–164.

Mason, E.S. and Asher, R.E. 1973. *The World Banks since Bretton Woods*. Washington, D.C.: The Brookings Institution.

McNamara, R.S. 1968. "Foreward" to A.A. Walters, *The Economics of Road User Charges*. World Bank staff occasional papers no. 5.

McNamara, R.S. 1978. "Foreward," *World Development Report*.

McNamara, R.S. 2003. "On the Occasion of the OED's 30th Anniversary," in *World Bank Operations Evaluation Department*, ed. Grasso, Wasty and Weaving. Washington, D.C.: The World Bank, ix.

Mikesell, R.F. 1994. *The Bretton Woods Debates*. Princeton, NJ: Princeton University.

Miliband, R. 1973. *The State in Capitalist Society*. London: Quartet Books.

Munasinghe, M. and Saunders, R.J. 1989. "Reforming Electric Power Policy in Developing Countries". World Bank working paper 106, January.

Nankani, G. 2005. "Acting Strategically and Building Trust," in *At the Frontlines of Development*, ed. Gill and Pugatch. Washington, D.C.: The World Bank, 67–86.

Neustadt, R.E. 1990. *Presidential Power and the Modern Presidents*. New York: The Free Press.

Newbery, D.M. 1999. *Privatisation, restructuring, and Regulation of Network Utilities*. Cambridge, MA: The MIT Press.

Newbery, D.M. and Green, R. 1996. "Regulation, Public Ownership and Privatisation of the English Electricity Industry," in *International Comparisons of Electricity Regulations*, ed. R.J. Gilbert and E.P. Kahn. New York: Cambridge University Press, 25–81.

North, D.C. 1990. *Institutions, Institutional Change, and Economic Performance*. New York: Cambridge University Press.

OED. 2003. *Power for Development: A Review of the World Bank Group's experience with Private Participation in the Electricity Sector*. The World Bank.

OED. 2005. *The Effectiveness of World Bank Support for Community-Based and Driven Development*. The World Bank.

Oliver, R.W. 1995. *George Woods and the World Bank*. Boulder: Lynne Rienner.

OPCS (Operations Policy and Country Strategy). 2007. "Strengthening the World Bank's Group Response and Long-Term Engagement in Fragile States," March 30.

Picciotto, R. 2003. "The Logic of Renewal: Evaluation at the World Bank, 1992–2002," in *World Bank Operations Evaluation Department*, ed. Grasso, Wasty and Weaving, Washington, D.C.: The World Bank, 61–71.

Piercy, J. 1997. "The Challenge of Privatisation: Meshing Social Policy and Development Goals," an interview with Jan Piercy, January, at http://usinfo.state.gov/journals/ites/0197/ijee/ej5f1.htm.

Piercy, J. 2003. "Panel Discussion: Perspectives on Evaluation in the Bank Today," in *World Bank Operations Evaluation Department*, ed. Grasso, Wasty and Weaving, Washington, D.C.: The World Bank, 95–102.

Please, S. 1984. *The Hobbled Giant*. Boulder, CO: Westview Press.

Pollack, M.A. 1997. "Delegation, Agency, and Agenda Setting in the European Community." *International Organization*, 51 (1): 99–134.

Pollitt, C. and Bouckaert, G. 2000. *Public Management Reforms*. New York: Oxford University Press.

Pomerantz, P. 2005. "A Little Luck and a Lot of Trust," in *At the Frontlines of Development*, ed. Gill and Pugatch, Washington, D.C.: The World Bank, 49–63.

Poortman, C. 2005. "Leadership, Learning, and Luck: Reflections on the Balkan States," in *At the Frontlines of Development*, ed. Gill and Pugatch, Washington, D.C.: The World Bank, 199–212.

Press Release. 2005. "Statement by Group of Executive Directors on the World Bank's Selection Process," March 23, no.2005/397/S.

Qureshi, M.A. 1981. "Remarks at a Farewell Reception," the John F. Kennedy Center for the Performing Acts, June 28, in *A Collection of Farewell Speeches on the Occasion of the Retirement of Robert S. McNamara*, Washington, D.C.: The World Bank.

Ravallion, M. 2007. "Research in Practice at the World Bank," at http://econ.worldbank.org/WBSITE/EXTERNAL/EXTDEC/0,,contentMDK:21496094~pagePK:64165401~piPK:64165026~theSitePK:469372,00.html, October.

Razafindrabe, A. 1981. "Statement before the Board of Executive Directors," in *A Collection of Farewell Speeches on the Occasion of the Retirement of Robert S. McNamara*, Washington, D.C The World Bank, June 30.

Ritzen, J. 2005. *A Chance for the World Bank*. London: Anthem Press.

Ritzen, J. 2007. "In Search of World Governance: Books on the Bank." *Global Governance*, 13, 575–579.

Rovani, Y. 2003. "Building up the Capacity and Influence in the Bank and Outside, 1986–92," in *World Bank Operations Evaluation Department*, eds. Grasso, Wasty and Weaving, Washington, D.C.: The World Bank, 31–40.

Rowen, H. 1986. "Conable Outlines World Bank Goals for Poor Nations." *Washington Post*, October 1.

Rowen, H. 1987. "World Bank to Trim Jobs in Reorganization'. *Washington Post*, January 22.

Salop, J. 2003. "Panel Discussion," in *World Bank Operations Evaluation Department*, eds. Grasso, Wasty and Weaving, Washington, D.C.: The World Bank, 97–98.

Shihata, I. 1991. *The World Bank in a Changing World*. Volume I & II. The Hague: Martinus Nijhoff.

Shihata, I. 2000. *The World Bank in a Changing World*. Volume III. The Hague: Martinus Nijhoff.

Simon, H.A. 1976. *Administrative Behaviour*. New York: The Free Press.

Squire, L. 2000. 'Why the World Bank Should be Involved in Development Research," in *The World Bank*, eds. Gilbert and Vines. New York: Cambridge University Press, 108–131.

Stek, P. 2003. "Evaluation at the World Bank and Implications for Bilateral Donors." *Evaluation*, 9 (4): 491–497.

Stern, E. 1981. "Remarks at a Farewell Reception," the John F. Kennedy Centre for the Performing Acts, June 28, in *A Collection of Farewell Speeches on the Occasion of the Retirement of Robert S. McNamara*. Washington, D.C.: The World Bank.

Stern, N. and Ferreira, F. 1997. "The World Bank as 'Intellectual Actor'," in *The World Bank: Its First Half Century*, eds. Kapur, Lewis, and Webb. Washington, D.C.: The Brookings Institution, 523–609.

Stiglitz, J.E. 1999. "The World Bank at the Millennium." *Economic Journal*, 109: F577–597.

———. 2002. *Globalisation and its Discontents*. New York: W.W. Norton & CO.

Stout, S. 2003. "On Joining OED," in *World Bank Operations Evaluation Department*, eds. Grasso, Wasty, and Weaving, Washington, D.C.: The World Bank, 149–150.

Sud, I. 2005. "Reflections on Development," in *At the Frontlines of Development*, ed. Gill and Pugatch, Washington, D.C.: The World Bank, 243–269.

Task Force. 2005. "Organisational Effectiveness." The World Bank, February 15.

Thomas M.A. 2007. "The Governance Bank." *International Affairs*, 83 (4): 730–745.

Thornburgh, D., Gainer, R.L., and Walker, C.H. 2000. "Report to Shengman Zhang, Managing Director and Chairman of the Oversight Committee on Fraud and Corruption: Concerning Mechanisms to Address Problems of Fraud and Corruption." Washington, D.C.: The World Bank.

———. 2003. "Report Concerning the Proposed Strategic Plan of the World Bank's Department of Institutional Integrity and the Adequacy of the Bank's Mechanisms and Resources for Implementing that Strategy," Washington, D.C.: The World Bank, July 9.

Toussaint, E. 2008. *The World Bank: A Critical Primer*. London: Pluto.

Turvey, R. and Anderson, D. 1977 *Electricity economics: essay and case studies*, Baltimore: John Hopkins University Press

Van der Tak, H.G. 1966. "The Economic Choice between Hydroelectric and Thermal Power Development." World Bank staff occasional papers no. 1.

Volcker, P.A.; Gaviria, G.; Githongo, J.; Heineman, B.W.; Van Gerven, W.; and Vereker, J. 2007. "Independent Panel Review of the World Bank Group Department of Institutional Integrity." Washington, D.C., September 13.

Wade, R. 1997. "Greening the Bank," in *The World Bank: Its First Half Century*. V. 2, eds. Kapur, Lewis, and Webb. Washington, D.C.: The Brookings Institution Press, 611–734.

Wade, R.H. 2002. "US Hegemony and the World Bank." *Review of International Political Economy*, 9 (2): 215–243.

Weiner, M.L. 2003. "Institutionalising the Evaluation Function at the World Bank, 1975–84," in *World Bank Operations Evaluation Department*, eds. Grasso, Wasty and Weaving. Washington, D.C.: The World Bank, 17–25.

Willoughby, C. 2003. "First Experiments in Operations Evaluation: Roots, Hopes, and Gaps," in *World Bank Operations Evaluation Department: The First 30 Years*, eds. Grasso, Wasty, and Weaving. Washington, D.C.: The World Bank, 3–15.

Wilson, W. 1981. *Congressional Government*. Baltimore: Johns Hopkins University Press.

Winters, A. 2006. "Q & A with Alan Winters on Development Research at the Bank," at http://econ.worldbank.org/WBSITE/EXTERNAL/EXTDEC/EXTRESEARCH/0,,contentMDK:20924295~pagePK:64165401~piPK:64165026~theSitePK:469382,00.html, June 30.

Wolfensohn, J.D. 2005. "Press Briefing with James D. Wolfensohn," April 14, Washington, D.C. at http://web.worldbank.org/WBSITE/EXTERNAL/NEWS/0,,contentMDK:20449796~menuPK:34476~pagePK:34370~piPK:34424~theSitePK:4607,00.html.

Wolfowitz, P. 2006. "Good Governance and Development: A Time for Action," speech Jakarta, April 11.

Woods, G.D. 1966. "The Development Decade in the Balance." *Foreign Affairs* 44 (2): 206–215.

Woods, N. 2006. *The Globalisers: the IMF, the World Bank, and Their Borrowers*. Ithaca: Cornell University Press.

World Development Report (WDR), various years.

World Bank. 1971. "Electric Power," December.

———. 1983. *The Energy Transition in Developing Countries.*

———.1993a. "Conference on Power Sector Reforms in India," Jaipur, October 29–31.

———.1993b. "Power Supply in Developing Countries," No. 17638.

———.1993c. "Strategic Options for Power Sector Reform in China," July 8–10.

———. 1993d. "The World Bank's Role in the Electric Power Sector," January.

———. 1994. "Governance: The World Bank's Experience," May.

———. 1996. "Bosnia and Herzegovina: Towards Economic Recovery," April 2.

———. 1999. "Civil Service Reform," April 1.

———. 2000. "Reforming Public Institutions and Strengthening Governance," November.

———. 2001. "Assessment of the Strategic Compact," March 13.

———. 2003a. "Accountability at the World Bank."

———. 2003b. "Implementing the World Bank Group Infrastructure Action Plan," September 12.

World Bank 2003, "Code of Conduct for Board Officials," Board Report, no. 27102, October 8, 2003.

———. 2005. "Capacity Building in Africa: An OED Evaluation of World Bank Support."

———. 2006a. "Strengthening Bank Group Engagement on Governance and Anticorruption," feedback from initial consultation, August 30.

———. 2006b. "Strengthening Bank Group Engagement on Governance and Anticorruption," paper for Development Committee Meeting, Singapore, September 18.

World Bank 2007 "Report to the Executive Directors: Strengthening Bank Group Engagement on Governance and Anticorruption," March 28.

———. 2008a. "Improving Public Sector Governance Portfolio, Quality Enhancement Review," July.

———. 2008b. *Public Sector Reform*, IEG, World Bank.

Xu Yi-chong. 2005. "Models, Templates and Currents." *Review of International Political Economy,* 12 (4): 647–673.

Xu Yi-chong and Weller P. 2008 "'To Be, But not To Be Seen': Exploring the Impact of International Civil Servants", *Public Administration*, 86(1): 35–52.

Zhang, Shengman. 2003. "Reflection on the 30th Anniversary of OED," in *World Bank Operations Evaluation Department: the First 30 Years*, eds. Grasso, Wasty, and Weaving. Washington, D.C.: The World Bank, 91–93.

Zhang, Shengman. 2004. "Opening Ceremony for Stari Most (Moster Bridge)," at http://web. worldbank.org/WBSITE/EXTERNAL/COUNTRIES/ECAEXT/BOSNIAHERZEX TN/0,,contentMDK:20251716~menuPK:362049~pagePK:2865066~piPK:2865079~theSi tePK:362026,00.html.

———. 2005. "Memorandum to the Executive Directors," February 15.

———. 2006. *One Step at a Time*. Shanghai: Wenhui Press (in Chinese and translated by one of the authors).

Zoellick, R.B. 2007. "An Inclusive & Sustainable Globalisation," October 10. Annual Report. World Bank Annual Report various years.

INDEX